DICKENS ON ENGLAND AND THE ENGLISH

DICKENS
ON ENGLAND
AND THE
ENGLISH

Malcolm Andrews

BARNES & NOBLE
BOOKS
10 East 53d St., New York 10022
(a division of Harper & Row Publishers, Inc.)

First published in the United States in 1979 by
HARPER & ROW PUBLISHERS, INC
BARNES & NOBLE IMPORT DIVISION
10 East 53rd Street, New York 10022

© The Harvester Press Limited, 1979

Library of Congress Cataloging in Publication Data

Andrews, Malcolm.
  Dickens on England and the English.

  Includes index.
  1. Dickens, Charles, 1812-1870—Knowledge—
England. 2.   England—Social life and customs—19th
century. I. Title.
PR4592.E54A5   1979   823'.8   78-27539
ISBN 0-06-490186-6

Printed and bound in Great Britain by
Redwood Burn Limited, Trowbridge and Esher

For my Mother and Father

Contents

List of Illustrations

List of Abbreviations

a. *Dickens's Writings*

In the following list I have arranged the fiction in order of date of publication, for those who like to be reminded of Dickens chronology. The date in brackets refers to the first volume publication.

Except where otherwise stated all references to Dickens's writings are to the New Oxford Illustrated edition, 21 vols. 1947-58.

i. Major Fiction	Abbreviated To
Sketches by Boz (1836)	SB
Pickwick Papers (1837)	PP
Oliver Twist (1838)	OT
Nicholas Nickelby (1839)	NN
The Old Curiosity Shop (1841)	OCS
Barnaby Rudge (1841)	BR
Martin Chuzzlewit (1844)	MC
Christmas Books	CB
(incorporating *A Christmas Carol*, 1843;	
The Chimes, 1844; *The Cricket on the*	
Hearth, 1845; *The Battle of Life*, 1846;	
The Haunted Man, 1848)	
Dombey and Son (1848)	D&S
David Copperfield (1850)	DC
Bleak House (1853)	BH
Hard Times (1854)	HT
Little Dorrit (1857)	LD
A Tale of Two Cities (1859)	TTC
Great Expectations (1861)	GE
Our Mutual Friend (1865)	OMF
The Mystery of Edwin Drood (1870)	ED

References will include chapter number in large Roman, and page number in Arabic: e.g. '*OCS* XXXVIII, 281-2'.

ii. Miscellaneous Writings

Master Humphrey's Clock & *A Child's History of England*	MHC & CHE
American Notes & Pictures *From Italy*	AN & PI
Christmas Stories	CS

The Uncommercial Traveller &	UT & RP
Reprinted Pieces	

The Nonesuch Edition of the   NCP
Collected Papers, 2 vols (1938)
References give the title of Dickens's article, where and when
first published, followed by vol. and page no. in this edition:
e.g. ' "Insularities", *HW** 19 January 1856: *NCP* I, 624'
*HW is the abbreviation for Dickens's weekly magazine *House-*
hold Words (1850-9): *AYR* for its successor *All The Year Round*
(1859—)

The Speeches of Charles Dickens   Speeches
ed. K. J. Fielding (Oxford 1960)
References give page no. in this edition, followed by location
and date of speech: e.g. *'Speeches*, 19-20: Boston, 1 February
1842'.

iii. Letters

The Nonesuch Edition of *The*   *Letters N*
Letters, ed. W. Dexter, 3 vols (1938)

The Pilgrim Edition of *The Letters*   *Letters P*
of Charles Dickens, ed. M. House &
G. Storey, (Oxford 1965—)
For both Nonesuch and Pilgrim *Letters* references give vol.
& page no. of the edition, followed by name of recipient of
letter and date: e.g. *'Letters N* II, 797. Forster: 15 August
1856'. A date enclosed in square brackets denotes conjectural
date on part of editors.

The Heart of Charles Dickens: Letters from   *Letters C*
Dickens to Angela Burdett Coutts, ed.
E. Johnson (1952)
Since the recipient is the same throughout this edition,
references are condensed to page no. and date: e.g. *Letters*
C , 50-1: 16 September 1843'.

b. *Biographical and Critical Studies*

John Forster *The Life of Charles Dickens*   Forster
ed. J. W. T. Ley (1928)

Edgar Johnson *Charles Dickens: His Tragedy*   Johnson
and Triumphs, 2 vols. (1952)

Humphry House *The Dickens World* (1941)   House

Philip Collins *Dickens and Crime* (1962:   Collins: *Crime*
rev. 1963)

Philip Collins *Dickens and Education*   Collins:
(1963: rev. 1964)   *Education*

Dickens: The Critical Heritage, ed.   *Crit. H.*
Philip Collins (1971)

Acknowledgements

By permission of the Oxford University Press:
The Speeches of Charles Dickens, ed. K.J. Fielding,
© Oxford University Press 1960

The Pilgrim Edition of *The Letters* of Charles Dickens, ed.
M. House & G. Storey
© Oxford University Press 1965—.

By permission of Jonathan Cape Ltd: Quotation from *Letters
from Charles Dickens to Angela Burdett Coutts, 1841-1865*,
edited by Edgar Johnson (1953).

Thanks are due to the following for permission to reproduce
or for supplying copies of illustrations:

The Dickens House—London (plates 1, 2 & 14)

Mary Evans Picture Library—London (plates 3, 7, 8, 15, 16,
18-20, 27, 29, 31)

The Mansell Collection—London (plates 4-6, 9-13, 17, 21-26,
28, 30 & 32)

Introduction

> In the old days, a long, long while ago, before Our Saviour was born on earth and lay asleep in a manger, these Islands were in the same place, and the stormy sea roared round them, just as it roars now. But the sea was not alive, then, with great ships and brave sailors, sailing to and from all parts of the world. It was very lonely. The Islands lay solitary, in the great expanse of water. The foaming waves dashed against their cliffs, and the bleak winds blew over their forests; but the winds and waves brought no adventurers to land upon the Islands, and the savage Islanders knew nothing of the rest of the world, and the rest of the world knew nothing of them.

Those bleak islands of long long ago must have been very difficult for the proud Victorian imagination to grasp: surely the rest of the world in 1850, even if it knew nothing else, could hardly help being aware of Britain's power and prestige? This fanciful passage is from the opening chapter of Dickens's *A Child's History of England*, an inordinately bloodthirsty chronicle of his country's emergence from barbarism and Catholicism (usually synonymous conditions in Dickens's mind) that closes more or less with the Glorious Revolution of 1688. For the record of what Dickens thought of his country in his own age we have, of course, his letters, speeches, journalistic writings, and above all, his novels. But from all this vast range of material there emerges no clearly ordered perspective on Victorian England as had emerged from his simplified *Child's History* of England's past.

Dickens's writings offer us a portrait of England in the nineteenth century that has extraordinary richness and complexity. Aldous Huxley once observed that nations are, to a very large extent, invented by their poets and novelists. In his own day Dickens was recognised as a master of the knowledge of English life: 'he is so thoroughly English, and is now part and parcel of that mighty aggregate of national fame which we feel bound to defend on all points against attack'. This review appeared in 1850, soon after *David Copperfield* had come to an end, when Dickens was on the crest of his career. Even a century and a quarter later, it is hard to think of any other English writer whose imaginative world remains so fully assimilated into the national identity. There may be finer novelists, greater masters of their craft, but few if any, whose books yield such an abundance of particularised national life.

'I am certain,' Ruskin remarked in *Modern Painters,* 'that whatever is to be truly great and affecting must have on it the strong stamp of the native land. Not a law this, but a necessity, from the intense hold on their country of the affections of all truly great men.... If we are now to do anything great, good, awful, religious, it must be got out of our own little island, and out of these very times, railroads and all'. Ruskin's emphasis on the national and the contemporary is a familiar one in the earlier nineteenth century. Bulwer Lytton's elegantly polemical *England and the English* (1833) also insisted that 'everything great in art must be national'. Dickens's earliest success was largely due to his answering this kind of need. The 'Every-Day Life and Every-Day People' that his *Sketches by Boz* were designed to illustrate opened up scenes from the national life that had always been considered 'low' material for the writer, in the same way that genre painting was traditionally low in the artistic canon. This was something new. Although Dickens was not the first in this field, he was its earliest and perhaps greatest genius. An obituary tribute to him in 1870 suggested that his first novel marked a cultural watershed:

> He did with the pen what some of the old Dutch painters — Ostade, and Teniers, and Jan Steen — had done with the pencil, revealing not only the picturesque effects, but the interesting moral characteristics, that lie in the commonest and even the basest forms of plebeian life. This was a reaction, about thirty-four years ago, as many of us can well remember, against the high-flown affectation of classic and aristocratic elegance which pervaded the romances of Sir Edward Bulwer-Lytton. Just when Ernest Maltravers had posed himself in a sublime attitude of transcendental nobility, Mr. Pickwick, of Goswell-

street, in his gaiters and spectacles, with Sam Weller at his heels, toddled forward and took possession of the stage.

Mr. Pickwick of Goswell-street is a version of that jovial, early eighteenth-century creation, Mr. John Bull, the personification of the national character. Partially in search of the national character, the American writer Washington Irving visited England in 1815 and recorded his impressions in his *Sketch Book* (1820):

> Men are apt to acquire peculiarities that are continually ascribed to them. The common orders of English seem wonderfully captivated with the *beau ideal* which they have formed of John Bull, and endeavour to act up to the broad caricature that is perpetually before their eyes.

The image is evidently still strong in the Regency period — Dickens's early childhood years. But Irving is also aware that the English are finding it harder to live up to the caricature, so changed are their economic and social conditions. John Bull's family mansion is in decay — 'complete suites of rooms apparently deserted and time-worn; and towers and turrets...tottering to decay'. Times are hard. Even that familiar figure has changed:

> Instead of that jolly round corporation, and snug rosy face, which he used to present, he has of late become as shrivelled and shrunk as a frost-bitten apple.

In the hero of Dickens's first novel *Pickwick Papers* this emaciated figure is given a literary blood transfusion. But even there one sometimes becomes aware of him as a stately anachronism, towed (rather like Turner's 'Fighting Temeraire' exhibited three years later) into Victorian England by the wily, devoted Sam Weller. Later still, when Dickens reintroduces Pickwick in his weekly magazine *Master Humphrey's Clock* (1840-1), the plump figure and fixed beam radiate all the good health and spirits of someone who has passed through the hands of the Forest Lawn cosmeticians.

The Pickwick world is itself glamourised by Dickens's own nostalgia for the Regency years of his childhood.

Even while he was celebrating the Pickwickian Christmas in rural Dingley Dell, he knew that another, grimmer world was beckoning, just as surely as Dodson and Fogg were preparing the hero's recall to London to face criminal proceedings and later the debtors' prison. Indeed, halfway through the writing of *Pickwick Papers* Dickens began work on the sombre *Oliver Twist*. The rest of his career as a novelist in reflecting the changing England of his time seems so often poised between his fondness for the fading, softly-focussed Pickwickian idyll and his recognition of the hard-edged, brutal contemporary world. The countryside slips away from his novels and the city crowds into his pages, as surely as industrialisation spreads through mid-nineteenth-century England.

So if we take representative Dickensian England to be the early Pickwickian world of stagecoach rides, cosy inns and plum puddings (and this is an enduring image) we are faithful principally to our own dreams: 'The world would not take another Pickwick from me now', Dickens relfects in 1849.

David Copperfield (1850) is the last of his picaresque novels. The Victorian city seems to close in upon the Pickwick world. All levels of society are packed together into a few square miles of bricks and mortar. Born in prison, Little Dorrit slips timidly back and forth through the dark London streets. Fog, thickest at Chancery, steals over the city and even out to the bleak estuary marshes, where, on a raw afternoon, Pip is nearly frightened to death by the convict from the prison Hulks. In the industrial north, Coketown's grimy uniformity presses its inhabitants into lives of despairing monotony. Dickens voices a despair himself in the 1850s at the condition of England, at the stifled lives of her poor and the buttoned-up lives of her rich and powerful. There is a failure of energy and fancy, and of compassion and generosity. The ingenious Daniel Doyce in *Little Dorrit* has to leave England to find support, moral and financial, for his inventions. Magwitch, on the other hand, who earned his fortune as a convict in Australia, must measure his wealth by English standards, and buys vicarious gentility in providing Pip's nearly fatal great expectations. Passion, creativity, and what Dickens called 'the graces of the imagination' seem to have deserted England in the last fifteen years or so of his life.

The relationship of Dickens to his country is therefore a continually changing one, and it is the aim of this book to present, through a selection from the full range of his writings, some of the aspects of that relationship. The book itself started life as an anthology, like its companion volume on America and the Americans, and soon ran into the obvious problem, the vast amount of eligible material: Dickens wrote very little that was not to do with England and the English. But he also wrote very little that specifically examined the state of England or the English character in the way that *American Notes* gathered together and organised his impressions of that country. Partly as a consequence of this, my own choice of material may often seem too arbitrary, or, as a Charybdis to this Scylla, too familiar: hence the commentary, which is designed to give some navigational aid to the reader. Although the commentary is much more extensive than an anthology conventionally requires, I have still tried throughout to observe the title's emphasis and present Dickens *on* the English, rather than undertake a fuller study of Dickens *and* the English, after the model of, say, Philip Collins's *Dickens and Crime*. So Dickens is given room to speak for himself at greater length than the purposes of the latter kind of study allow or intend. This is especially the case in my earlier chapters, concerned principally with Dickens on England — her countryside, her capital, and the industrial changes. The last two chapters, dealing more with the condition and character of the English as Dickens views them, are for obvious reasons more speculative, and the proportion of commentary to quotation is accordingly modified.

Dickens, for better or worse, is beginning to rival Shakespeare in terms of the amount of published critical discussion of his work. One would, incidentally, love to hear him sometimes on one or two of his own literary critics, whose earnest exegeses will probably be more fatal than anything else to his posthumous vitality. But fortunately he has also had some fine critics. I am indebted to many studies of particular aspects of Dickens's relationship with his country, and in the course of the book I have mentioned a number from whom I have drawn directly, or to whom I wanted to direct the reader for more information and discussion. But, as is often the case, the more pervasive help goes proportionately unacknowledged; so I would like here to record my larger debts to a handful of studies: Humphry House's *The Dickens World*, Philip Collins's two studies *Dickens and Crime* and *Dickens and Education*, George Ford's *Dickens and His Readers*, Edgar Johnson's biography *Charles Dickens: His Tragedy and Triumph*, and those two classic essays in modern Dickens criticism Edmund Wilson's 'Dickens: The Two Scrooges' and George Orwell's 'Charles Dickens'.

My debt of gratitude extends also to the secretaries of Eliot College at the University of Kent, under the supervision of Miss Sally Hewett, whose industry, patience and ability to decipher my handwriting went beyond the call of duty.

My final acknowledgement is recorded in the book's dedication.

CHAPTER I

Home Thoughts

> Oh for Jack Straw's! Oh for Jack! oh for Topping! — oh for
> Charley, Mamey, Katey — the study, the Sunday's dinner, the
> anything and everything connected with our life at Home!
>
> *(Letters P* III, 94. Maclise: 27 February 1842)

However difficult it may be to define 'Home' — or even
to identify it — no writer has done more to persuade us
of its beneficent influence than Dickens, whose own
childhood home was for a while destroyed by impro-
vidence and poverty, and whose adult home dis-
integrated through deep emotional incompatibilities. The
nostalgic passage above is from a letter Dickens wrote
during his 1842 visit to America. 'Jack Straw's' was (and
is) a Hampstead pub, 'Jack' was his closest friend John
Forster, 'Topping' was his groom, 'Charley, Mamey,
Katey' his children; the Devonshire Terrace 'study' was
where he had brought to life little Nell, Quilp, and
Barnaby Rudge; and 'Sunday's dinner', like his famous
Christmases, was the fragrant occasion for the full family
gathering.

We would probably all compose our notion of home
from such features, seeing it as an aggregate of familiar
people and places.

> 'When I talk of homes', pursued Nicholas, 'I talk of mine.... If
> it were defined by any particular four walls and a roof, God
> knows I should be sufficiently puzzled to say whereabouts it lay;
> but that is not what I mean. When I speak of home, I speak of
> the place where, in default of a better, those I love are gathered
> together; and if that place were a gipsy's tent, or a barn, I
> should call it by the same good name notwithstanding'.
>
> *(NN,* XXXV, 443)

Home is more than one's house, even though, as

1

Nicholas Nickleby suggests, its centre may well be identified with all that is enclosed and sheltered by those particular walls. It can also be more than one's neighbourhood. Indeed the further one strays from that familiar house, the more comprehensive can 'home' become, until it begins to embrace notions of a national character and culture. Again, writing from America, Dickens confides:

> Apart from my natural desire to be among my friends and to be at home again, I have a yearning after our English Customs and english manners, such as you cannot conceive.
>
> *(Letters P* III, 120. Fonblanque: 12[&?21] March 1842)

Dickens himself is the great painter of English manners, and for better or worse, the image of his country that emerges from his books has become indelibly a part of the national character. He has, for instance, given us notions of a cosy domesticity which is not just sentimental decoration, but central to his moral creed. His daughter Mamie recalls this trait in her father:

> From his earliest childhood, throughout his earliest married life to the day of his death, his nature was home-loving. He was a "home man" in every respect. When he became celebrated at a very early age, as we know, all his joys and sorrows were taken home; and he found there sympathy and the companionship of his "own familiar friends". In his letters to these latter, in his letters to my mother, to my aunt, and, later on, to us his children, he never forgot anything that he knew would be of interest about his work, his successes, his hopes or fears. And there was a sweet simplicity in his belief that such news would most certainly be acceptable to all, that is wonderfully touching and child-like coming from a man of genius.
>
> His care and thoughtfulness about home matters, nothing being deemed too small or trivial to claim his attention and consideration, were really marvellous when we remember his active, eager, restless, working brain. No man was so inclined naturally to derive his happiness from home affairs. He was full of the kind of interest in a house which is commonly confined to women, and his care of and for us as wee children did most certainly "pass the love of women!" His was a tender and most affectionate nature.
>
> (Mamie Dickens, *My Father As I Recall Him* 1896, pp.11-12)

Alongside this testimony one should put the rather different — certainly more complex — recollections of Dickens's other daughter, Kate. Gladys Storey records a scene in Kate Perugini's old age:

> We frequently sat for long periods in silence. It was apparent that her mind was busily occupied with some train of thought. After a time she would look up and give utterance to what appeared to be a decision — a summing-up of her deliberations.
>
> "I loved my father better than any man in the world — in a different way of course," she observed after one of these long silences. "I loved him for his faults." Rising from her chair and walking towards the door, she added: "My father was a wicked man — a very wicked man." And left the room.
>
> On her return she continued:
>
> "My poor mother was afraid of my father. She was never allowed to express an opinion — never allowed to say what she felt." Following another considerable silence, she said: "Ah! We were *all* very wicked not to take her part; Harry does not take this view, but he was only a boy at the time, and does not realize the grief it was to our mother, after having all her children, to go away and leave us. My mother never rebuked me. I never saw her in a temper. We like to think of our geniuses as great characters — but we can't."
>
> (Gladys Storey, *Dickens and Daughter* 1939, pp.218-9)

However confused Dickens's private domestic life may have been, home remained a significant source of his creative inspiration:

> that common household lamp in which my feeble fire is all enshrined, and at which my flickering torch is lighted up.
> (*Speeches*, 19. Boston: 1 February 1842)

We would expect, therefore, that his portraits of England would be infused with this domestic spirit; and so they are. Again and again, to banish or keep at bay the world's wickedness Dickens conjures in a wealth of outward forms this spirit of home. Here are some of the feminine embodiments of this spirit:

> [Rose Maylie] was not past seventeen. Cast in so slight and exquisite a mould; so mild and gentle; so pure and beautiful; that earth seemed not her element, nor its rough creatures her

fit companions. The very intelligence that shone in her deep blue eye, and was stamped upon her noble head, seemed scarcely of her age, or of the world; and yet the changing expression of sweetness and good humour, the thousand lights that played about the face, and left no shadow there; above all, the smile, the cheerful, happy smile, were made for Home, and fireside peace and happiness.

(*OT*, XXIX, 212)

Pleasant little Ruth [Pinch]! Cheerful, tidy, bustling, quiet little Ruth! No doll's house ever yielded greater delight to its young mistress, than little Ruth derived from her glorious dominion over the triangular parlour and the two small bedrooms.

To be Tom's housekeeper. What dignity! Housekeeping, upon the commonest terms, associated itself with elevated responsibilities of all sorts and kinds; but housekeeping for Tom implied the utmost complication of grave trusts and mighty charges. Well might she take the keys out of the little chiffonier which held the tea and sugar; and out of the two little damp cupboards down by the fireplace, where the very black beetles got mouldy, and had the shine taken out of their backs by envious mildew; and jingle them upon a ring before Tom's eyes when he came down to breakfast! Well might she, laughing musically, put them up in that blessed little pocket of hers with a merry pride! For it was such a grand novelty to be mistress of anything, that if she had been the most relentless and despotic of all little housekeepers, she might have pleaded just that much for her excuse, and have been honourably acquitted.

(*MC*, XXXIX, 599)

Then Dot [Peerybingle] . . . arranged the great chair in the chimney-corner for her husband; filled his pipe and gave it him; and took her usual little stool beside him on the hearth.

She always *would* sit on that little stool. I think she must have had a kind of notion that it was a coaxing, wheedling little stool.

She was, out and out, the very best filler of a pipe, I should say, in the four quarters of the globe. To see her put that chubby little finger in the bowl, and then blow down the pipe to clear the tube, and, when she had done so, affect to think that there was really something in the tube, and blow a dozen times, and hold it to her eye like a telescope, with a most provoking twist in her capital little face, as she looked down it, was quite a brilliant thing. As to the tobacco, she was perfect mistress of the subject; and her lighting of the pipe, with a wisp of paper, when the Carrier had it in his mouth — going so very near his nose, and yet not scorching it — was Art, high Art.

And the Cricket and the kettle, turning up again, acknowledged it! The bright fire, blazing up again, acknowledged

it! The little Mower on the clock, in his unheeded work,
acknowledged it! The Carrier, in his smoothing forehead and
expanding face acknowledged it, the readiest of all.

And as he soberly and thoughtfully puffed at his old pipe;
and as the Dutch clock ticked; and as the red fire gleamed; and
as the Cricket chirped; that Genius of his Hearth and Home (for
such the Cricket was) came out, in fairy shape, into the room,
and summoned many forms of Home about him. Dots of all
ages, and all sizes, filled the chamber. Dots who were merry
children, running on before him gathering flowers in the fields;
cosy Dots, half shrinking from, half yielding to, the pleading of
his own rough image; newly-married Dots, alighting at the
door, and taking wondering possession of the household keys;
motherly little Dots, attended by fictitious Slowboys, bearing
babies to be christened; matronly Dots, still young and blooming, watching Dots of daughters, as they danced at rustic balls;
fat Dots, encircled and beset by troops of rosy grandchildren;
withered Dots, who leaned on sticks, and tottered as they crept
along.

(*The Cricket on The Hearth, CB,* 180)

Dickens's idealised domestic heroines are extraordinarily
efficient in managing the home. It is one of their primary
attractions for him, and a virtue which he regards as
profoundly English. When he was staying in Genoa in
1845, his English cook one day announced that she was
engaged to a Frenchman. He was apprehensive for her
on several counts, not least because of the likelihood of
great cultural incompatibility:

It is a great venture on her part, for she is well brought up, quite
delicate in her ideas, full of English notions of comfort and
cleanliness and decency — and must, for some time at all
events, live in some miserable rooms in some miserable
neighbourhood, of which you can form no idea without seeing
the ordinary residences of an Italian Town. I do not remember a
single English person of her own station who will be here, after
we have left.

(*Letters N* I, 673. Maclise: 9 May 1845)

Comfort, cleanliness and decency — as we shall see later,
Dickens was to grow impatient with some of the more
torpid consequences of these valued 'English notions',
and indeed with some of their more aggressive expo-

nents: there is, for example, Mrs. Joe in *Great Expectations*, whose cleanliness and decency are decidedly
*un*comfortable:

> Mrs. Joe was a very clean housekeeper, but had an exquisite art
> of making her cleanliness more uncomfortable and unacceptable
> than dirt itself. Cleanliness is next to Godliness, and some
> people do the same by their religion.
>
> (*GE*, IV, 20)

But however emphasized or abused these notions may
be, there is little doubt in Dickens that love of home is
the cornerstone to individual moral health and to
national stability. Emerson remarked in *English Traits*
(1856) that 'Domesticity is the tap-root which enables the
nation to branch wide and high. The motive and end of
their trade and empire is to guard the independence and
privacy of their homes. Nothing so much marks their
manners as the concentration on their household ties'.
Dickens would not have dissented from this view,
though he might have felt a need to qualify the general
sentiment in favour of the poor:

> And let me linger in this place, for an instant, to remark that if
> ever household affections and loves are graceful things, they are
> graceful in the poor. The ties that bind the wealthy and the
> proud to home may be forged on earth, but those which link the
> poor man to his humble hearth are of the truer metal and bear
> the stamp of Heaven. The man of high descent may love the
> halls and lands of his inheritance as a part of himself: as trophies
> of his birth and power; his associations with them are associ-
> ations of pride and wealth and triumph; the poor man's
> attachment to the tenements he holds, which strangers have
> held before, and may to-morrow occupy again, has a worthier
> root, struck deep into a purer soil. His household gods are of
> flesh and blood, with no alloy of silver, gold, or precious stone;
> he has no property but in the affections of his own heart; and
> when they endear bare floors and walls, despite of rags and toil
> and scanty fare, that man has his love of home from God, and
> his rude hut becomes a solemn place.
>   Oh! if those who rule the destinies of nations would but
> remember this – if they would but think how hard it is for the
> very poor to have engendered in their hearts, that love of home
> from which all domestic virtues spring, when they live in dense

and squalid masses where social decency is lost, or rather never
found, —if they would but turn aside from the wide
thoroughfares and great houses, and strive to improve the
wretched dwellings in bye-ways where only Poverty may walk,
— many low roofs would point more truly to the sky, than the
loftiest steeple that now rears proudly up from the midst of
guilt, and crime, and horrible disease, to mock them by its
contrast... In love of home, the love of country has its rise; and
who are the truer patriots or the better in time of need — those
who venerate the land, owning its wood, and stream, and earth,
and all that they produce? or those who love their country
boasting not a foot of ground in all its wide domain!

(OCS, XXXVIII, 281-2)

Young couples setting out in life together can do no
better than cultivate these 'domestic virtues':

> Before marriage and afterwards, let them learn to centre all their
> hopes of real and lasting happiness in their own fireside: let
> them cherish the faith that in home, and all the English virtues
> which the love of home engenders, lies the only true source of
> domestic felicity; let them believe that round the household
> gods, contentment and tranquility cluster in their gentlest and
> most graceful forms; and that many weary hunters of happiness
> through the noisy world, have learnt this truth too late, and
> found a cheerful spirit and a quiet mind only at home at last.

(Sketches of Young Couples, SB, 604)

For one young couple in particular this model is recommended. In 1840 the young Queen Victoria was married
to Prince Albert:

> To that one young couple on whose bright destiny the thoughts
> of nations are fixed, may the youth of England look, and not in
> vain, for an example. From that one young couple, blessed and
> favoured as they are, may they learn that even the glare and
> glitter of a court, the splendour of a palace, and the pomp and
> glory of a throne, yield in their power of conferring happiness,
> to domestic worth and virtue. From that one young couple may
> they learn that the crown of a great empire, costly and jewelled
> though it be, gives place in the estimation of a Queen to the
> plain gold ring that links her woman's nature to that of tens of
> thousands of her humble subjects, and guards in her woman's
> heart one secret store of tenderness, whose proudest boast shall
> be that it knows no Royalty save Nature's own, and no pride of
> birth but being the child of heaven.!

(Ibid., p. 603)

Dickens's favourite fictional child, David Copperfield,
has two marriages, to Dora and Agnes. This involves his
exchanging a childlike incompetent housekeeper, for a
highly competent one, and a romantic love, for a
domestic, sisterly love. Dickens's own emotional and
domestic life was to involve curious permutations of
David's situation: he replaced his wife Kate with the
combination of sisterly housekeeper (Georgina Hogarth)
and very young mistress (Ellen Ternan). Here is David's
child-wife, trying very hard:

> Sometimes, of an evening, when I was at home and at work —
> for I wrote a good deal now, and was beginning in a small way
> to be known as a writer — I would lay down my pen, and watch
> my child-wife trying to be good. First of all, she would bring out
> the immense account-book, and lay it down upon the table,
> with a deep sigh. Then she would open it at the place where Jip
> had made it illegible last night, and call Jip up to look at his
> misdeeds. This would occasion a diversion in Jip's favour, and
> some inking of his nose, perhaps, as a penalty. Then she would
> tell Jip to lie down on the table instantly, 'like a lion' — which
> was one of his tricks, although I cannot say the likeness was
> striking — and, if he were in an obedient humour, he would
> obey. Then she would take up a pen, and begin to write, and
> find a hair in it. Then she would take up another pen, and begin
> to write, and find that it spluttered. Then she would take up
> another pen, and begin to write, and say in a low voice 'Oh, it's
> a talking pen, and will disturb Doady!' And she would then give
> it up as a bad job, and put the account-book away, after
> pretending to crush the lion with it.
>   Or, if she were in a very sedate and serious state of mind, she
> would sit down with the tablets, and a little basket of bills and
> other documents, which looked more like curl-papers than
> anything else, and endeavour to get some result out of them.
> After severely comparing one with another, and making entries
> on the tablets, and blotting them out, and counting all the
> fingers on her left hand over and over again, backwards and
> forwards, she would be so vexed and discouraged, and would
> look so unhappy, that it gave me pain to see her bright face
> clouded — and for me! — and I would go softly to her, and say:
>   'What's the matter, Dora?'
>   Dora would look up hopelessly, and reply, 'They won't come
> right. They make my head ache so. And they won't do anything
> I want!'
>   Then I would say, 'Now let us try together. Let me show you,
> Dora.'

Then I would commence a practical demonstration, to which Dora would pay profound attention, perhaps for five minutes; when she would begin to be dreadfully tired, and would lighten the subject by curling my hair, or trying the effect of my face with my shirt-collar turned down. If I tacitly checked this playfulness, and persisted, she would look so scared and disconsolate, as she became more and more bewildered, that the remembrance of her natural gaiety when I first strayed into her path, and of her being my child-wife, would come reproachfully upon me; and I would lay the pencil down, and call for the guitar.

(DC, XLIV, 644-45)

Then there is Agnes Wickfield, waiting demurely in the wings:

Mr. Wickfield tapped at a door in a corner of the panelled wall, and a girl of about my own age came quickly out and kissed him. On her face, I saw immediately the placid and sweet expression of the lady whose picture had looked at me down-stairs. It seemed to my imagination as if the portrait had grown womanly, and the original remained a child. Although her face was quite bright and happy, there was a tranquillity about it, and about her — a quiet, good, calm spirit, — that I never have forgotten; that I never shall forget.

This was his little housekeeper, his daughter Agnes, Mr. Wickfield said. When I heard how he said it, and saw how he held her hand, I guessed what the one motive of his life was.

She had a little basket-trifle hanging at her side, with keys in it; and she looked as staid and as discreet a housekeeper as the old house could have. She listened to her father as he told her about me, with a pleasant face; and when he had concluded, proposed to my aunt that we should go up-stairs and see my room. We all went together, she before us. A glorious old room it was, with more oak beams, and diamond panes; and the broad balustrade going all the way up to it.

I cannot call to mind where or when, in my childhood, I had seen a stained glass window in a church. Nor do I recollect its subject. But I know that when I saw her turn round, in the grave light of the old staircase, and wait for us, above, I thought of that window; and I associated something of its tranquil brightness with Agnes Wickfield ever afterwards.

(DC, XV, 223)

The beautiful Agnes is 'quiet, good, calm...staid and discreet' compared with the volatile, playful, childish

Dora: thereby David is to learn the penalties for his 'undisciplined heart'. One may well feel that none of Dickens's fictional heroines can really be called as a witness for the defence against his own daughter's charge: 'My father did not understand women', (Gladys Storey, *op.cit.*, p. 100). For all his idealised portraits of happy family life, Dickens realised in later years that incompatibility within a marriage could become a torment too painful to enforce on people, simply for the sake of preserving certain religious and social conventions. Stephen Blackpool's circumstances in *Hard Times* provide an example of the iniquities in the prevailing Divorce Laws in England to which Dickens called attention on several occasions:

> The Law of Divorce is in such condition that from the tie of marriage there is no escape to be had, no absolution to be got, except under certain proved circumstances not necessary to enter upon here, and then only on payment of an enormous sum of money. Ferocity, drunkenness, flight, felony, madness, none of these will break the chain, without the enormous sum of money. The husband who, after years of outrage, has abandoned his wife, may at any time claim her for his property and seize the earnings on which she subsists. The most profligate of women, an intolerable torment, torture, and shame to her husband, may nevertheless, unless he be a very rich man, insist on remaining handcuffed to him, and dragging him away from any happier alliance, from youth to old age and death. Out of this condition of things among the common people, out of the galling knowledge of the impossibility of relief — aggravated, in cottages and single rooms, to a degree not easily imaginable by ill-assorted couples who live in houses of many chambers, and who, both at home and abroad, can keep clear of each other and go their respective ways — vices and crimes arise which no one with open eyes and any fair experience of the people can fail often to trace, from the Calendars of Assizes, back to this source.
>
> ('The Murdered Person', *HW* 11 October 1856: *NCP* I, 663)

This is an appropriate point at which to turn from home-makers to home-breakers:

> Domestic happiness, thou only bliss
> Of Paradise that has surviv'd the fall!

Though few now taste thee unimpair'd and pure,
Or, tasting, long enjoy thee . . .
Thou art the nurse of virtue — in thine arms
She smiles, appearing, as in truth she is,
Heav'n born, and destin'd to the skies again.
Thou art not known where pleasure is ador'd,
That reeling goddess with the zoneless waist
And wand'ring eyes, still leaning on the arm
Of novelty, her fickle frail support;
For thou art meek and constant, hating change,
And finding, in the calm of truth-tried love,
Joys that her stormy raptures never yield.
Forsaking thee, what shipwreck have we made
Of honour, dignity, and fair renown!
Till prostitution elbows us aside
In all our crowded streets; and senates seem
Conven'd for purposes of empire less
Than to release th' adultress from her bond.

William Cowper's paean to domestic happiness in the third Book of *The Task* (1785) strikes many of the Dickensian keynotes — the nurse of virtue, the bulwark against change. It also introduces the great threats to domestic security—adultery and prostitution. There are two women who violate domestic happiness in *David Copperfield*, Little Emily and Martha Endell, school friends, both orphaned early in life. Their lives end in remorseful degradation, and both of them draw from Dickens some of his most extravagantly melodramatic writing. As Philip Collins points out in *Dickens and Crime* the conventional melodramatic treatment of the fallen women in the fiction sorts oddly with Dickens's own more sophisticated approach to the care and management of real-life Marthas. He had for some years before *David Copperfield* been managing a Home for Fallen Women. This was one of the many philanthropic enterprises inaugurated and funded by Angela Burdett Coutts. A house was bought in Shepherds Bush, London, and named Urania Cottage. In the first six years of the project there were between fifty and sixty inmates, between the ages of fourteen and twenty-six. In a *Household Words* article in 1853 Dickens described the kind of girls admitted to the Home:

It was (and is) established in a detached house with a garden. The house was never designed for any such purpose, and is only adapted to it, in being retired and not immediately overlooked. It is capable of containing thirteen inmates besides two Superintendents. Excluding from consideration ten young women now in the house, there have been received in all, since November eighteen hundred and forty-seven, fifty-six inmates. They have belonged to no particular class, but have been starving needle-women of good character, poor needlewomen who have robbed their furnished lodgings, violent girls committed to prison for disturbances in ill-conducted workhouses, poor girls from Ragged Schools, destitute girls who have applied at Police offices for relief, young women from the streets; young women of the same class taken from the prisons after undergoing punishment there as disorderly characters, or for shoplifting, or for thefts from the person: domestic servants who have been seduced, and two young women held to bail for attempting suicide. No class has been favoured more than another; and misfortune and distress are a sufficient introduction. It is not usual to receive women of more than five or six-and-twenty; the average age in the fifty-six cases would probably be about twenty. In some instances there have been great personal attractions; in others, the girls have been very homely and plain. The reception has been wholly irrespective of such sources of interest. Nearly all have been extremely ignorant.

('Home for Homeless Women', *HW* 23 April 1853: *NCP* I, 426-7)

In 1847, the year of the Home's opening, Dickens issued an 'Appeal to Fallen Women'; reminding them of the wretched consequences of their lives, and how, once fallen, they enter a vicious circle. The Home offers a chance to break that circle by preparing them to be conscientious housewives:

In this home they will be taught all household work that would be useful to them in a home of their own and enable them to make it comfortable and happy. In the home, which stands in a pleasant country lane and where each may have her little flower-garden if she pleases, they will be treated with the greatest kindness: will lead an active, cheerful, healthy life: will learn many things it is profitable and good to know, and being entirely removed from all who have any knowledge of their past career will begin life afresh and be able to win a good name and character.

(*Letters C*, 99: 28 October 1847)

When they are morally and physically rehabilitated, emigration (usually to Australia) is organised for them, where they can enter into good service and work towards happily married lives. Dickens's plans for the actual running of the Home were admirably enlightened. The girls were not to be bullied out of their viciousness, but 'tempted to virtue':

> What they would be taught in the house, would be grounded in religion, most unquestionably. It must be the basis of the whole system. But it is very essential in dealing with this class of persons to have a system of training established, which, while it is steady and firm, is cheerful and hopeful. Order, punctuality, cleanliness, the whole routine of household duties — as washing, mending, cooking — the establishment itself would supply the means of teaching practically, to everyone. But then I would have it understood by all — I would have it written up in every room — that they were not going through a monotonous round of occupation and self-denial, which began and ended there, but which began, or was resumed, under that roof, and would end, by God's blessing, in happy homes of their own.
>
> (*Ibid.*, p.80: 26 May 1846)

Domestic happiness and efficiency lie at the heart of Dickens's system of rehabilitation, both as a novelist and as a practical social reformer. The place of the virtuous woman was properly in the home. For the man there were, of course, different standards. In April of 1848 Emerson dined with Dickens, Carlyle and Forster, and at one point the conversation turned to the sexual mores of the age. Carlyle and Dickens agreed that chastity in the male sex was as good as gone: in England it was so rare that they could name all the exceptions. Dickens remarked:

> incontinence is so much the rule in England, that if his own son were particularly chaste, he should be alarmed on his account, as if he could not be in good health.
>
> (Emerson, *Journals* Harvard U.P., 1973, Vol.X ed. M. Sealts, p.551)

In Emerson's own country there was a rather more independent breed of woman emerging, typified by Mrs.

Amelia Bloomer, who gave her name to that famous article of 'rational dress' for women and made herself a familiar figure behind the lectern in many parts of America. Dickens was, perhaps inevitably, disconcerted by this:

> Personally, we admit that our mind would be disturbed, if our own domestic well-spring were to consider it necessary to entrench herself behind a small table ornamented with a water-bottle and tumbler, and from that fortified position to hold forth to the public.... We should put the question thus to Mrs. Bellows. 'Apple of our eye, we will freely admit your inalienable right to step out of your domestic path into any phase of public appearance and palaver that pleases you best; but we doubt the wisdom of such a sally. Beloved one, does your sex seek influence in the civilised world? Surely it possesses influence therein to no mean extent, and has possessed it since the civilised world was. Should we love our Julia (assuming for the sake of argument, the Christian name of Mrs. Bellows to be Julia), — should we love our Julia better, if she were a Member of Parliament, a Parochial Guardian, a High Sheriff, a Grand Juror, or a woman distinguished for her able conduct in the chair? Do we not, on the contrary, rather seek in the society of our Julia, a haven of refuge from Members of Parliament, Parochial Guardians, High Sheriffs, Grand Jurors, and able chairmen? Is not the home-voice of our Julia as the song of a bird, after considerable bow-wowing out of doors? And is our Julia certain that she has a small table and water-bottle Mission round the corner, when here are nine (say, for the sake of argument, nine) little Bellowses to mend, or mar, at home? Does our heart's best treasure refer us to the land across the Atlantic for a precedent? Then let us remind our Julia, with all respect for the true greatness of that great country, that it is not generally renowned for its domestic rest, and that it may have yet to form itself for its best happiness on the domestic patterns of other lands'.
>
> ('Sucking Pigs', *HW* 8 November 1851: *NCP I*, 386-7)

Domestic security is also impaired by the father figures (more often than not widowers) in Dickens's fiction, who forsake their paternal responsibilities and lean too heavily on the frail shoulders of their little daughters: e.g. Madeline Bray's father in *Nicholas Nickleby*, Little Nell's grandfather, Agnes Wickfield's father, William Dorrit, and the truculent Old Barley in *Great Expectations*. The harm inadvertently done by the selfishness and apathy of these figures is often more subtle and damaging than the havoc created by the more stereotyped fallen women. As has been remarked many times, the amount of happy, loving families in Dickens's fiction is actually very small considering his reputation as the great celebrator of the domestic idyll. For every Cratchit household there is an abundance of Old Wickfields and Mrs. Joes. As Dickens unhappily remarked once:

> the greater part of my observation of Parents and children had shown selfishness in the first, almost invariably.
> *(Letters N* I, 588. T.J.Thompson: 29 March 1844)

Recognizing that from the love of home both the domestic virtues and the love of one's country spring, could Dickens, as a writer better serve his countrymen than by concentrating his imaginative powers on the home? 'He set in motion the secret springs of sympathy by touching the domestic affections', G. H. Lewes observed in 1872. Throughout his life Dickens sought for a place at the hearth of every home. In 1845 he was hatching an idea for a periodical to be called *The Cricket* (the little creature that lives by the hearth). This he planned to contain 'a vein of glowing, hearty, generous, mirthful, beaming reference in everything to Home, and Fireside':

> I would come out, sir, with a prospectus of the Cricket that should put everybody in a good temper, and make such a dash at people's fenders and armchairs as hasn't been made for many a long day. I could approach them in a different mode under this name, and in a more winning and immediate way, than under any other. I would at once sit down upon their very hobs; and take a personal and confidential position with them which should separate me, instantly, from all other periodicals periodically published, and supply a distinct and sufficient reason for my coming into existence. And I would chirp, chirp, chirp away in every number until I chirped it up to well, you shall say how many hundred thousand!
> . . .Seriously, I feel a capacity in this name and notion which appears to give us a tangible starting-point, and a real, defined, strong genial drift and purpose. I seem to feel that it is an aim and name which people would readily and pleasantly connect with *me*; and that, for a good course and a clear one, instead of making circles pigeon-like at starting, here we should be safe. I

think the general recognition would be likely to leap at it; and of the helpful associations that could be clustered round the idea at starting, and the pleasant tone of which the working of it is susceptible, I have not the smallest doubt ....

(*Letters N* I, 684-5. Forster: [June 1845])

Two years later, the same sentiments occurred in his Address in the Cheap Edition of his Works:

To become, in his new guise, a permanent inmate of many English homes, where, in his old shape, he was only known as a guest, or hardly known at all; to be well thumbed and soiled in a plain suit that will bear a great deal, by children and grown people, at the fireside and on the journey: to be hoarded on the humble shelf where there are few books, and to lie about in libraries like any familiar piece of household stuff that is easy of replacement: and to see and feel this — not to die first, or grow old and passionless: must obviously be among the hopes of a living author, venturing on such an enterprise. Without such hopes it never could be set on foot. I have no fear of being mistaken in acknowledging that they are mine; that they are built, in simple earnestness and grateful faith, on my experience, past and present, of the cheering-on of very many thousands of my countrymen and countrywomen, never more numerous or true to me than now; and that hence this Cheap Edition is projected.

('Address in the Cheap Edition of *Pickwick Papers*' 1847: *NCP* I, 65-6)

Dickens recognises that he and his writings are already associated primarily with the hearth and home, and that he, of all writers, has been granted special access to that English sanctum sanctorum. Three years later he launched his periodical *Household Words* with these hopes:

We aspire to live in the Household affections, and to be numbered among the Household thoughts, of our readers. We hope to be the comrade and friend of many thousands of people, of both sexes, and of all ages and conditions, on whose faces we may never look. We seek to bring into innumerable homes, from the stirring world around us, the knowledge of many social wonders, good and evil, that are not calculated to render any of us less ardently persevering in ourselves, less tolerant of one another, less faithful in the progress of mankind, less thankful for the privilege of living in the summer-dawn of time.

('Address in the First Number of *Household Words*', 30 March 1850: *NCP* I, 223)

Dickens became the laureate of the hearth and home. 'There is no contemporary English writer whose works are read so generally through the whole house, who can give pleasure to the servants as well as the mistress, to the older children as well as to the master', observed one contemporary reviewer.

The greatest celebration of the spirit of home is, of course, the Dickensian Christmas. How better to live in the Household affections and thoughts than by creating immortal images of that most homely of festivities? At home and abroad, for over a century after his death, Dickens's name is intimately associated with Christmas. Christmas is the occasion for all the living generations of the family to reunite, and for all hard feelings to dissolve in warm conviviality:

> Who can be insensible to the outpourings of good feeling, and the honest interchange of affectionate attachment, which abound at this season of the year? A Christmas family-party! We know nothing in nature more delightful! There seems a magic in the very name of Christmas. Petty jealousies and discords are forgotten; social feelings are awakened, in bosoms to which they have long been strangers; father and son or brother and sister, who have met and passed with averted gaze, or a look of cold recognition, for months before, proffer and return the cordial embrace, and bury their past animosities in their present happiness. Kindly hearts that have yearned towards each other, but have been withheld by false notions of pride and self-dignity, are again reunited, and all is kindness and benevolence! Would that Christmas lasted the whole year through (as it ought), and that the prejudices and passions which deform our better nature, were never called into action among those to whom they should ever be strangers!
>
> ("A Christmas Dinner", *SB*, 221)

Christmas is a very cosy occasion. G.K. Chesterton remarked of Dickens's Christmas sentiment: 'It has cosiness, that is the comfort that depends upon a discomfort surrounding it'. Snow outside, blazing fires and hot punch indoors. The defect of this sentiment, Chesterton continues, was that Dickens tended some-times to 'pile up the cushions until none of the characters could move'. But the euphoria was irresistible. 'Christ-mas somehow felt warmer after reading that book', one of Dickens's first biographers recalled in 1858 — 'that book' was *Pickwick Papers:*

> As brisk as bees, if not altogether as light as fairies, did the four Pickwickians assemble on the morning of the twenty-second day of December, in the year of grace in which these, their faithfully-recorded adventures, were undertaken and accom-plished. Christmas was close at hand, in all his bluff and hearty honesty; it was the season of hospitality, merriment and open-heartedness; the old year was preparing, like an ancient philosopher, to call his friends around him, and amidst the sound of feasting and revelry to pass gently and calmly away. Gay and merry was the time, and gay and merry were at least four of the numerous hearts that were gladdened by its coming
>
> And numerous indeed are the hearts to which Christmas brings a brief season of happiness and enjoyment. How many families, whose members have been dispersed and scattered far and wide, in the restless struggles of life, are then reunited, and meet once again in that happy state of companionship and mutual good-will, which is a source of such pure and unalloyed delight, and one so incompatible with the cares and sorrows of the world, that the religious belief of the most civilised nations, and the rude traditions of the roughest savages, alike number it among the first joys of a future condition of existence, provided for the blest and happy! How many old recollections, and how many dormant sympathies, does Christmas time awaken!
>
> We write these words now, many miles distant from the spot at which, year after year, we met on that day a merry and joyous circle. Many of the hearts that throbbed so gaily then, have ceased to beat; many of the looks that shone so brightly then, have ceased to glow; the hands we grasped have grown cold; the eyes we sought have hid their lustre in the grave; and yet the old house, the room, the merry voices and smiling faces, the jest, the laugh, the most minute and trivial circumstances connected with those happy meetings, crowd upon our mind at each recurrence of the season, as the last assemblage had been but yesterday! Happy, happy Christmas, that can win us back to the delusions of our childish days; that can recall to the old man the pleasures of his youth; that can transport the sailor and the traveller, thousands of miles away, back to his own fireside and his quiet home!
>
> (*PP*, XXVIII, 374 - 5)

Dickens was in his early twenties when he wrote this celebration of Christmas. Fifteen years later he reflects on 'What Christmas is as we Grow Older':

Time was, with most of us, when Christmas Day encircling all our limited world like a magic ring left nothing out for us to miss or seek; bound together all our home enjoyments, affections, and hopes; grouped everything and every one around the Christmas fire; and made the little picture shining in our bright young eyes, complete.

Time came, perhaps, all too soon, when our thoughts over-leaped that narrow boundary; when there was some one (very dear, we thought then, very beautiful, and absolutely perfect) wanting to the fulness of our happiness; when we were wanting too (or we thought so, which did just as well) at the Christmas hearth by which that some one sat; and when we interwined with every wreath and garland of our life, that some one's name.

That was the time for the bright visionary Christmases which have long arisen from us to show faintly, after summer rain, in the palest edges of the rainbow! That was the time for the beautified enjoyment of the things that were to be, and never were, and yet the things that were so real in our resolute hope that it would be hard to say, now, what realities achieved since, have been stronger!

...is our life here, at the best, so constituted that, pausing as we advance at such a noticeable milestone in the track as this great birthday, we look back on the things that never were, as naturally and full as gravely as on the things that have been and are gone, or have been and still are? If it be so, and so it seems to be must we come to the conclusion that life is little better than a dream, and little worth the loves and striving that we crowd into it?

No! Far be such miscalled philosophy from us, dear Reader, on Christmas Day! Nearer and closer to our hearts be the Christmas spirit, which is the spirit of active usefulness, perseverance, cheerful discharge of duty, kindness and for-bearance! It is in the last virtues especially, that we are, or should be, strengthened by the unaccomplished visions of our youth; for, who shall say that they are not our teachers to deal gently with the impalpable nothings of the earth!

Therefore as we grow older, let us be more thankful that the circle of our Christmas associations and of the lessons that they bring, expands! Let us welcome every one of them, and summon them to take their places by the Christmas hearth.

Welcome, old aspirations, glittering creatures of an ardent fancy, to your shelter underneath the holly! We know you, and have not outlived you yet. Welcome, old projects and old loves, however fleeting, to your nooks among the steadier lights that turn round us. Welcome, all that was ever real to our hearts; and for the earnestness that made you real, thanks to heaven! Do we build no Christmas castles in the clouds now? Let our thoughts, fluttering like butterflies among these flowers of children, bear witness. Before this boy, there stretches out a Future, brighter than we ever looked on in our old romantic time, but bright with honour and with truth. Around this little head on which the sunny curls lie heaped, the graces sport, as prettily, as airily, as when there was no scythe within the reach of time to shear away the curls of our first-love. Upon another girl's face near it — placider but smiling bright — a quiet and contented little face, we see Home fairly written. Shining from the word, as rays shine from a star, we see how, when our graves are old, other hopes than ours are young, other hearts than ours are moved; how other ways are smoothed; how other happiness blooms, ripens, and decays — no, not decays, for other homes and other bands of children, not yet in being nor for ages yet to be, arise, and bloom and ripen to the end of all!

("What Christmas is as we Grow Older", *CS*, 21-3)

It is the Pickwickian Christmas that we associate most strongly with Dickens. It is the manner in which it is celebrated there that has become associated with a typically English festivity. "Hospitality, merriment, open-heartedness; Gay and merry...pure and unalloyed delight". This is the keynote. Christmas 'As we Grow Older' changes. The Christmas spirit then is the 'spirit of active usefulness, perseverance, cheerful discharge of duty, kindness and forbearance...earnestness'. It is an altogether more sober affair. We may be reminded of that crucial difference between David Copperfield's child-wife and Agnes. The difference between the two Christmases points up not only the discrepancy between the childhood and adult vision, but also the changes that had stolen over England from the Regency days to the mid-century. Our 'old romantic time' in the last Christmas passage is perhaps an echo of the pre-Victorian years of Dickens's childhood, the good old days. When, in that same *Pickwick Papers* chapter, Dickens fancifully personified Christmas, it was as 'quite a country gentleman of the old school'[1]. But over the years, this robust, genial unalloyed delight is checked by, among other things, the moral pieties of Evangelical reform, and by the 'disciplined heart' of Dickens himself. In spite of change, though, home remained as central as ever. Mamie Dickens recalled the Gad's Hill Christmases of the 1860s:

> But I think that our Christmas and New Year's tides at "Gad's Hill" were the happiest of all. Our house was always filled with guests, while a cottage in the village was reserved for the use of the bachelor members of our holiday party. My father himself, always deserted work for the week, and that was almost our greatest treat. He was the fun and life of those gatherings, the true Christmas spirit of sweetness and hospitality filling his large and generous heart. Long walks with him were daily treats to be remembered. Games passed our evenings merrily. "Proverbs", a game of memory, was very popular, and it was one in which either my aunt or myself was apt to prove winner. Father's annoyance at our failure sometimes was very amusing, but quite genuine. "Dumb Crambo" was another favorite, and one in which my father's great imitative ability showed finely. I remember one evening his dumb showing of the word "frog" was so extremely laughable that the memory of it convulsed Marcus Stone, the clever artist, when he tried some time later to imitate it.
>
> One very severe Christmas, when the snow was so deep as to make out-door amusement or entertainment for our guests impossible, my father suggested that he and the inhabitants of the "bachelors" cottage, should pass the time in unpacking the French chalet, which had been sent to him by Mr. Fechter, and which reached Higham Station in a large number of packing cases. Unpacking these and fitting the pieces together gave them interesting employment, and some topics of conversation for our luncheon party.
>
> Our Christmas Day dinners at "Gad's Hill" were particularly bright and cheery, some of our nearest neighbours joining our home party. The Christmas plum pudding had its own special dish of coloured "repousse" chine, ornamented with holly. The pudding was placed on this with a sprig of real holly in the centre, lighted, and in this state placed in front of my father, its

1. A description oddly deleted after the novel's first edition: see Penguin English Library *Pickwick Papers* (ed. R. Patten) p. 994

arrival being always the signal for applause. A prettily decorated table was his special pleasure, and from my earliest girlhood the care of this devolved upon me. When I had everything in readiness, he would come with me to inspect the result of my labours, before dressing for dinner, and no word except of praise ever came to my ears.

He was a wonderfully neat and rapid carver, and I am happy to say taught me some of his skill in this. I used to help him in our home parties at "Gad's Hill" carving at a side table, returning to my seat opposite him as soon as my duty was ended. On Christmas Day we all had our glasses filled, and then my father, raising his, would say, "Here's to us all. God Bless us"! a toast which was rapidly and willingly drunk. His conversation, as may be imagined, was often extremely humorous, and I have seen the servants who were waiting at table, convulsed often with laughter at his droll remarks and stories. Now, as I recall these gatherings, my sight grows blurred with the tears that rise to my eyes. But I love to remember them, and to see, if only in memory, my father at his own table, surrounded by his own family and friends — a beautiful Christmas spirit.

(Mamie Dickens, *op.cit.*, 35 - 9)

Such a Christmas spirit he must have seemed to several thousands more. When news of his death on June 9th 1870 spread rapidly around London, a little ragged girl in Drury Lane was heard to exclaim: 'Dickens dead? Then will Father Christmas die too?'

Dickens and Christmas, the Household affections and thoughts, the domestic virtues and their angelic little incarnations — all of these belong together. The national identity owed largely to Dickens whatever international reputation it had as home-loving people:

Every traveller has a home of his own, and he learns to appreciate it the more from his wandering. If he has no home, he learns the same lesson unselfishly by turning to the homes of other men. He may have his experiences of cheerful and exciting pleasures abroad; but home is best, after all, and its pleasures are the most heartily and enduringly prized.

(*Speeches*, 173: London, 30 December 1854)

'Home' wrote the American poet Robert Frost, 'is the place where, when you have to go there, they have to take you in'. But here, from *Little Dorrit*, is Arthur Clennam's heart-breaking welcome home after some twenty years abroad:

> He crossed by St. Paul's and went down, at a long angle, almost to the water's edge, through some of the crooked and descending streets which lie (and lay more crookedly and closely then) between the river and Cheapside. Passing, now the mouldy hall of some obsolete Worshipful Company, now the illuminated windows of a Congregationless Church that seemed to be waiting for some adventurous Belzoni to dig it out and discover its history; passing silent warehouses and wharves— and here and there a narrow alley leading to the river, where a wretched little bill, FOUND DROWNED, was weeping on the wet wall; he came at last to the house he sought. An old brick house, so dingy as to be all but black, standing by itself within a gateway. Before it, a square court-yard where a shrub or two and a patch of grass were as rank (which is saying much) as the iron railings enclosing them were rusty; behind it, a jumble of roots. It was a double house, with long, narrow, heavily-framed windows. Many years ago, it had had it in its mind to slide down sideways; it had been propped up, however, and was leaning on some half-dozen gigantic crutches: which gymnasium for the neighbouring cats, weather-stained, smoke-blackened, and overgrown, with weeds, appeared in these latter days to be no very sure reliance.
>
> 'Nothing changed,' said the traveller, stopping to look round. 'Dark and miserable as ever. A light in my mother's window, which seems never to have been extinguished since I came home twice a year from school, and dragged my box over this pavement. Well, well, well!'
>
> (*LD*, III, 31)

He is admitted to the house, with a cold reception, by the ancient and grotesque retainer Jeremiah Flintwinch:

> 'How weak am I,' said Arthur Clennam, when he was gone, 'that I could shed tears at this reception! I who have never experienced anything else; who have never expected anything else.'
>
> He not only could, but did. It was a momentary yielding of a nature that had been disappointed from the dawn of its perceptions, but had not quite given up all its hopeful yearnings yet. He subdued it, took up the candle and examined the room. The old articles of furniture were in their old places; the Plagues of Egypt, much the dimmer for the fly and smoke plagues of

London, were framed and glazed upon the walls. There was the old cellaret with nothing in it, lined with lead, like a sort of coffin in compartments; there was the old dark closet, also with nothing in it, of which he had been many a time the sole contents, in days of punishment, when he had regarded it as the veritable entrance to that bourne to which the tract had found him galloping. There was the large, hard-featured clock on the side-board, which he used to see bending its figured brows upon him with a savage joy when he was behind-hand with his lessons, and which, when it was wound up once a week with a iron handle, used to sound as if it were growling in ferocious anticipation of the miseries into which it would bring him. But here was the old man come back, saying, 'Arthur, I'll go before and light you'.

Arthur followed him up the staircase, which was panelled off into spaces like so many mourning tablets, into a dim bed-chamber, the floor of which had gradually so sunk and settled, that the fireplace was in a dell. On a black bier-like sofa in this hollow, propped up behind with one great angular black bolster, like the block at a state execution in the good old times, sat his mother in a widow's dress.

She and his father had been at variance from his earliest remembrance. To sit speechless himself in the midst of rigid silence, glancing in dread from the one averted face to the other, had been the peacefullest occupation of his childhood. She gave him one glassy kiss, and four stiff fingers muffled in worsted.

(*Ibid.*, pp.32-3)

This homecoming is a kind of sacrilege. It is an entry into death rather than the rejuvenation of the Dickensian Christmas idyll.

The chapter began with Dickens's nostalgic cry from America. We can close it with the description, from *Martin Chuzzlewit*, of the ship from America nearing the English shore, and the feelings of the passengers Martin and Mark Tapley as they catch sight of their homeland after a year away:

It was mid-day, and high water in the English port for which the Screw was bound, when, borne in gallantly upon the fulness of the tide, she let go her anchor in the river.

Bright as the scene was: fresh, and full of motion; airy, free, and sparkling; it was nothing to the life and exultation in the breasts of the two travellers, at sight of the old churches, roofs, and darkened chimney stacks of Home. The distant roar, that swelled up hoarsely from the busy streets, was music in their ears; the lines of people gazing from the wharves, were friends held dear; the canopy of smoke that overhung the town was brighter and more beautiful to them than if the richest silks of Persia had been waving in the air. And though the water going on its glistening track, turned, ever and again, aside to dance and sparkle round great ships, and heave them up; and leaped from off the blades of oars, a shower of diving diamonds; and wantoned with the idle boats, and swiftly passed, in many a sportive chase, through obdurate old iron rings, set deep into the stone-work of the quays; not even it was half so buoyant, and so restless, as their fluttering hearts, when yearning to set foot, once more, on native ground.

A year had passed, since those same spires and roofs had faded from their eyes. It seemed, to them, a dozen years. Some trifling changes, here and there, they called to mind; and wondered that they were so few and slight. In health and fortune, prospect and resource, they came back poorer men than they had gone away. But it was home. And though home is a name, a word, it is a strong one; stronger than magician ever spoke, or spirit answered to, in strongest conjuration.

(*MC*, XXXV, 548)

CHAPTER II

In Search of the Picturesque

> English landscape. The beautiful prospect, trim fields, clipped hedges, everything so neat and orderly—gardens, houses, roads. Where are the people who do all this?
>
> ('Memorandum Book': in *Letters N* III, 788)

Where indeed? The foreign visitor to England is invariably struck by the neat, swept appearance of the countryside. Emerson remarked in *English Traits* that 'England is a garden. Under an ash-coloured sky, the fields have been combed and rolled till they appear to have been finished with a pencil instead of a plough'. It is a domesticated landscape. Behind Dickens's puzzlement lies affection; for the well-ordered domestic ideal that he spent a lifetime promoting in social relations seems to have spilled over into the natural landscape of his own country.

As we consider the ways in which Dickens responded to the various features of the English landscape, and how that response in turn shaped some of those distinctive images of the English countryside that we associate with his writings, we may find it helpful to recall certain conventions of taste in the earlier nineteenth century to which Dickens makes interesting reactions.

The English were slow to recognise the scenic pleasures peculiar to their own country. The home tourist movement began in earnest only fifty years before the birth of Dickens, and, in the last third of the eighteenth century, established itself as the middle-class answer to the aristocrat's Grand Tour of Europe. Patriotic writers on the Lake District and the Scottish Highlands were soon comparing Britain's native landscapes with the

Alps, and discovered abundant delights to compensate for the humbler scale of their mountain regions. Theories of the Picturesque developed, introducing an adjective to match the authoritative Sublime and Beautiful which were the common currency of the tourist handbooks and which were more accurate as descriptions of, respectively, spectacular Alpine scenery and the serenity of the Italian Campagna. By the end of the eighteenth century, Picturesque came to be applied more and more to the modest but rich and infinitely varied character of the English countryside.

The early English tourist movement is also associated with that decisive shift of attention in the middle and latter part of the eighteenth century, particularly in poetry and painting, away from a sophisticated metropolitan and cosmopolitan culture towards remoter regions, and the humbler features of the national life. The latter shift may be said, indeed, to have helped prepare the way, in terms of public taste, for Dickens's first publication that sketched with such picturesque effectiveness middle and lower class life in London, the *Sketches by Boz*. Thomas Gray's elegiac celebration of the poor, obscure, 'unhonour'd Dead' lying in a small country churchyard typified this new interest in the middle of the eighteenth century. Towards the end of the century the poets Goldsmith and Crabbe (both early favourites of Dickens), Burns and Cowper, in their various ways, brought into clearer focus the rural poor set in the natural landscape: and ideas of a moral and spiritual integrity that is 'incorporated with the beautiful and permanent forms of nature' formed one of the central premises of Wordsworth's *Lyrical Ballads* in 1798 and 1800. Wordsworth also, whether he liked it or not, was one of the main contributors to the growing popularity (and populousness) of his own Lake District,[1] and in 1842 published an excellent *Guide* to the history and scenic beauties of the region.

1. See, for instance, his protests against the coming of the railway into his Lake District, mentioned below p. 68.

Dickens inherits much from the Romantics, (the preoccupation with childhood, for example) but he is neither a
worshipper of Nature as a moral guardian, nor particularly responsive to the more spectacular landscape of
his native country. He always has less appetite for
natural scenery than for human incident: the Dickensian
'picturesque' is largely confined to the human scene. But
his response to the English countryside, though unob-
trusive, is in many ways a profound one.

He was a very energetic traveller throughout Britain. In
his earlier years it was mainly for professional reasons,
connected with his duties as a political correspondent for
the *Morning Chronicle*, reporting local elections all round
the country:

> I went into the gallery of the House of Commons as a
> Parliamentary reporter when I was a boy not eighteen, . . . I have
> pursued the calling of a reporter under circumstances of which
> many of my brethren at home in England here, many of my
> modern successors, can form no adequate conception. I have
> often transcribed for the printer from my shorthand notes,
> important public speeches in which the strictest accuracy was
> required, and a mistake in which would have been to a young
> man severely compromising, writing on the palm of my hand,
> by the light of a dark lantern, in a post chaise and four,
> galloping through a wild country, all through the dead of night,
> at the then surprising rate of fifteen miles an hour . . . I have
> been, in my time, belated on miry by-roads, towards the small
> hours, in a wheelless carriage, with exhausted horses and
> drunken postboys, and have got back in time for publication, to
> be received with never-forgotten compliments by the late Mr
> Black [Editor of the *Chronicle*] coming in the broadest of Scotch
> from the broadest of hearts I ever knew.
>
> (*Speeches*, 346–47: London, 20 May 1865)

There was little enough time in these circumstances for
any sightseeing, even though the experience later yielded
splendid material for the Eatanswill episodes in *Pickwick
Papers*.

It was, however, as a relatively leisured tourist that he
later paid visits to the traditional Picturesque spots of
Britain: the West country, North Wales, the Lake District
and the Scottish Highlands. A Highlands tour in July

1841, which he took with his wife Kate and a few
eccentric friends and servants, proved to be an amusing
blend of wild scenery and wilder anecdotes that taxed
even his powers of description:

> It is impossible to say what a glorious scene it was. It rained as it
> never does rain anywhere but here. We conveyed Kate up a
> rocky pass to go and see the island of the Lady of the Lake, but
> she gave in after the first first five minutes, and we left her, very
> picturesque and uncomfortable, with Tom holding an umbrella
> over her head, while we climbed on. When we came back she
> had gone into the carriage. We were wet through to the skin,
> and came on in that four and twenty miles. Fletcher is very good
> natured, and of extraordinary use in these outlandish parts. His
> habit of going into kitchens and bars, disconcerting at Broad-
> stairs, is here of great service. Not expecting us till six, they
> hadn't lighted our fires when we arrived here; and if you had
> seen him (with whom the responsibility of the omission rested)
> running in and out of the sitting-room and the two bed-rooms
> with a great pair of bellows, with which he distractedly blew
> each of the fires out in turn, you would have died of laughing.
> He had on his head a great highland cap, on his back a white
> coat, and cut such a figure as even the inimitable can't
> depicter . . . .
> The Inns, inside and out, are the queerest places imaginable
> from the road, this one looks like a white wall, with windows in
> it by mistake. We have a good sittingroom though, on the first
> floor: as large (but not as lofty) as my study. The bedrooms are
> of that size which renders it impossible for you to move, after
> you have taken your boots off, without chipping pieces out of
> your legs. There isn't a basin in the Highlands which will hold
> my face; not a drawer which will open after you have put your
> clothes in it; not a waterbottle capacious enough to wet your
> toothbrush. The huts are wretched and miserable beyond all
> description. The food (for those who can pay for it) "not bad",
> as M would say: oatcake, mutton, hotch potch, trout from the
> loch, small beer bottled, marmalade, and whiskey. Of the last
> named article I have taken about a pint today. The weather is
> what they call "soft" — which means that the sky is a vast
> water-spout that never leaves off emptying itself; and the liquor
> has no more effect than water . . .I don't bore you with accounts
> of Ben this and that, and Lochs of all sorts of names, but this is a
> wonderful region. The way the mists were stalking today, and
> the clouds lying down upon the hills; the deep glens, the high
> rocks, the rushing waterfalls, and the roaring rivers down in
> deep gulfs below; were all stupendous. This house is wedged
> round by great heights that are lost in the clouds; and the loch,

twelve miles long, stretches out its dreary length before the
windows. In my next, I shall soar to the sublime, perhaps; in
this here present writing I confine myself to the ridiculous.

(*Letters P* II, 322-3. Forster: 5 July 1841)

It is interesting to see Dickens here associating the
Picturesque with the discomfort suffered by poor Kate.
He seems to have had little patience with one of the
traditional constituents of Picturesque that found aesthetic delights in scenes of rustic poverty — in, for example,
the colourful squalor of gipsy encampments. 'I am sorry
to remind you what fast friends picturesqueness and
Typhus often are', he once observed. He is horrified by
the Naples slums in an 1845 visit to Italy:

The condition of the common people here is abject and
shocking. I am afraid the conventional idea of the picturesque is
associated with such misery and degradation that a new
picturesque will have to be established as the world goes
onward.

(*Letters N* I, 658. Forster: 11 February 1845)

For one thing, the Picturesque challenges that precious
English — and at least *early* Dickensian — love of the
comfortable. Walter Scott had commented on this amusing incompatibility in *Waverley* when, in Chapter 8, his
hero arrives at Tully-Veolan hamlet and sees the rustic
village girls:

Nor could a lover of the picturesque have challenged either the
elegance of their costume, or the symmetry of their shape;
although, to say the truth, a mere Englishman, in search of the
comfortable, a word peculiar to his native tongue, might have
wished the clothes less scanty, the feet and legs somewhat
protected from the weather, the head and complexion shrouded
from the sun, or perhaps might even have thought the whole
person and dress considerably improved, by a plentiful appli-
cation of spring water, with a *quantum sufficit* of soap.

It is ironic, nonetheless, how many of the attributes of
the Picturesque have been absorbed into the popular
ideas associated with the epithet 'Dickensian'.

But we must return to the rigours of the Dickensian

Highlands. As he promised Forster, he now tries his hand at some 'sublime' description in the approach to Glencoe:

> All the way, the road had been among moors and mountains with huge masses of rock, which fell down God knows where, sprinkling the ground in every direction, and giving it the aspect of the burial place of a race of giants. Now and then we passed a hut or two, with neither window nor chimney, and the smoke of the peat fire rolling out at the door. But there were not six of these dwellings in a dozen miles; and anything so bleak and wild, and mighty in its loneliness, as the whole country, it is impossible to conceive. Glencoe itself is perfectly *terrible*. The pass is an awful place. It is shut in on each side by enormous rocks from which great torrents come rushing down in all directions. In amongst these rocks on one side of the pass (the left as we came) there are scores of glens, high up, which form such haunts as you might imagine yourself wandering in, in the very height and madness of a fever. They will live in my dreams for years — I was going to say as long as I live, and I seriously think so. The very recollection of them makes me shudder . . . . Well, I will not bore you with my impressions of these tremendous wilds, but they really are fearful in their grandeur and amazing solitude. Wales is a mere toy compared with them.
>
> (*Letters P* II, 324. Forster: 9 July 1841)

The party had to retrace its steps the next day:

> I was not at all ill pleased to have to come again through that awful Glencoe. If it had been tremendous on the previous day, yesterday it was perfectly horrific. It had rained all night, and was raining then, as it only does in these parts. Through the whole glen, which is ten miles long, torrents were boiling and foaming, and sending up in every direction spray like the smoke of great fires. They were rushing down every hill and mountain side, and tearing like devils across the path and down into the depths of the rocks. Some of the hills looked as if they were full of silver, and had cracked in a hundred places. Others as if they were frightened and had broken out into a deadly sweat. In others there was no compromise or division of streams, but one great torrent came roaring down with a deafening noise, and a rushing of water that was quite appalling.
>
> (*Ibid.*, p. 326. Forster: 11 July 1841)

It is significant that the one or two points here where the description is most effective — the torrents like devils,

and the hills frightened into a sweat — are those where
Dickens animates the natural scene: literally, it comes to
life.

One might well wish Dickens had recorded more of the
remoter spectacular scenery of Britain:

> I think of trying with Horne ...a kind of adaptation of an old
> idea I once had (when I was making my name) of a fanciful and
> picturesque Beauties of England and Wales .... Don't you think
> a Series of Places *well* chosen, and described *well*, with their
> peculiarities and popularities thoroughly seized, would be a
> very promising Series?
>
> (*Letters N* II, 335. Wills: 30 July 1851)

It surely would; but, unless one counts the 'Uncommercial Traveller' series in *All The Year Round* in the early
1860s, nothing much seems to have come from this
promising notion of 1851.

Partially in search of the Picturesque, Dickens visited
that most popular of all tourist attractions, the Lake
District, in 1857 during a tour with Wilkie Collins:

> I have arranged with Collins that he and I will start next
> Monday on a ten or twelve days' expedition to out-of-the-way
> places, to do (in inns and coast-corners) a little tour in search of
> an article and in avoidance of railroads. I must get a good name
> for it, and I propose it in five articles, one for the beginning of
> every number in the October part [of *Household Words*].
>
> (*Ibid.*, pp. 873-4. Forster: [August 1857])

The articles, written by Dickens and Collins together,
were published under the title *The Lazy Tour of Two Idle
Apprentices*. The *Tour* is generally more effective in
narrative of colourful incidents than in description of
scenery — an impression which further confirms the
view that his favourite kind of tour is one in which he
has the most congenial companionship, rather than the
most spectacular landscapes. In this sense an excursion
to Cornwall late in 1842 was deemed to have been an
enormous success:

> Blessed star of morning, such a trip as we had into Cornwall,
> just after Longfellow went away! The "we", means Forster,

Maclise, Stanfield (the renowned Marine Painter) and the Inimitable Boz. We went down into Devonshire by the Railroad, and there we hired an open carriage from an Innkeeper, patriotic in all Pickwick matters; and went on with Post Horses. Sometimes we travelled all night; sometimes all day; sometimes both. I kept the joint stock purse; ordered all the dinners and drinks, paid all the turnpikes; conducted facetious conversations with the postboys; and regulated the pace at which we travelled. Stanfield (an old sailor) consulted an enormous map on all disputed points of wayfaring: and referred moreover to a pocket compass and other scientific instruments. The luggage was in Forster's department; and Maclise, having nothing particular to do, sang songs. Heavens! If you could have seen the necks of bottles — distracting in their immense varieties of shape — peering out of the carriage pockets! If you could have witnessed the deep devotion of the postboys — the wild attachment of the Hostlers — the maniac glee of the waiters. If you could have followed us into the earthy old Churches we visited, and into the strange caverns on the gloomy sea-shore, and down into the depths of Mines, and up to the tops of giddy heights where the unspeakably green water was roaring I don't know how many hundred feet below! If you could have seen but one gleam of the bright fires by which we sat in the big rooms of ancient Inns at night, until long after the small hours had come and gone — or smelt but one steam of the *hot* punch (not white, dear Felton, like that amazing compound I sent you a taste of, but a rich, genial, glowing brown) which came in every evening in a huge broad china bowl! I never laughed in my life as I did on this journey. It would have done you good to hear me. I was choaking and gasping and bursting the buckle off the back of my stock all the way. And Stanfield (who is very much of your figure and temperament, but fifteen years older) got into such apoplectic entanglements that we were often obliged to beat him on the back with Portmanteaus before we could recover him. Seriously, I do believe there never was such a trip. And they made such sketches, those two men, in the most romantic of our halting places, that you would have sworn we had the Spirit of Beauty with us, as well as the Spirit of Fun.

(*Letters P* III, 414-6. Felton: 31 December 1842)

An important incidental to such tours, especially when the weather was so good, was the experience of the country inns of Britain, of which Dickens has left us so many rich impressions. The Cornwall trip evidently satisfied essential requirements here: ancient inns, bright fires, big rooms, and huge bowls of steaming hot punch.

Hospitality in mellow surroundings represents an ideal in these matters:

> The candles were brought, the fire was stirred up, and a fresh log of wood thrown on. In ten minutes' time, a waiter was laying the cloth for dinner, the curtains were drawn, the fire was blazing brightly, and everything looked (as everything always does, in all decent English inns) as if the travellers had been expected and their comforts prepared, for days beforehand.
>
> (*PP*, LI, 716)

The Maypole Inn in *Barnaby Rudge* (based on the King's Head pub at Chigwell in Essex) is one of the most ancient of all Dickens's inns, and a true specimen of the architectural Picturesque:

> ...the Maypole was really an old house, a very old house, perhaps as old as it claimed to be, and perhaps older, which will sometimes happen with houses of an uncertain, as with ladies of a certain age. Its windows were old diamond-pane lattices, its floors were sunken and uneven, its ceilings blackened by the hand of time, and heavy with massive beams. Over the doorway was an ancient porch, quaintly and grotesquely carved; and here on summer evenings the more favoured customers smoked and drank — ay, and sang many a good song too, sometimes — reposing on two grim-looking high backed settles, which, like the twin dragons of some fairy tale, guarded the entrance to the mansion.
>
> In the chimneys of the disused rooms, swallows had built their nests for many a long year, and from earliest spring to latest autumn whole colonies of sparrows chirped and twittered in the eaves. There were more pigeons about the dreary stable yard and out-buildings than anybody but the landlord could reckon up. The wheeling and circling flights of runts, fantails, tumblers, and pouters, were perhaps not quite consistent with the grave and sober character of the building, but the monotonous cooing, which never ceased to be raised by some among them all day long, suited it exactly, and seemed to lull it to rest. With its overhanging stories, drowsy little panes of glass, and front bulging out and projecting over the pathway, the old house looked as if it were nodding in its sleep. Indeed, it needed no very great stretch of fancy to detect in it other resemblances to humanity. The bricks of which it was built had originally been a deep dark red, but had grown yellow and discoloured like an old man's skin; the sturdy timbers had

decayed like teeth; and here and there the ivy, like a warm garment to comfort it in its age, wrapt its green leaves closely round the time-worn walls.

It was a hale and hearty age though, still: and in the summer or autumn evenings, when the glow of the setting sun fell upon the oak and chestnut trees of the adjacent forest, the old house, partaking of its lustre, seemed their fit companion, and to have many good years of life in him yet.

(*BR*, I, 1-2)

But ripe old houses, bright fires and hearty hospitality are not the rule, and the number of 'decent English inns' in Dickens is curiously small when we consider the *beau ideal* that we preserve of the Dickensian inn. It is with qualified nostalgia that Dickens recalls the trials and rewards of the old coaching days:

I dare say most of us had experience of the extinct 'fast coaches', the 'Wonders', 'Taglionis' and 'Tallyhos', of other days. I dare say most of us remember certain modest post-chaises, dragging us down interminable roads through slush and mud, to little country towns with no visible populations except half a dozen men in smock frocks smoking pipes under the lee of the Town Hall; half a dozen women with umbrellas and pattens, and a washed-out dog or so shivering under the gables to complete the desolate picture. We can all discourse I dare say, if so minded, upon our recollections of the 'Talbot', the 'King's Head', or the 'Lion' of those days. We have all been to that room on the ground floor on one side of the old inn yard, not quite free from a certain smell of tobacco, where the cruets on the sideboard were usually absorbed by the skirts of the box coats that hung from the wall where, driving-seats were laid out at every turn like so many human mantraps, where country members framed and glazed were eternally presenting that petition which somehow or other made their glory in the country, though nothing else had ever come of it. Where the *Book of Roads*, the first and last thing always required, was always missing, and generally wanted the first and last dozen leaves, and where one man was always arriving at some unusual hour in the middle of the night, and requiring his breakfast at a similarly singular period of the day. I have no doubt we could all be very eloquent on the comforts of our favourite hotel, wherever it was, — its beds, its stables, its vast amount of posting, its excellent cheese, its head waiter, its capital dishes, its pigeon-pies, or its 1820 port. Or possibly we could recall our chaste and innocent admiration of its landlady, or our fraternal regard for its handsome chambermaid.

(*Speeches*, 172: London 30 December 1854)

Memory is, in general, rather kinder than it was to the narrator of Dickens's 1855 Christmas story *The Holly-Tree*, when his imagination rambles over past experiences of the public-houses — those 'monuments of British submission to rapacity and extortion':

This reminiscence brought the Welsh Inns in general before me; with the women in their round hats, and the harpers with their white beards (venerable, but humbugs, I am afraid), playing outside the door while I took my dinner. The transition was natural to the Highland Inns, with the oatmeal bannocks, the honey, the venison steaks, the trout from the loch, the whisky, and perhaps (having the materials so temptingly at hand) the Athol brose. Once was I coming south from the Scottish Highlands in hot haste, hoping to change quickly at the station at the bottom of a certain wild historical glen, when these eyes did with mortification see the landlord come out with a telescope and sweep the whole prospect for the horses; which horses were away picking up their own living, and did not heave in sight under four hours. Having thought of the loch-trout, I was taken by quick association to the Angler's Inns of England (I have assisted at innumerable feats of angling by lying in the bottom of the boat, whole summer days, doing nothing with the greatest perseverance; which I have generally found to be as effectual towards the taking of fish as the finest tackle and the utmost science), and to the pleasant white, clean, flower-pot-decorated bedrooms of those inns, overlooking the river, and the ferry, and the green ait, and the church-spire, and the country bridge; and to the peerless Emma with the bright eyes and the pretty smile, who waited, bless her! with a natural grace that would have converted Blue-Beard. Casting my eyes upon my Holly-Tree fire, I next discerned among the glowing coals the pictures of a score or more of those wonderful English posting-inns which we are all so sorry to have lost, which were so large and so comfortable, and which were such monuments of British submission to rapacity and extortion. He who would see these houses pining away, let him walk from Basingstoke, or even Windsor, to London by way of Hounslow, and moralise on their perishing remains; the stables crumbling to dust; unsettled labourers and wanderers bivouacking in the out-houses; grass growing in the yards; the rooms, where erst so many hundred beds of down were made up, let off to Irish lodgers at eighteen pence a week, a little ill-looking beer-shop shrinking in the tap of former days, burning coach-house gates for firewood, having one of its two windows bunged up as if it had received punishment in a fight with the Railroad; a low bandy-legged, brick-making bulldog standing in the doorway.

('The Holly-Tree', *CS*, 112-3)

The end of the coaching days made many a change. This description suggests that in those latter days the poor Home Counties stage-coach commuter is less likely to be rewarded with full-flavoured hospitality than is the more adventurous tourist in his pursuit of the remote Picturesque.

It is not really surprising that a writer so centred on the hearth and home should have found little or no dramatic use for the sort of grand natural scenery so appealing to the tourist. Rural pleasures in Dickens's fiction are on a smaller scale altogether, and serve a rather restricted range of purposes. In the early works, the unspoilt countryside is the proper setting for physical and spiritual recovery (a dilute form of the Wordsworthian ideal). In this context sublime, exhilarating scenery is wholly out of place. For example, Oliver Twist's place of recovery, under the protection of the Maylies, is about the nearest Dickens comes to describing his version of an earthly paradise. The Maylies live at Chertsey in Surrey, but as Spring comes they close up their house and leave with Oliver for a cottage at some distance in the country (the place is unspecified):

Who can describe the pleasure and delight, the peace of mind and soft tranquillity, the sickly boy felt in the balmy air, and among the green hills and rich woods, of an inland village! Who can tell how scenes of peace and quietude sink into the minds of pain-worn dwellers in close and noisy places, and carry their own freshness, deep into their jaded hearts! Men who have lived in crowded, pent-up streets, through lives of toil, and who have never wished for change; men, to whom custom has indeed been second nature, and who have come almost to love each brick and stone that formed the narrow boundaries of their daily walks; even they, with the hand of death upon them, have been known to yearn at last for one short glimpse of Nature's

face; and, carried far from the scenes of their old pains and
pleasures, have seemed to pass at once into a new state of
being. Crawling forth, from day to day, to some green sunny
spot, they have had such memories wakened up within them by
the sight of the sky, and hill and plain, and glistening water,
that a foretaste of heaven itself has soothed their quick decline,
and they have sunk into their tombs, as peacefully as the sun
whose setting they watched from their lonely chamber window
but a few hours before, faded from their dim and feeble sight!
The memories which peaceful country scenes call up are not of
this world, nor of its thoughts and hopes. Their gentle influence
may teach us how to weave fresh garlands for the graves of
those we loved: may purify our thoughts, and bear down before
it old enmity and hatred; but beneath all this, there lingers, in
the least reflective mind, a vague and half-formed consciousness
of having held such feelings long before, in some remote and
distant time, which calls up solemn thoughts of distant times to
come, and bends down pride and worldliness beneath it.

It was a lovely spot to which they repaired. Oliver, whose
days had been spent among squalid crowds, and in the midst of
noise and brawling, seemed to enter on a new existence there.
The Rose and honeysuckle clung to the cottage walls; the ivy
crept round the trunks of the trees; and the garden-flowers
perfumed the air with delicious odours. Hard by, was a little
churchyard; not crowded with tall unsightly gravestones, but
full of humble mounds, covered with fresh turf and moss:
beneath which the old people of the village lay at rest . . . .

And when Sunday came, how differently the day was spent
from any way in which he had ever spent it yet! and how
happily too; like all the other days in that most happy time!
There was the little church, in the morning, with the green
leaves fluttering at the windows: the birds singing without: and
the sweet-smelling air stealing in at the low porch, and filling
the homely building with its fragrance. The poor people were so
neat and clean, and knelt so reverently in prayer, that it seemed
a pleasure, not a tedious duty, their assembling there together;
and though the singing might be rude, it was real, and sounded
more musical (to Oliver's ears at least) than any he had ever
heard in church before. Then, there were the walks as usual,
and many calls at the clean houses of the labouring men; and at
night, Oliver read a chapter or two from the Bible, which he had
been studying all the week, and in the performance of which
duty he felt more proud and pleased, than if he had been the
clergyman himself.

In the morning, Oliver would be a-foot by six o'clock,
roaming the fields, and plundering the hedges far and wide for
nosegays of wild flowers, with which he would return laden,

home; and which took great care and consideration to arrange,
to the best advantage, for the embellishment of the breakfast-
table. There was fresh groundsel, too, for Miss Maylie's birds,
with which Oliver, who had been studying the subject under
the able tuition of the village clerk, would decorate the cages, in
the most approved taste. When the birds were made all spruce
and smart for the day, there was usually some little commission
of charity to execute in the village; or, failing that, there was rare
cricket-playing, sometimes on the green; or failing that, there
was always something to do in the garden, or about the plants,
to which Oliver (who had studied this science also, under the
same master, who is a gardener by trade) applied himself with
hearty goodwill, until Miss Rose made her appearance; when
there were a thousand commendations to be bestowed on all he
had done.

(*OT*, XXXII, 237-9)

This is a generalised and idealised picture, of course, but
it is one that is central to Dickens's imagination. It is a
scene that is echoed throughout his works, and, because
its features are so frequently and ardently impressed on
his reader's imagination, it has come to define one of the
most popular images, at home and abroad, of the typical
English country village. Just the year before *Oliver Twist*
appeared Dickens had published a polemical pamphlet
entitled *Sunday Under Three Heads* attacking contemporary
moves in Parliament to restrict the opportunities for
public recreation on Sundays. The third 'Head' presents
a picture of what Sunday ought to be:

I was travelling in the west of England a summer or two back,
and was induced by the beauty of the scenery, and the seclusion
of the spot, to remain for the night in a small village, distant
about seventy miles from London. The next morning was
Sunday; and I walked out, towards the church. Groups of
people — the whole population of the little hamlet apparently —
were hastening in the same direction. Cheerful and good-
humoured congratulations were heard on all sides, as
neighbours overtook each other, and walked on in company.
Occasionally I passed an aged couple, whose married daughter
and her husband were loitering by the side of the old people,
accommodating their rate of walking to their feeble pace, while a
little knot of children hurried on before; stout young labourers
in clean round frocks; and buxom girls with healthy, laughing
faces, were plentifully sprinkled about in couples, and the

whole scene was one of quiet and tranquil contentment, irresistibly captivating. The morning was bright and pleasant, the hedges were green and blooming, and a thousand delicious scents were wafted on the air, from the wild flowers which blossomed on either side of the footpath. The little church was one of those venerable simple buildings which abound in the English counties; half overgrown with moss and ivy, and standing in the centre of a little plot of ground, which, but for the green mounds with which it was studded, might have passed for a lovely meadow.

> *(Sunday Under Three Heads, UT & RP, 658-9)*

In the evening of that day he comes across a game of cricket in the meadow beyond the churchyard, a recreation not only unchecked by the clergyman, but even encouraged. One of the most potent influences on Dickens's fond pictures of English countryside was the American writer Washington Irving, whose impressions of England during a visit in 1815 were recorded in his *Sketch Book* (1820), a great favourite among Dickens's early reading. Compare this passage from one of Irving's sketches 'Rural Life in England', with the two previous passages:

> A great part of the island is rather level, and would be monotonous, were it not for the charms of culture: but it is studded and gemmed, as it were with castles and palaces, and embroidered with parks and gardens. It does not abound in grand and sublime prospects, but rather in little home scenes of rural repose and sheltered quiet. Every antique farmhouse and moss-grown cottage is a picture; and as the roads are continually winding, and the view is shut in by groves and hedges, the eye is delighted by a continual succession of small landscapes of captivating loveliness.
>
> The great charm, however, of English scenery is the moral feeling that seems to pervade it. It is associated in the mind with ideas of order, of quiet, of sober, well-established principles, of hoary usage and reverend custom. Everything seems to be the growth of regular and peaceful existence. The old church of remote architecture, with its low, massive portal, its gothic tower, its windows rich with tracery and painted glass, in scrupulous preservation, its stately monuments of warriors and worthies of the olden times, ancestors of the present lords of the soil: its tombstones, recording successive generations of sturdy yeomanry, whose progeny still plough the same fields, and

kneel at the same altar — the parsonage, a quaint, irregular pile, partly antiquated, but repaired and altered in the tastes of various ages and occupants — the stile and footpaths leading from the churchyard, across pleasant fields, and along shady hedgerows, according to an immemorial right of way — the neighbouring village, with its venerable cottages, its public green sheltered by trees, under which the forefathers of the present race have sported — the antique family mansion, standing apart in some little rural domain, but looking down with a protecting air on the surrounding scene: all these common features of English landscape evince a calm and settled security and hereditary transmission of home-bred virtues and local attachments, that speak deeply and touchingly for the moral character of the nation.

It is a pleasing sight of a Sunday morning, when the bell is sending its sober melody across the quiet fields, to behold the peasantry in their best finery, with ruddy faces and modest cheerfulness, thronging tranquilly along the green lanes to church; but it is still more pleasing to see them in the evenings, gathering about their cottage doors, and appearing to exult in the humble comforts and embellishments which their own hands have spread around them.

Hazlitt complained that Irving's portrait of England was anachronistic and dependent on fanciful literary inspiration rather than on contemporary social realities. But it is frequently just this idealised way of describing the country that Dickens perpetuates in his own writing. For example, Irving's description is remarkably close, in particular details and general sentiment, to the ancient village in which little Nell is to spend her last days in *The Old Curiosity Shop:*

> They admired everything — the old grey porch, the mullioned windows, the venerable gravestones dotting the green churchyard, the ancient tower, the very weathercock; the brown thatched roofs of cottage, barn, and homestead, peeping from among the trees; the stream that rippled by the distant watermill; the blue Welsh mountains far away.
>
> (*OCS*, XLVI, 347)

For Nell such a setting is "A quiet, happy place — a place to live and learn to die in!" Here is the link with the *Oliver Twist* passage, where, even before the description has begun to particularise the honey-suckle on the cottages and the little church with its 'humble mounds' (reminding us of Thomas Gray's elegised country churchyard), the reader is prompted to associate the scene with heaven, with ideas of an eternal paradise spreading away on either side of human existence. The last few sentences of that first paragraph represent Dickens's intimations of immortality from recollections of early childhood.

This is the kind of rural setting that carries a full weight of significance in Dickens's world, and becomes more than a backdrop for the human drama. As Irving remarked, this kind of English scenery seems instinct with 'moral feeling'. What signalises the *Oliver Twist* setting is not exhilarating natural energy and freshness, but a calm mellow domesticity. In such a landscape nothing threatens: the natural imagery is all pleasantly expressive of a desire to co-operate with the human scene.

Some twenty years later, in his Chapter on the 'Turnerian Picturesque' in volume IV of *Modern Painters*, Ruskin endeavoured to define the character of the English Picturesque as it might strike the traveller returning from the Continent:

> ...that marvellous smallness both of houses and scenery, so that a ploughman in the valley has his head on a level with the tops of all the hills in the neighbourhood; and a house is organized into a complete establishment — parlour, kitchen, and all, with a knocker to its door, and a garret window to its roof, and a bow to its second story, on a scale of 12 feet wide by 15 feet high, so that three such at least would go into the granary of an ordinary Swiss cottage; and also our serenity of perfection, our peace of conceit, everything being done that vulgar minds can conceive as wanting to be done; the spirit of well-principled housemaids everywhere, exerting itself for perpetual propriety and renovation, so that nothing is old, but only "old-fashioned", and contemporary, as it were, in date and impressiveness only with last year's bonnets.

Smallness, serenity, and the spirit of well-principled housemaids — it is precisely this spirit that animates many of Dickens's favoured country settings. His poor are neat and clean, the caged birds spruce and smart, the gardens are well tended. Like Christmas, it has a special cosiness — 'one at least of the essentials' of which, Chesterton declared, was 'smallness, smallness in preference to largeness, smallness for smallness' sake'.

A well-ordered life and a country setting is the twin reward for many of Dickens's heroes and heroines. Here is Esther Summersons's first sight of her own 'Bleak House' where, through the kindess of her old guardian, she is to start her married life with Allan Woodcourt:

> We went on by a pretty little orchard, where the cherries were nestling among the green leaves and the shadows of the apple-trees were sporting on the grass, to the house itself, — a cottage, quite a rustic cottage of doll's rooms; but such a lovely place, so tranquil and so beautiful, with such a rich and smiling country spread around it; with water sparkling away into the distance, here all overhung with summer-growth, there turning a humming mill; at its nearest point glancing through a meadow by the cheerful town, where cricket-players were assembling in bright groups, and a flag was flying from a white tent that rippled in the sweet west wind. And still, as we went through the pretty rooms, out at the little rustic verandah doors, and underneath the tiny wooden colonnades, garlanded with woodbine, jasmine and honeysuckle, I saw, in the papering on the walls, in the colours of the furniture, in the arrangement of all the pretty objects, my little tastes and fancies, my little methods and inventions which they used to laugh at while they praised them, my odd ways everywhere.
>
> (*BH*, LXIV, 856)

Consider how often all the objects are described as little. The cottage is hardly more than a doll's house. The scale — Ruskin's 'marvellous smallness' again — is evidently important to ensure happiness. It is the toymaker's dream, this miniature version of the adult world. We are to recognise it as the restoration of her lost childhood to poor Esther who, years ago, and with full consciousness of the act's symbolic significance, buried her doll.

The association of virtue with benign ordered country settings is persistent. In his plans for the Home for Fallen Women Dickens reminded Miss Coutts that 'The cultivation of little gardens, if they be no bigger than graves, is a great resource, and a great reward' (*Letters C*, 87: 5 October 1846). He was perhaps aware of the recommendations, three years earlier, of the Report from the Parliamentary Select Committee on the Labouring Poor which pointed out that 'Many striking instances have been stated...where the possession of an allotment has been the means of reclaiming the criminal, reforming the dissolute, and of changing the whole moral character and conduct'. Choice countryside settings are also important to Dickens for more private sentimental reasons, as Forster suggested :

> Excepting always the haunts and associations of his childhood, Dickens had no particular sentiment of locality.
>
> (Forster, 521)

Dickens's feelings about Rochester confirm this:

> As I peered about its odd corners with interest and wonder when I was a very little child, few people can find a greater charm in that ancient city than I do.
>
> (*Letters N* III, 442. W. Rye: 3 November 1865)

He spent his happiest childhood years at Chatham and in the rolling countryside around Rochester. That fictional pastoral haven, Dingley Dell, is only about fifteen miles from Rochester. It is not surprising, therefore, that the idealised rural scenery, little inland villages and seaside 'watering-places' — fictional or real — so often bear the Kentish stamp; for this is home to Dickens. When, with very mixed feelings, he completed *David Copperfield*, a curious nostalgia took possession of him:

> I have just finished Copperfield and don't know whether to laugh or cry... I have an idea of wandering somewhere for a day or two — to Rochester, I think, where I was a small boy — to get all this fortnight's work out of my head.
>
> (*Letters N* II, 241. Coutts: 23 October 1850)

A few years later he was to buy Gad's Hill Place, the place that inspired a very particular sentiment of locality:

> It is so old-fashioned, plain, and comfortable. On the summit of

Gad's Hill, with a noble prospect at the side and behind, looking down into the Valley of the Medway. Lord Darnley's Park at Cobham (a beautiful place with a noble walk through a wood) is close by it; and Rochester is within a mile or two. It is only an hour and a quarter from London by the Railway. To Crown all, the sign of the Sir John Falstaff is over the way, and I used to look at it as a wonderful Mansion (which God knows it is not), when I was a very odd little child with the first faint shadows of all my books in my head — I suppose.

(*Ibid.*, p. 743. Coutts: 9 February 1856)

The antiquity of the place is itself a recommendation. When one adds its associations with Falstaff and with Dickens's own childhood one can see how irresistible it must have been for him. The countryside around Chatham and Gravesend he knew well, both its beauties and its more formidable aspects. The Kent marsh country by the Thames estuary is superbly evoked in his early chapters of *Great Expectations*, when, as in some nightmare, the landscape's misty images seem to dissolve, solidify and shape themselves to the 'oppressed conscience' of the young Pip:

Ours was the marsh country, down by the river, within, as the river wound, twenty miles of the sea. My first most vivid and broad impression of the identity of things, seems to me to have been gained on a memorable raw afternoon towards evening. At such a time I found out for certain, that this bleak place overgrown with nettles was the churchyard; and that Philip Pirrip, late of this parish, and also Georgiana wife of the above, were dead and buried; and that Alexander, Bartholomew, Abraham, Tobias, and Roger, infant children of the aforesaid, were also dead and buried; and that the dark flat wilderness beyond the churchyard, intersected with dykes and mounds and gates, with scattered cattle feeding on it, was the marshes; and that the low leaden line beyond was the river; and that the distant savage lair from which the wind was rushing, was the sea; and that the small bundle of shivers growing afraid of it all and beginning to cry, was Pip.

(*GE*, I, 1)

Later he returns to the marshland, bringing stolen food for the convict:

It was a rimy morning, and very damp. I had seen the damp lying on the outside of my little window, as if some goblin had been crying there all night, and using the window for a pocket-handkerchief. Now I saw the damp lying on the bare hedges and spare grass, like a coarser sort of spiders' webs; hanging itself from twig to twig and blade to blade. On every rail and gate, wet lay clammy, and the marsh-mist was so thick, that the wooden finger on the post directing people to our village — a direction which they never accepted, for they never came there — was invisible to me until I was quite close under it. Then, as I looked up at it, while it dripped, it seemed to my oppressed conscience like a phantom devoting me to the Hulks.

The mist was heavier yet when I got out upon the marshes, so that instead of my running at everything, everything seemed to run at me. This was very disagreeable to a guilty mind. The gates and dykes and banks came bursting at me through the mist, as if they cried as plainly as could be, 'A boy with Somebody-else's pork Pie! Stop him!' The cattle came upon me with like suddenness, staring out of their eyes, and steaming out of their nostrils, 'Halloa, young thief!' One black ox, with a white cravat on — who even had to my awakened conscience something of a clerical air — fixed me so obstinately with his eyes, and moved his blunt head round in such an accusatory manner as I moved round, that I blubbered out to him, 'I couldn't help it, sir! It wasn't for myself I took it!' Upon which he put down his head, blew a cloud of smoke out of his nose, and vanished with a kick-up of his hindlegs, and a flourish of his tail.

(GE, III, 14)

Brighter and more buoyant in setting is the little Kentish seaside village of Broadstairs, which 'beats all watering places' Dickens claimed. He and his family spent many a summer there. He describes the view from his study in the gaunt cliff-top mansion that came to be known as 'Bleak House':

Half awake and half asleep, this idle morning in our sunny window on the edge of a chalk-cliff in the old-fashioned watering-place to which we are a faithful resorter, we feel a lazy inclination to sketch its picture.

The place seems to respond. Sky, sea, beach, and village, lie as still before us as if they were sitting for the picture. It is dead low-water. A ripple plays among the ripening corn upon the cliff, as if it were faintly trying from recollection to imitate the sea; and the world of butterflies hovering over the crop of radish-seed are as restless in their little way as the gulls are in their larger manner when the wind blows. But the ocean lies winking in the sunlight like a drowsy lion — its glassy waters scarcely curve upon the shore — the fishing-boats in the tiny harbour are all stranded in the mud — our two colliers (our watering-place has a maritime trade employing that amount of shipping) have not an inch of water within a quarter of a mile of them, and turn, exhausted, on their sides, like faint fish of an antediluvian species. Rusty cables and chains, ropes and rings, undermost parts of posts and piles and confused timber-defences against the waves, lie strewn about, in a brown litter of tangled sea-weed and fallen cliff which looks as if a family of giants had been making tea here for ages, and had observed an untidy custom of throwing their tea-leaves on the shore.

We have a pier — a queer old wooden pier, fortunately without the slightest pretensions to architecture, and very picturesque in consequence. Boats are hauled up upon it, ropes are coiled all over it; lobster-pots, nets, masts, oars, spars, sails, ballast, and rickety capstans, make a perfect labyrinth of it. For ever hovering about this pier, with their hands in their pockets, or leaning over the rough bulwark it opposes to the sea, gazing through telescopes which they carry about in the same profound receptacles, are the Boatmen of our watering-place. Looking at them, you would say that surely these must be the laziest boatmen in the world. They lounge about, in obstinate and inflexible pantaloons that are apparently made of wood, the whole season through.

('Our English Watering Place', *HW* 2 August 1851: *UT & RP*, 391-95)

The old city of Rochester, consecrated in Dickens's imagination through those childhood associations, haunts his work. It provides the settings for early chapters in his first novel *Pickwick Papers* and for most of his last novel *Edwin Drood*. Separated by thirty-five years, these two views of Rochester (disguised as 'Cloisterham' in *Edwin Drood*) and its environs offer interesting contrasts:

Bright and pleasant was the sky, balmy the air, and beautiful the appearance of every object around, as Mr Pickwick leant over the balustrades of Rochester Bridge, contemplating nature, and waiting for breakfast. The scene was indeed one which might well have charmed a far less reflective mind, than that to which it was presented.

On the left of the spectator lay the ruined wall, broken in many places, and in some, overhanging the narrow beach below in rude and heavy masses. Huge knots of sea-weed hung upon the jagged and pointed stones, trembling in every breath of wind; and the green ivy clung mournfully round the dark and ruined battlements. Behind it rose the ancient castle, its towers roofless, and its massive walls crumbling away, but telling us proudly of its own might and strength, as when, seven hundred years ago, it rang with the clash of arms, or resounded with the noise of feasting and revelry. On either side, the banks of the Medway, covered with corn-fields and pastures, with here and there a windmill, or a distant church, stretched away as far as the eye could see, presenting a rich and varied landscape, rendered more beautiful by the changing shadows which passed swiftly across it, as the thin and half-formed clouds skimmed away in the light of the morning sun. The river, reflecting the clear blue of the sky, glistened and sparkled as it flowed noiselessly on; and the oars of the fishermen dipped into the water with a clear and liquid sound as the heavy but picturesque boats glided slowly down the stream.

(*PP*, V, 57)

From Mr Pickwick's wide-ranging contemplation of nature, the focus narrows in *Edwin Drood* to the old city itself:

An ancient city, Cloisterham, and no meet dwelling-place for any one with hankerings after the noisy world. A monotonous, silent city, deriving an earthy flavour throughout from its Cathedral crypt, and so abounding in vestiges of monastic graves, that the Cloisterham children grow small salad in the dust of abbots and abbesses and make dirt-pies of nuns and friars; while every ploughman in its outlying fields renders to once puissant Lord Treasurers, Archbishops, Bishops, and such-like, the attention which the Ogre in the story-book desired to render to his unbidden visitor, and grinds their bones to make his bread.

A drowsy city, Cloisterham, whose inhabitants seem to suppose, with an inconsistency more strange than rare, that all its changes lie behind it, and that there are no more to come. A queer moral to derive from antiquity, yet older than any traceable antiquity. So silent are the streets of Cloisterham (though prone to echo on the smallest provocation), that of a summer-day the sunblinds of its shops scarce dare to flap in the south wind; while the sun-browned tramps, who pass along and stare, quicken their limp a little, that they may the sooner get beyond the confines of its oppressive respectability. This is a feat not difficult of achievement, seeing that the streets of Cloisterham city are little more than one narrow street by which you get into it and get out of it: the rest being mostly disappointing yards with pumps in them and no thoroughfare — exception made of the Cathedral-close, and a paved Quaker settlement, in colour and general conformation very like a Quakeress's bonnet, up in a shady corner.

In a word, a city of another and a bygone time is Cloisterham, with its hoarse Cathedral bell, its hoarse rooks hovering about the Cathedral tower, its hoarser and less distinct rooks in the stalls far beneath. Fragments of old wall, saint's chapel, chapter-house, convent and monastery, have got incongruously or obstructively built into many of its houses and gardens, much as kindred jumbled notions have become incorporated into many of its citizens' minds. All things in it are of the past.

(*ED*, III, 18-19)

The Picturesque manner of the Pickwick description reminds one of tourist handbooks: it offers a stage set painted in bold primary colours. In *Edwin Drood* the spirit of the place has assumed a distinct peronality, (like the marsh country in *Great Expectations)*, and become a force to be reckoned with in the human drama of the novel. Cloisterham is a part of early English history that has survived as a kind of anachronism into the nineteenth century, long past any possibility of change. It hardly supports life anymore: its vital centre seems to be its Cathedral crypt. As its name implies, it is a retreat from the 'noisy world', but it is in no sense a place that offers moral or physical refreshment for the return to this world (as did old-fashioned Dingley Dell), nor is it one that fortifies the spirit for its journey to the next world, as little Nell's ancient village had done. It is rather the image of an England decaying from within, fossilizing through its 'oppressive respectability'.

Whether applied to people or places, much of what is old in the earlier novels is recommended to the readers' affections as well seasoned and morally dependable — think of Wardle and his old Manor Farm at Dingley Dell, or indeed, later, of Gad's Hill's appealingly 'old-fashioned' quality. Much of what is old in the later novels is represented as the source of confusion, prejudice and

moral atrophy. But if Dickens's reverence for things old
and tried was waning, what he saw as a new source of
energy for England was hardly reassuring. His picturesque rural scenes can, for a while, provide an earthly
paradise, with that carefully harmonised relationship
between domestic man and the natural setting. But no
Victorian could ignore the forces that were endangering
the survival of these same sequestered spots. Ironically,
the most feared intruder into the pastoral corners of
England was the very means by which suffocated city
dwellers could gain a day's respite in fields and fresh air.

CHAPTER III

Constant Shiftings and Changes

> ...we have fallen upon strange times, and live in
> days of constant shiftings and changes.
>
> ('Familiar Epistle', *SB*, 686)

The spread of industrialisation over England in the nineteenth century contributed more than anything else to these shiftings and changes; and there was nothing that so effectively symbolised these changes as the railway train. Dickens's own attitude towards it has strange but characteristic ambiguities. As might be expected, his descriptions frequently endow the engine with an animal life, so that, paradoxically, this product of British ingenuity that promised so much for the future is greeted as some kind of monster from the primaeval past. It is a descriptive habit that Dickens exploits for comic effect in giving the opinion of that veteran of the coaching days, old Tony Weller:

> "And as to the ingein, — a nasty, wheezin', creakin', gaspin', puffin', bustin' monster, alvays out o' breath, vith a shiny green-and-gold back, like a unpleasant beetle in that 'ere gas magnifier."
>
> (*MHC & CHE*, 80)

It is the same kind of primitive response as the American Indians' alarm at the 'Iron Horse' that invaded their quiet prairies. An early description occurs in *Dombey and Son*. In the course of a train journey from London to Leamington Mr Dombey's broodings over the death of his son are finely merged with the raucous presence of the train and the disturbing new perspectives on familiar landscapes that high-speed travel offers:

> He found no pleasure or relief in the journey. Tortured by these thoughts he carried monotony with him, through the rushing

51

landscape, and hurried headlong, not through a rich and varied country, but a wilderness of blighted plans and gnawing jealousies. The very speed at which the train was whirled along mocked the swift course of the young life that had been borne away so steadily and so inexorably to its foredoomed end. The power that forced itself upon its iron way — its own — defiant of all paths and roads, piercing through the heart of every obstacle, and dragging living creatures of all classes, ages, and degrees behind it, was a type of the triumphant monster, Death!

Away, with a shriek, and a roar, and a rattle, from the town, burrowing among the dwellings of men and making the streets hum, flashing out into the meadows for a moment, mining in through the damp earth, booming on in darkness and heavy air, bursting out again into the sunny day so bright and wide; away, with a shriek, and a roar, and a rattle, through the fields, through the woods, through the corn, through the hay, through the chalk, through the mould, through the clay, through the rock, among objects close at hand and almost in the grasp, ever flying from the traveller, and a deceitful distance ever moving slowly within him: like as in the track of the remorseless monster, Death!

Through the hollow, on the height, by the heath, by the orchard, by the park, by the garden, over the canal, across the river, where the sheep are feeding, where the mill is going, where the barge is floating, where the dead are lying, where the factory is smoking, where the stream is running, where the village clusters, where the great cathedral rises, where the bleak moor lies, and the wild breeze smooths or ruffles it at its inconstant will; away, with a shriek, and a roar, and a rattle, and no trace to leave behind but dust and vapour; like as in the track of the remorseless monster, Death!

Breasting the wind and light, the shower and sunshine, away, and still away, it rolls and roars, fierce and rapid, smooth and certain, and great works and massive bridges crossing up above, fall like a beam of shadow an inch broad, upon the eye, and then are lost. Away, and still away, onward and onward ever: glimpses of cottage-homes, of houses, mansions, rich estates, of husbandry and handicraft, of people, of old roads and paths that look deserted, small, and insignificant as they are left behind; and so they do, and what else is there but such glimpses, in the track of the indomitable monster, Death!

Away, with a shriek, and a roar, and a rattle, plunging down into the earth again, and working on in such a storm of energy and perseverance, that amidst the darkness and whirlwind the motion seemed reversed, and to tend furiously backward, until a ray of light upon the wet wall shows its surface flying past like a fierce stream. Away once more into the day, and through the day, with a shrill yell of exultation, roaring, rattling, tearing on,

spurning everything with its dark breath, sometimes pausing for
a minute where a crowd of faces are, that in a minute more are
not; sometimes lapping water greedily, and before the spout at
which it drinks has ceased to drip upon the ground, shrieking,
roaring, rattling through the purple distance!

(D & S, XX, 280-1)

The prose catches the rhythms of the train ride, its
lurching rapidity, and its remorseless levelling powers
that associate it closely with social as well as physical
changes to the country. A few years later, Dickens
experiments again with these rhythms, in describing a
journey by express train from London to Folkestone. The
versatility of his prose is remarkable. How many other
English writers before Dickens, given the experience of
railway travel, could have rendered it with such alarming
and illuminating zest?

Ah! The fresh air is pleasant . . . though it does blow over these
interminable streets, and scatter the smoke of this vast wilderness of chimneys. Here we are — no, I mean there we were,
for it has darted far into the rear — in Bermondsey where the
tanners live. Flash! The distant shipping in the Thames is gone.
Whirr! The little streets of new brick and red tile, with here and
there a flagstaff growing like a tall weed out of the scarlet beans,
and, everywhere, plenty of open sewer and ditch for the
promotion of the public health, have been fired off in a volley.
Whizz! Dust-heaps, market-gardens, and waste grounds. Rattle!
New Cross Station. Shock! There we were at Croydon. Burr-
r-r! The tunnel.

I wonder why it is that when I shut my eyes in a tunnel I
begin to feel as if I were going at an Express pace the other way.
I am clearly going back to London now . . . . No! After long
darkness, pale fitful streaks of light appear. I am still flying on
for Folkestone. The streaks grow stronger — become continuous
— become the ghost of day — become the living day — became
I mean — the tunnel is miles and miles away, and here I fly
through sunlight, all among the harvest and the Kentish hops....

Bang! We have let another Station off, and fly away
regardless. Everything is flying. The hop-gardens turn grace-
fully towards me, presenting regular avenues of hops in rapid
flight, then whirl away. So do the pools and rushes, haystacks,
sheep, clover in full bloom delicious to the sight and smell,
corn-sheaves, cherry-orchards, apple-orchards, reapers, glean-
ers, hedges, gates, fields that taper off into little angular corners,

cottages, gardens, now and then a church. Bang, bang! A
double-barrelled Station! Now a wood, now a bridge, now a
landscape, now a cutting, now a — Bang! a single-barrelled
Station — there was a cricket-match somewhere with two white
tents, and then four flying cows, then turnips — now the wires
of the electric telegraph are all alive, and spin, and blurr their
edges, and go up and down, and make the intervals between
each other most irregular: contracting and expanding in the
strangest manner. Now we slacken. With a screwing, and a
grinding, and a smell of water thrown on ashes, now we stop!

('A Flight', *HW* 30 August 1851: *UT & RP*, 476-7)

However exhilarating individual journeys were, the
railway brought about changes that were much more
radical for the early Victorians. In his role as the
Uncommercial Traveller (the title given to a series of
papers Dickens wrote for his 1860s magazine *All the Year
Round*) he records a change of particularly sentimental
significance from his own experience. 'Dullborough' is
the name he gives to his childhood home town of
Chatham:

It lately happened that I found myself rambling about the scenes
among which my earliest days were passed; scenes from which I
departed when I was a child, and which I did not revisit until I
was a man. This is no uncommon chance, but one that befalls
some of us any day; perhaps it may not be quite uninteresting to
compare notes with the reader respecting an experience so
familiar and a journey so uncommercial.

I call my boyhood's home (and I feel like a Tenor in an English
Opera when I mention it) Dullborough. Most of us come from
Dullborough who come from a country town.

As I left Dullborough in the days when there were no
railroads in the land, I left it in a stage-coach. Through all the
years that have since passed, have I ever lost the smell of the
damp straw in which I was packed — like game — and
forwarded, carriage paid, to the Cross Keys, Wood Street,
Cheapside, London? There was no other inside passenger, and I
consumed my sandwiches in solitude and dreariness, and it
rained hard all the way, and I thought life sloppier than I
expected to find it.

With this tender remembrance upon me, I was cavalierly
shunted back into Dullborough the other day, by train. My
ticket had been previously collected, like my taxes, and my
shining new portmanteau had had a great plaster stuck upon it,
and I had been defied by Act of Parliament to offer an objection

to anything that was done to it, or me, under a penalty of not less than forty shillings or more than five pounds, compoundable for a term of imprisonment. When I had sent my disfigured property on to the hotel, I began to look about me; and the first discovery I made, was, that the Station had swallowed up the playing-field.

It was gone. The two beautiful hawthorn-trees, the hedge, the turf, and all those buttercups and daisies, had given place to the stoniest of jolting roads: while, beyond the Station, an ugly dark monster of a tunnel kept its jaws open, as if it had swallowed them and were ravenous for more destruction. The coach that had carried me away, was melodiously called Timpson's Blue-Eyed Maid, and belonged to Timpson, at the coach-office up-street; the locomotive engine that had brought me back, was called severely No. 97, and belonged to S.E.R., and was spitting ashes and hot water over the blighted ground.

When I had been let out at the platform-door, like a prisoner whom his turnkey grudgingly released, I looked in again over the low wall, at the scene of departed glories. Here in the haymaking time, had I been delivered from the dungeons of Seringapatam, an immense pile (of haycock), by my own countrymen, the victorious British (boy next door and his two cousins), and had been recognised with ecstasy by my affianced one (Miss Green), who had come all the way from England (second house in the terrace) to ransom me, and marry me. Here, had I first heard in confidence, from one whose father was greatly connected, being under Government, of the existence of a terrible banditti, called 'The Radicals', whose principles were, that the Prince Regent wore stays, and that nobody had a right to any salary, and that the army and navy ought to be put down — horrors at which I trembled in my bed, after supplicating that the Radicals might be speedily taken and hanged. Here, too, had we, the small boys of Boles's, had that cricket match against the small boys of Coles's, when Boles and Coles had actually met upon the ground, and when, instead of instantly hitting out at one another with the utmost fury, as we had all hoped and expected, those sneaks had said respectively, 'I hope Mrs Boles is well', and 'I hope Mrs Coles and the baby are doing charmingly'. Could it be that, after all this, and much more, the Playing-field was a Station, and No. 97 expectorated boiling water and red hot cinders on it, and the whole belonged by Act of Parliament to S.E.R.?

('Dullborough Town', *UT & RP*, 116-17)

The train here has encroached upon hallowed ground. When Dickens returned to the area in later years, to establish his home at Gad's Hill, he tried to recapture memories of those 'Blue-Eyed Maid' journeys by arranging coach-rides in the old fashion for his summer visitors, who would, doubtless, have treasured memories of the Pickwickian stage-coach journeys thirty years before. But *Pickwick Papers* was itself just as much an essay in nostalgia as it was a comic portrait of contemporary manners. Though its action is backdated to the late 1820s, it appeared in 1836, the same year as the opening of the first London railway Station at London Bridge, and two years before the completion of the line to Birmingham which Mr Dombey was to travel. Here are the Pickwickians setting off from London to Dingley Dell in the heart of Kent on a bright frosty December morning:

> The guard and Mr Weller disappear for five minutes: most probably to get the hot brandy and water, for they smell very strongly of it, when they return, the coachman mounts to the box, Mr Weller jumps up behind, the Pickwickians pull their coats round their legs and their shawls over their noses, the helpers pull the horse-cloths off, the coachman shouts out a cheery 'All right,' and away they go.
>
> They have rumbled through the streets, and jolted over the stones, and at length reach the wide and open country. The wheels skim over the hard and frosty ground: and the horses, bursting into a canter at a smart crack of the whip, step along the road as if the load behind them: coach, passengers, cod-fish, oyster barrels, and all: were but a feather at their heels. They have descended a gentle slope, and enter upon a level, as compact and dry as a solid block of marble, two miles long. Another crack of the whip, and on they speed, at a smart gallop: the horses tossing their heads and rattling the harness, as if in exhilaration at the rapidity of the motion: while the coachman, holding whip and reins in one hand, takes off his hat with the other, and resting it on his knees, pulls out his handkerchief, and wipes his forehead: partly because he has a habit of doing it, and partly because it's as well to show the passengers how cool he is, and what an easy thing it is to drive four-in-hand, when you have had as much practice as he has. Having done this very leisurely (otherwise the effect would be materially impaired), he replaces his handkerchief, pulls on his hat, adjusts his gloves, squares his elbows, cracks the whip again, and on they speed, more merrily than before.
>
> A few small houses, scattered on either side of the road, betoken the entrance to some town or village. The lively notes of

the guard's key-bugle vibrate in the clear cold air, and wake up the old gentleman inside, who, carefully letting down the window-sash half-way, and standing sentry over the air, takes a short peep out, and then carefully pulling it up again, informs the other inside that they're going to change directly; on which the other inside wakes himself up, and determines to postpone his next nap until after the stoppage. Again the bugle sounds lustily forth, and rouses the cottager's wife and children, who peep out at the house-door, and watch the coach till it turns the corner, when they once more crouch round the blazing fire, and throw on another log of wood against father comes home; while father himself, a full mile off, has just exchanged a friendly nod with the coachman, and turned round to take a good long stare at the vehicle as it whirls away.

And now the bugle plays a lively air as the coach rattles through the ill-paved streets of a country-town; and the coachman, undoing the buckle which keeps his ribands together, prepares to throw them off the moment he stops ....The coachman throws down the reins and gets down himself, and the other outside passengers drop down also: except those who have no great confidence in their ability to get up again: and they remain where they are, and stamp their feet against the coach to warm them — looking, with longing eyes and red noses, at the bright fire in the inn bar, and the sprigs of holly with red berries which ornament the window.

But the guard has delivered at the corn-dealer's shop the brown paper packet he took out of the little pouch which hangs over his shoulder by a leathern strap; and has seen the horses carefully put to ....and he and Mr Weller, are all right behind, and the coachman is all right in front, and the old gentleman inside, who has kept the window down full two inches all this time, has pulled it up again, and the cloths are off, and they are all ready for starting....The coachman shouts an admonitory 'Now then, gen'l'm'n!' the guard re-echoes it . . . . Mr Winkle cries 'All right;' and off they start. Shawls are pulled up, coat collars are re-adjusted, the pavement ceases, the houses disappear, and they are once again dashing along the open road, with the fresh clear air blowing in their faces, and gladdening their very hearts within them.

(PP, XXVIII, 375-8)

The rhythms are markedly different from the *Dombey* passage. Moreover, in spite of the brisk pace of travel, there is no loss of contact with the countryside and people passed by. The energy here enchances vitality whereas in the *Dombey* passage it was gathering a headlong momentum towards death. The imagery of death again dominates the nightmarish description of Mugby Junction, the remote railway station that gives its name to the title of Dickens's 1866 Christmas Story:

> A place replete with shadowy shapes, this Mugby Junction in the black hours of the four-and-twenty. Mysterious goods trains, covered with palls and gliding on like vast weird funerals, conveying themselves guiltily away from the presence of the few lighted lamps, as if their freight had come to a secret and unlawful end. Half-miles of coal pursuing in a Detective manner, following when they lead, stopping when they stop, backing when they back. Red-hot embers showering out upon the ground, down this dark avenue, and down the other, as if torturing fires were being raked clear; concurrently, shrieks and groans and grinds invading the ear, as if the tortured were at the height of their suffering. Iron-barred cages full of cattle jangling by midway, the drooping beasts with horns entangled, eyes frozen with terror, and mouths too: at least they have long icicles (or what seem so) hanging from their lips. Unknown languages in the air, conspiring in red, green, and white characters. An earthquake, accompanied with thunder and lightning going up express to London. Now, all quiet, all rusty, wind and rain in possession, lamps extinguished, Mugby Junction dead and indistinct, with its robe drawn over its head, like Caesar.
>
> ('Mugby Junction', *CS*, 476-7)

The reluctant compromise with such changes is vividly captured by Dickens when he describes a melancholy scene at a railway station:

> I was returning from Manchester to London by the Mail Train, when I suddenly fell into another train — a mixed train — of reflection, occasioned by the dejected and disconsolate demeanour of the Post Office Guard. We were stopping at some station where they take in water, when he dismounted slowly from the little box in which he sits in ghastly mockery of his old condition with pistol and blunderbuss beside him, ready to shoot the first highwayman (or railwayman) who shall attempt to stop the horses, which now travel (when they travel at all) *inside* and in a portable stable invented for the purpose — he dismounted, I say, slowly and sadly, from his post, and looking mournfully about him as if in dismal recollection of the old roadside public-house — the blazing fire — the glass of foaming ale — the buxom handmaid and admiring hangers-on of

tap-room and stable, all honoured by his notice; and, retiring a little apart, stood leaning against a signal-post, surveying the engine with a look of combined affliction and disgust which no words can describe. His scarlet coat and golden lace were tarnished with ignoble smoke; flakes of soot had fallen on his bright green shawl — his pride in days of yore — the steam condensed in the tunnel from which we had just emerged, shone upon his hat like rain. His eye betokened that he was thinking of the coachman; and as it wandered to his own seat and his own fast-fading garb, it was plain to see that he felt his office and himself had alike no business there, and were nothing but an elaborate practical joke.

('Familiar Epistle', *SB*, 686-7)

All this clearly means more than simply a change in methods of transportation. The tremor of the steam engine is felt at the roots of the national culture:

The old stage-coachman was a farmer's friend. He wore top-boots, understood cattle, fed his horses upon corn, and had a lively personal interest in malt. The engine-driver's garb, and sympathies, and tastes belong to the factory. His fustian dress, besmeared with coal-dust and begrimed with soot; his oily hands, his dirty face, his knowledge of machinery, all point him out as one devoted to the manufacturing interest. Fire and smoke and red-hot cinders follow in his wake. He has no attachment to the soil, but travels on a road of iron, furnace wrought. His warning is not conveyed in the fine old Saxon dialect of our glorious forefathers, but in a fiendish yell. He never cries 'ya-hip!' with agricultural lungs; but jerks forth a manufactured shriek from a brazen throat.

('The Agricultural Interest', *Morning Chronicle* 9 March 1844: *NCP* I, 21-2)

But it would be wrong to assume that Dickens found no occasion for welcoming the coming of the railways to England. For one thing, as perhaps the passage before last showed, he found the train to be 'a wonderfully suggestive place to me when I am alone'. But he also believed in the value of technological progress in principle, because it held such promise for the kind of social reforms he continually promoted. In this context a nice general point is made and pertinently illustrated in the course of a speech given at Birmingham in 1844. Dickens is extolling the benefits of the new Polytechnic Institutions in Britain that offered educational opportunities for the factory labourers — an innovation, like the railways, that in those days excited considerable controversy:

> ... it surely cannot be allowed that those who labour day by day, surrounded by machinery, shall be permitted to degenerate into machines themselves; but, on the contrary, they should assert their common origin in that Creator, from whose wondrous hands they came, and unto whom, responsible and thinking men, they will return.
>
> There is, indeed, no difference in the main with respect to the dangers of ignorance, and the advantages of knowledge, between those who hold different opinions; for, it is to be observed, that those who are most distrustful of the advantages of education, are always the first to exclaim against the results of ignorance. This fact was pleasantly illustrated on the railway, as I came here. In the same carriage with me there sat an ancient gentleman (I feel no delicacy in alluding to him, for I know that he is not in the room, having got out far short of Birmingham), who expressed himself most mournfully as to the ruinous effects and rapid spread of railways, and was most pathetic upon the virtues of the slow-going old stage coaches. Now I, entertaining some little lingering kindness for the road, made shift to express my concurrence with the old gentleman's opinion, without any great compromise of my own. Well, we got on tolerably comfortably together; and when the engine, with a frightful screech dived into the darkness, like some strange aquatic monster, the old gentleman said this would never do, and I agreed with him. When it parted from each successive station with a shock and a shriek, as if it had had a double tooth drawn, the old gentleman shook his head, and I shook mine. When he burst forth against such new fangled notions, and said no good could come from them, I did not contest the point. But I invariably found that when the speed of the engine was abated, or there was the slightest prolongation of our stay at any station, the old gentleman was up in arms, and his watch was instantly out of his pocket, denouncing the slowness of our progress. Now I could not help comparing this old gentleman to that ingenious class of persons who are in the constant habit of declaiming against the vices and crimes of society and at the same time are the first and foremost to assert that vice and crime have not their common origin in ignorance and discontent.
>
> (*Speeches*, 61-2: Birmingham 28 February 1844)

Dickens's ironic detachment is skilfully conveyed. He

maintains critical independence without seeming con-
descendingly superior, an attitude that very often charac-
terises his fluctuating reactions to radical changes of this
kind.

Perhaps the single most complex and energetic
response of all is Dickens's description of the railway's
transformation of the London suburb of Staggs's Gardens in *Dombey and Son:*

> There was no such place as Staggs's Gardens. It had vanished
> from the earth. Where the old rotten summerhouses once had
> stood, palaces now reared their heads, and granite columns of
> gigantic girth opened a vista to the railway world beyond. The
> miserable waste ground, where the refuse-matter had been
> heaped of yore, was swallowed up and gone; and in its frowsy
> stead were tiers of warehouses, crammed with rich goods and
> costly merchandise. The old by-streets now swarmed with
> passengers and vehicles of every kind: the new streets that had
> stopped disheartened in the mud and waggon-ruts, formed
> towns within themselves, originating wholesome comforts and
> conveniences belonging to themselves, and never tried nor
> thought of until they sprung into existence. Bridges that had led
> to nothing, led to villas, gardens, churches, healthy public
> walks. The carcasses of houses, and beginnings of new
> thoroughfares, had started off upon the line at steam's own
> speed, and shot away into the country in a monster train.
>
> As to the neighbourhood which had hesitated to acknowledge
> the railroad in its straggling days, that had grown wise and
> penitent, as any Christian might in such a case, and now
> boasted of its powerful and prosperous relation. There were
> railway patterns in its drapers' shops, and railway journals in
> the windows of its newsmen. There were railway hotels,
> office-houses, lodging-houses, boarding-houses; railway plans,
> maps, views, wrappers, bottles, sandwich-boxes, and timet-
> ables; railway hackney-coach and cabstands; railway omnibuses,
> railway streets and buildings, railway hangers-on and parasites,
> and flatterers out of all calculation. There was even railway time
> observed in clocks, as if the sun itself had given in. Among the
> vanquished was the master chimney-sweeper, whilome
> incredulous at Staggs's Gardens, who now lived in a stuccoed
> house three stories high, and gave himself out, with golden
> flourishes upon a varnished board, as contractor for the
> cleansing of railway chimneys by machinery.
>
> To and from the heart of this great change, all day and night,
> throbbing currents rushed and returned incessantly like its life's
> blood. Crowds of people and mountains of goods, departing

and arriving scores upon scores of times in every four-and-twenty hours, produced a fermentation in the place that was always in action. The very houses seemed disposed to pack up and take trips. Wonderful Members of Parliament, who, little more than twenty years before, had made themselves merry with the wild railroad theories of engineers, and given them the liveliest rubs in cross-examination, went down into the north with their watches in their hands, and sent on messages before by the electric telegraph, to say that they were coming. Night and day the conquering engines rumbled at their distant work, or, advancing smoothly to their journey's end, and gliding like tame dragons into the allotted corners grooved out to the inch for their reception, stood bubbling and trembling there, making the walls quake, as if they were dilating with the secret knowledge of great powers yet unsuspected in them, and strong purposes not yet achieved.

But Staggs's Gardens had been cut up root and branch. Oh woe the day when 'not a rood of English ground' — laid out in Staggs's Gardens — is secure!

(D & S, XV, 217-19)

Staggs's Gardens has welcomed the railway eventually, and been properly rewarded by an exhilarating injection of vitality into what was before a decaying corner of the city. 'Remorseless monsters' seem here to have become 'tame dragons', their energies harnessed and directed to ensure the prosperity of their masters. The passing away of Staggs's Gardens hardly seems an occasion for regret, and one wonders whether Dickens's last paragraph can be anything else but ironic. He misquotes the opening of Wordsworth's 1844 sonnet on the projected Kendal and Windermere Railway. Wordsworth wrote two letters to the *Morning Post* in December of that same year (two years before *Dombey and Son* appeared) protesting eloquently against allowing the railways to invade the Lake District: 'But be it remembered . . .that the staple of the country is its beauty and its character of retirement. Let then the beauty be undisfigured and the retirement unviolated, unless there be reason for believing that rights and interests of a higher kind and more apparent than those which have been urged in behalf of the projected intrusion will compensate the sacrifice'.

It was one thing to deplore the railways' intrusion into

regions of natural beauty, but quite another to complain of its wiping out an old, decaying city suburb. On the other hand, in the chapter immediately following this description, the death of little Paul Dombey occurs, in which Dickens clearly asks us to lament the passing away of the 'old-fashioned' child who could never have taken his place in Mr Dombey's flourishing commercial world. Tensions between the old and the new, the frail and the robust, are so curiously figured in this novel that it would be unwise to isolate the Staggs's Gardens description.

In a *Household Words* article a few years later, Dickens describes the effects of the upheaval around Camden Town in north London (an area to which he had come as a small boy with his family nearly thirty years before) when the railway Terminus at Euston is in preparation. It is the fictional Staggs's Gardens, and Dickens sees it as 'a picture of our moral state':

> ... what put the neighbourhood off its head, and wrought it to that feverish pitch that it has ever since been unable to settle down to any one thing, and will never settle down again? THE RAILROAD has done it all.
>
> Why, only look at it! What with houses being pulled down and houses being built up, is it possible to imagine a neighbourhood less collected in its intellects? There are not fifty houses of any sort in the whole place that know their own mind a month. Now, a shop says, 'I'll be a toy-shop.' To-morrow it says, 'No I won't; I'll be a milliner's.' Next week it says, 'No I won't; I'll be a stationer's.' Next week it says, 'No I won't; I'll be a Berlin wool repository.' Take the shop directly opposite my house. Within a year, it has gone through all these changes, and has likewise been a plumber's painter's and glazier's, a tailor's, a broker's, a school, a lecturing-hall, and a feeding-place, 'established to supply the Railway public with a first-rate sandwich and a sparkling glass of Crowley's Alton Ale for threepence.'
>
> ... Now, I don't complain of the whistle, I say nothing of the smoke and steam, I have got used to the red-hot burning smell from the Breaks which I thought for the first twelve-month was my own house on fire, and going to burst out; but, my ground of offence is the moral inoculation of the neighbourhood. I am convinced that there is some mysterious sympathy between my hat on my head, and all the hats in hat-boxes that are always going down the line. My shirts and stockings put away in a chest of drawers, want to join the multitude of shirts and

stockings that are always rushing everywhere, Express, at the rate of forty mile an hour. The trucks that clatter with such luggage, full trot, up and down the platform, tear into our spirits, and hurry us, and we can't be easy.

In a word, the Railway Terminus Works themselves are a picture of our moral state. They look confused and dissipated, with an air as if they were always up all night, and always giddy. Here, is a vast shed that was not here yesterday, and that may be pulled down to-morrow; there, a wall that is run up until some other building is ready; there, an open piece of ground, which is a quagmire in the middle, bounded on all four sides by a wilderness of houses, pulled down, shored up, broken-headed, crippled, on crutches, knocked about and mangled in all sorts of ways, and billed with fragments of all kinds of ideas. We are, mind and body, an unsettled neighbourhood.

('An Unsettled Neighbourhood', *HW* 11 November 1854: *NCP* I,
516-19)

Confusion and unsettlement in neighbourhoods `over- taken by the railway match the novel feelings induced in the passenger by rail travel itself:

I am never sure of time or place upon a Railroad. I can't read, I can't think, I can't sleep — I can only dream. Rattling along in the railway carriage in a state of luxurious confusion, I take it for granted I am coming from somewhere, and going somewhere else. I seek to know no more.

('Railway Dreaming', *HW* 10 May 1856: *NCP* I, 644-5)

Dickens, of course, benfitted as much as anyone from the railway. His Reading Tours up and down the country in the 1860s were greatly facilitated by rail travel. And even after the terrible Staplehurst derailment in 1865, his experience of which haunted him in every subsequent journey, he continued to use the trains extensively. Like so many of his contemporaries, Dickens came to rec- ognise the railway as both a practical convenience and the symbol of the new age, of changes and progress that were both alarming and exhilarating:

Not in vain the distance beacons. Forward, forward
let us range,
Let the great world spin for ever down the ringing
grooves of change

Tennyson uses it precisely as this symbol in 'Lockseley Hall' (though, as he confessed later, he had erroneously supposed that train wheels ran in grooves). It is the representative image of that new industrial world, to whose birthplace Mr Dombey is brought as that memorable train journey terminates in the approach to Leamington:

> Louder and louder yet, it shrieks and cries as it comes tearing on resistless to the goal; and now its way, still like the way of Death, is strewn with ashes thickly. Everything around is blackened. There are dark pools of water, muddy lanes, and miserable habitations far below. There are jagged walls and falling houses close at hand, and through the battered roofs and broken windows wretched rooms are seen, where want and fever hide themselves in many wretched shapes, while smoke and crowded gales, and distorted chimneys, and deformity of brick and mortar penning up deformity of mind and body, choke the murky distance. As Mr Dombey looks out of his carriage window, it is never in his thoughts that the monster who has brought him there has let the light of day in on these things; not made or caused them. It was the journey's fitting end, and might have been the end of everything; it was so ruinous and dreary.
>
> (*D & S*, XX, 281-2)

The first full impact of the Black Country on Dickens was made during a tour of the Midlands and North Wales in 1838. As he wrote to his wife from Shrewsbury, he and his illustrator Hablot Knight Browne had visited Kenilworth, Warwick and Stratford-on-Avon:

> ...where we sat down in the room where Shakespeare was born and left our autographs, and read those of other people, and so forth.
>
> We remained at Stratford all night, and found to our unspeakable dismay that father's plan of proceeding by Bridgenorth was impracticable as there were no coaches. So we were compelled to come here by way of Birmingham and Wolverhampton, starting at eight o'clock through a cold wet fog, and travelling when the day had cleared up, through miles of cinder-paths and blazing furnaces and roaring steam engines, and such a mass of dirt, gloom and misery as I never before witnessed.
>
> (*Letters P* I, 447. Mrs Dickens: 1 November 1838)

That was by coach. Some fifteen years later Dickens saw
the same scenes from a railway carriage, and published
this fine description of how the simple cosmetic of snow
can transform the industrial landscape:

> CAN this be the region of cinders and coal-dust, which we have
> traversed before now, divers times, both by night and by day,
> when the dirty wind rattled as it came against us charged with
> fine particles of coal, and the natural colour of the earth and all
> its vegetation might have been black, for anything our eyes
> could see to the contrary in a waste of many miles? Indeed it is
> the same country, though so altered that on this present day
> when the old year is near its last, the North-East wind blows
> white, and all the ground is white — pure white — insomuch
> that if our lives depended on our identifying a mound of ashes
> as we jar along this Birmingham and Wolverhampton Railway,
> we could not find a handful.
>
> The sun shines brightly, though it is a cold cold sun, this
> piercing day; and when the Birmingham tunnel disgorges us
> into the frosty air, we find the pointsman housed in no mere
> box, but in a resplendent pavilion, all bejewelled with dazzling
> icicles, the least a yard long. A radiant pointsman he should be,
> we think, invested by fairies with a dress of rainbow hues, and
> going round and round in some gorgeously playful manner on a
> gold and silver pivot. But, he has changed neither his stout
> great-coat, nor his stiff hat, nor his stiff attitude of watch; and as
> (like the ghostly dagger of Macbeth) he marshalls us the way
> that we were going, we observe him to be a mortal with a red
> face — red, in part from a seasonable joviality of spirit, and in
> part from frost and wind — with the encrusted snow dropping
> silently off his outstretched arm.
>
> So, away again over the moor, where the clanking serpents
> usually writhing above coal-pits, are dormant and whitened
> over — this being holiday time — but where those grave
> monsters, the blast-furnaces, which cannot stoop to recreation,
> are awake and roaring. Now, a smoky village; now, a chimney;
> now, a dormant serpent who seems to have been benumbed in
> the act of working his way for shelter into the lonely little
> engine-house by the pit's mouth; now, a pond with black specks
> sliding and skating; now, a drift with similar specks half sunken
> in it throwing snowballs; now, a cold white altar of snow with
> fire blazing on it; now, a dreary open space of mound and fell,
> snowed smoothly over, and closed in at last by sullen cities of
> chimneys.
>
> ('Fire and Snow', *HW* 21 January 1854: *NCP* I, 474-6)

But it was that first visit of 1838 to the Birmingham-Wolverhampton area that gave Dickens the basis for his remarkable description of England's Black Country through which Little Nell and her grandfather travel in *The Old Curiosity Shop*, before they reach the ancient rural village haven we noticed in the previous chapter:

A long suburb of red-brick houses, — some with patches of garden-ground, where coal-dust and factory smoke darkened the shrinking leaves and coarse rank flowers, and where the struggling vegetation sickened and sank under the hot breath of kiln and furnace, making them by its presence seem yet more blighting and unwholesome than in the town itself, — a long, flat straggling suburb passed, they came, by slow degrees, upon a cheerless region, where not a blade of grass was seen to grow, where not a bud put forth its promise in the spring, where nothing green could live but on the surface of the stagnant pools, which here and there lay idly sweltering by the black roadside.

Advancing more and more into the shadow of this mournful place, its dark depressing influence stole upon their spirits, and filled them with a dismal gloom. On every side, and far as the eye could see into the heavy distance, tall chimneys, crowding on each other, and presenting that endless repetition of the same dull, ugly, form, which is the horror of oppressive dreams, poured out their plague of smoke, obscured the light, and made foul the melancholy air. On mounds of ashes by the wayside, sheltered only by a few rough boards, or rotten penthouse roofs, strange engines spun and writhed like tortured creatures; clanking their iron chains, shrieking in their rapid whirl from time to time as though in torment unendurable, and making the ground tremble with their agonies. Dismantled houses here and there appeared, tottering to the earth, propped up by fragments of others that had fallen down, unroofed, windowless, blackened, desolate, but yet inhabited.

Men, women, children, wan in their looks and ragged in attire, tended the engines, fed their tributary fire, begged upon the road, or scowled half-naked from the doorless houses. Then, came more of the wrathful monsters, whose like they almost seemed to be in their wildness and their untamed air, screeching and turning round and round again; and still, before, behind, and to the right and left, was the same interminable perspective of brick towers, never ceasing in their black vomit, blasting all things living or inanimate, shutting out the face of day, and closing in on all these horrors with a dense dark cloud.

(*OCS*, XLV, 335-6)

As with the steam-train, Dickens's description converts these machines into savage animals — 'tortured creatures', 'wrathful monsters', — which are enslaving the human animals that tend them:

> In a large and lofty building, supported by pillars of iron, with great black apertures in the upper walls, open to the external air; echoing to the roof with the beating of hammers and roar of furnaces, mingled with the hissing of red-hot metal plunged in water, and a hundred strange unearthly noises never heard elsewhere; in this gloomy place, moving like demons among the flame and smoke, dimly and fitfully seen, flushed and tormented by the burning fires, and wielding great weapons, a faulty blow from any one of which must have crushed some workman's skull, a number of men laboured like giants. Others, reposing upon heaps of coals or ashes, with their faces turned to the black vault above, slept or rested from their toil. Others again, opening the white-hot furnace-doors, cast fuel on the flames, which came rushing and roaring forth to meet it, and licked it up like oil. Others drew forth, with clashing noise, upon the ground, great sheets of glowing steel, emitting an insupportable heat, and a dull deep light like that which reddens in the eyes of savage beasts.
>
> (*Ibid*., XLIV, 329-30)

It is a vision of Pandemonium, once again communicating the sense of raw energy barely kept in check. It helps us to realise how profoundly disturbing such sights were to the early Victorians. Their fears were compounded in the 1840s by the growing antagonism of the industrial labour force in these towns. One such scene was witnessed by Nell:

> But, night-time in this dreadful spot! — night, when the smoke was changed to fire; when every chimney spirted up its flame; and places, that had been dark vaults all day, now shone red-hot, with figures moving to and fro within their blazing jaws, and calling to one another with hoarse cries — night, when the noise of every strange machine was aggravated by the darkness; when the people near them looked wilder and more savage; when bands of unemployed labourers paraded the roads, or clustered by torch-light round their leaders, who told them, in stern language, of their wrongs, and urged them on to frightful cries and threats; when maddened men, armed with sword and firebrand, spurning the tears and prayers of women

who would restrain them rushed forth on errands of terror and destruction, to work no ruin half so surely as their own — night, when carts came rumbling by, filled with rude coffins (for contagious disease and death had been busy with the living crops); when orphans cried, and distracted women shrieked and followed in their wake — night, when some called for bread, and some for drink to drown their cares, and some with tears, and some with staggering feet, and some with bloodshot eyes, went brooding home — night, which, unlike the night that Heaven sends on earth, brought with it no peace, nor quiet, nor signs of blessed sleep — who shall tell the terrors of the night to the young wandering child!

> (*Ibid.*, XLV, 336)

The writing becomes shrill and mannered as it envisages the awful consequences of such scenes, and it becomes imperative to rescue Nell and take her on to that country village, secure in its pastoral antiquity, where she is to die in peace.

Dickens seems to have received, and certainly wishes to convey, a very different impression of Birmingham twelve years later when he congratulates her citizens on their working conditions:

> I have seen in the factories and workshops of Birmingham such beautiful order and regularity, and such great consideration for the work people provided, that they might justly be entitled to be considered educational too. I have seen in your splendid Town Hall, where the cheap concerts are going on there, also an admirable educational institution. I have seen the results in the demeanour of your working people, excellently balanced by a nice instinct, as free from servility on the one hand, as from self-conceit on the other.
>
> (*Speeches*, 160: Birmingham 6 January 1853)

Later in this same year, 1853, Dickens brought *Bleak House* to its conclusion. There, in the stalwart person of Mr. Rouncewell the ironmaster, he had created an enlightened, strong and energetic representative of industrial England. He also designed for him a telling confrontation with Sir Leicester Dedlock, whose feudal ideas represent the deadened world of the English ruling class. It is a strange variation on, if not a reversal of, the pattern of values set up in the *Old Curiosity Shop*, where the timeless antiquity of the little village is conceived as a sanctuary from the ferocious world portrayed in the Black Country chapters. This change in Dickens's attitudes in the 1850s is one we shall return to in later chapters.

Dickens's most fully developed study of industrial England is to be found in *Hard Times*, the novel begun in the year following the conclusion of *Bleak House*. The description of Coketown is one of Dickens's masterpieces:

> Coketown, to which Messrs. Bounderby and Gradgrind now walked, was a triumph of fact; it had no greater taint of fancy in it than Mrs. Gradgrind herself. Let us strike the keynote, Coketown, before pursuing our tune.
>
> It was a town of red brick, or of brick that would have been red if the smoke and ashes had allowed it; but as matters stood it was a town of unnatural red and black like the painted face of a savage. It was a town of machinery and tall chimneys, out of which interminable serpents of smoke trailed themselves for ever and ever, and never got uncoiled. It had a black canal in it, and a river that ran purple with ill-smelling dye, and vast piles of building full of windows where there was a rattling and a trembling all day long, and where the piston of the steam-engine worked monotonously up and down like the head of an elephant in a state of melancholy madness. It contained several large streets all very like one another, and many small streets stilll more like one another, inhabited by people equally like one another, who all went in and out at the same hours, with the same sound upon the same pavement, to do the same work, and to whom every day was the same as yesterday and to-morrow, and every year the counterpart of the last and the next.
>
> You saw nothing in Coketown, but what was severely workful. If the members of a religious persuasion built a chapel there — as the members of eighteen religious persuasions had done — they made it a pious warehouse of red brick, with sometimes (but this is only in highly ornamental examples) a bell in a birdcage on the top of it. The solitary exception was the New Church; a stuccoed edifice with a square steeple over the door, terminating in four short pinnacles like florid wooden legs. All the public inscriptions in the town were painted alike, in severe characters of black and white. The jail might have been the infirmary, the infirmary might have been the jail, the town-hall might have been either, or both, or anything else, for anything that appeared to the contrary in the graces of their

construction. Fact, fact, fact, everywhere in the material aspect
of the town; fact, fact, fact, everywhere in the immaterial.
(*HT*, Bk II, v, 22-3)

The accent here, and in the book as a whole (for this
description does indeed strike the keynote) is less on
physical misery and squalor in the living conditions of
Coketown's inhabitants, though these are bad enough,
than on their stifled spiritual and imaginative life.

The general design of Coketown, with its appalling
monotony and uniformity, its individual architectural
features, becomes the bricks-and-mortar version of the
same pernicious utilitarian philosophy that informs
Gradgrind's educational practice. Dickens's artistic
maturity enables his controlled descriptions of the physical environment to be resonantly expressive of the
nature of his disgust. What matters now is not the
physical presence of industrialisation; for that in itself is a
morally neutral process. It is how humans direct this
process, and how they balance means and ends that
Dickens recognises as the proper study of the novelist —
indeed of any concerned witness to these particular
'shiftings and changes' in the country. To throw one's
hands up in horror at the industrial scene, as the
description of the Black Country in *The Old Curiosity Shop*
had done, is hardly an adequate response to the
extraordinary scientific and technological innovations of
the nineteenth century.

Dickens is not as unequivocally hostile to the broader
Gradgrind philosophy as might be imagined, if only
Gradgrindism would make a little more room for the life
of the imagination:

> I often say to Mr. Gradgrind that there is reason and good
> intention in much that he does — but that he overdoes it.
> Perhaps by dint of his going his way and my going mine, we
> shall meet at last at some halfway house where there are flowers
> on the carpet, and a little standing room for Queen Mab's
> chariot among the Steam Engines.
> (Quoted in Johnson II, 797. To Henry Coles: 17 June 1854)

He knew that, as an imaginative writer, he had a

responsibility to 'consecrate' (in Emerson's terms) these formidable new creatures of England's technological ingenuity. He came to share the sentiments expressed in Wordsworth's sonnet 'Steamboats, Viaducts, and Railways' published in the second of his letters to the *Morning Post*:

> Motions and Means, on land and sea at war
> With old poetic feeling, not for this
> Shall ye, by poets even, be judged amiss!

> In spite of all that Beauty must disown
> In your harsh features, nature doth embrace
> Her lawful offspring in man's Art

What to the Dickens of *The Old Curiosity Shop* might have seemed a solecism, became, in 1848, the title of an article he wrote for *The Examiner*, 'The Poetry of Science'. He was giving an enthusiastic review to Robert Hunt's book *The Poetry of Science, or Studies of the Physical Phenomena of Nature*:

> The design of Mr. Hunt's volume is striking and good. To show that the facts of science are at least as full of poetry, as the most poetical fancies ever founded on an imperfect observation and a distant suspicion of them (as, for example, among the ancient Greeks); to show that if the Dryades no longer haunt the woods, there is, in every forest, in every tree, in every leaf, and in every ring on every sturdy trunk, a beautiful and wonderful creation, always changing, always going on, always bearing testimony to the stupendous workings of Almighty Wisdom, and always leading the student's mind from wonder on to wonder, until he is wrapt and lost in the vast worlds of wonder by which he is surrounded from his cradle to his grave; it is a purpose worthy of the natural philosopher, and salutary to the spirit of the age. To show that Science, truly expounding Nature, can, like Nature herself, restore in some new form whatever she destroys; that, instead of binding us, as some would have it, in stern utilitarian chains, when she has freed us from a harmless superstition, she offers to our contemplation something better and more beautiful, something which, rightly considered, is more elevating to the soul, nobler and more stimulating to the soaring fancy; is a sound, wise, wholesome object. If more of the learned men who have written on these themes had had it

in their minds, they would have done more good, and gathered upon their track many followers on whom its feeblest and most distant trace has only now begun to shine.

Science has gone down into the mines and coal-pits, and before the safety-lamp the Gnomes and Genii of those dark regions have disappeared. But in their stead, the process by which metals are engendered in the course of ages; the growth of plants which, hundreds of fathoms underground, and in black darkness, have still a sense of the sun's presence in the sky, and derive some portion of the subtle essence of their life from his influence; the histories of mighty forests and great tracts of land carried down into the sea, by the same process which is active in the Mississippi and such great rivers at this hour; are made familiar to us. Sirens, mermaids, shining cities glittering at the bottom of the quiet seas and in deep lakes, exist no longer; but in their place, Science, their destroyer, shows us whole coasts of coral reef constructed by the labours of minute creatures, points to our own chalk cliffs and limestone rocks as made of the dust of myriads of generations of infinitesimal beings that have passed away; reduces the very element of water into its constituent airs, and re-creates it at her pleasure.

('The Poetry of Science', *The Examiner* 9 December 1848: *NCP* I, 178-9)

These sentiments are echoed just over a year later when this assurance is made to the readers of his magazine *Household Words:*

The mightier inventions of this age are not, to our thinking, all material, but have a kind of souls in their stupendous bodies which may find expression in *Household Words*. The traveller whom we accompany on his railroad or his steamboat journey may gain, we hope, some compensation for incidents which these later generations have outlived, in new associations with the Power that bears him onward; with the habitations and the ways of life of crowds of his fellow creatures among whom he passes like the wind; even with the towering chimneys he may see, spurting out fire and smoke upon the prospect. The Swart giants, Slaves of the Lamp of Knowledge, have their thousand and one tales no less than the Genii of the East.

('A Preliminary Word' *HW* 30 March 1850: *NCP* I, 223-4)

By and large Dickens welcomes the 'mightier inventions' of his age, as is consistent with his impatient antagonism to the various contemporary 'revival' movements in English culture. In his article attacking the Pre-

Raphaelites, for instance, he takes what he understands
to be the logic of their movement — 'the great retrog-
ressive principle' — and extends it ad absurdum:

> A Society, to be called the Pre-Newtonian Brotherhood, was
> lately projected by a young gentleman, under articles to a Civil
> Engineer, who objected to being considered bound to conduct
> himself according to the laws of gravitation. But this young
> gentleman, being reproached by some aspiring companions
> with the timidity of his conception, has abrogated that idea in
> favour of a Pre-Galileo Brotherhood now flourishing, who
> distinctly refuse to perform any annual revolution round the
> sun, and have arranged that the world shall not do so any
> more.The course to be taken by the Royal Academy of Art in
> reference to this Brotherhood is not yet decided upon; but it is
> whispered that some other large educational Institutions in the
> neighbourhood of Oxford are nearly ready to pronounce in
> favour of it.
>   Several promising students connected with the Royal College
> of Surgeons have held a meeting, to protest against the
> circulation of the blood, and to pledge themselves to treat all the
> patients they can get, on principles condemnatory of that
> innovation. A Pre-Harvey Brotherhood is the result, from which
> a great deal may be expected — by the undertakers.
>
> ('Old Lamps for New Ones', *HW* 15 June 1850: *NCP* I, 295)

Among Dickens's last words on these matters is part of a
speech he gave in 1869, a few months before his death.
Appropriately, he is addressing the Birmingham citizens:

> I have no fear that the walls of the Birmingham and Midland
> Institute will ever tremble responsive to the croakings of the
> timid opponents of intellectual progress; but in this connexion
> generally I cannot forbear from offering a remark which is much
> upon my mind. It is commonly assumed — much too commonly
> — that this age is a material age, and that a material age is an
> irreligious age.
>   I confess, standing here in this responsible situation, that I do
> not understand this much-used and much-abused phrase, a
> 'material age', I cannot comprehend — if anybody can: which I
> very much doubt — its logical signification. For instance: has
> electricity become more material in the mind of any sane, or
> moderately insane man, woman, or child, because of the
> discovery that in the good providence of God it was made
> available for the service and use of man to an immeasurably
> greater extent than for his destruction?
>
> (*Speeches*, 403-4: Birmingham 27 September 1869)

In this spirit not only of acceptance but of positive welcome, even that daunting symbol of all England's contemporary shiftings and changes, the railway, begins to seem like a blessing from above instead of a creature from the infernal regions:

> Do I make a more material journey to the bedside of my dying parents or my dying child, when I travel there at the rate of sixty miles an hour, than when I travel thither at the rate of six? Rather, in the swift case, does not my agonized heart become over-fraught with gratitude to that Supreme Beneficence from whom alone can have proceeded the Wonderful means of shortening my suspense?
>
> *(Ibid.)*

CHAPTER IV

The World's Metropolis

> London is a vile place, I sincerely believe. I have never taken kindly to it, since I lived abroad. Whenever I come back from the country, now, and see that great canopy lowering over the house tops, I wonder what on earth I do there except on obligation.
>
> *(Letters N* II, 272. Bulwer Lytton: 10 February 1851)

At the same time, London was the greatest single quarry of raw material for Dickens's imagination to shape into fiction. Our image of London still owes more to Dickens than to any other writer. As Walter Bagehot wrote in 1858: 'He describes London like a special correspondent for posterity.' This achievement springs largely from the fact that Dickens was the first distinguished writer to hold a sustained focus on the way life is lived in a great modern city. London in the middle of the nineteenth century was not only the capital of England, but in many minds, at home and abroad, the capital of the world: 'The world's metropolis', as Mr Podsnap confidently calls it; or 'the great capital, mart, and business centre of the world', as Dickens described it in 1850. In the following year, London's prestige as the world's metropolis was confirmed by the opening of the Great Exhibition, which Dickens greeeted with little enthusiasm:

> I find I am "used up" by the exhibition. I don't say "there is nothing in it" — there's too much. I have only been twice; so many things bewildered me. I have a natural horror of sights, and the fusion of so many sights in one has not decreased it. I am not sure that I have seen anything but the fountain and perhaps the Amazon. It is a dreadful thing to be obliged to be false, but when anyone says "Have you seen—?" I say, "Yes" because if I don't, I know he'll explain it, and I can't bear that.

— Took all the school one day. The school was composed of a hundred "infants," who got among the horses' legs in crossing to the main entrance from the Kensington Gate, and came reeling out from between the wheels of coaches undisturbed in mind. They were clinging to horses, I am told, all over the park.

When they were collected and added up by the frantic monitors, they were all right. They were then regaled with cake, etc., and went tottering and staring all over the place; the greater part wetting their forefingers and drawing a wavy pattern on every accessible object. One infant strayed. He was not missed. Ninety and nine were taken home, supposed to be the whole collection, but this particular infant went to Hammersmith. He was found by the police at night, going round and round the turnpikes which he still supposed to be a part of the Exhibition. He had the same opinion of the police, also of Hammersmith workhouse, where he passed the night. When his mother came for him in the morning, he asked when it would be over? It was a great Exhibition, he said, but he thought it long.

(*Letters N* II, 327. Mrs. R. Watson: 11 July 1851)

Pip gives voice to some wry reflections on the vaunted greatness of London in *Great Expectations*. In that novel the action is backdated to the 1820s and '30s, so that Pip's first arrival in London, at the Cross Keys, Cheapside (exactly where the 'Blue-Eyed Maid' deposited the child from Dullborough) must have been mixed with Dickens's recollections of his own first impressions of the city:

We Britons had at that time particularly settled that it was treasonable to doubt our having and our being the best of everything: otherwise, while I was scared by the immensity of London, I think I might have had some faint doubts whether it was not rather ugly, crooked, narrow and dirty.

(*GE*, XX, 153)

The power and prestige of London as a great commercial centre was not its main attraction for Dickens. This had much more to do with his discovery that, within a comparatively small compass, all types of humanity were mixed together, old and young, weak and strong, rich and poor:

It is night. Calm and unmoved amidst the scenes that darkness favours, the great heart of London throbs in its Giant Breast. Wealth and beggary, vice and virtue, guilt and innocence, repletion and the direst hunger, all treading on each other and crowding together, are gathered round it. Draw but a little circle above the clustering housetops, and you shall have within its space everything, with its opposite extreme and contradiction, close beside. Where yonder feeble light is shining, a man is but this moment dead. The taper at a few yards' distance is seen by eyes that have this instant opened on the world. There are two houses separated by but an inch or two of wall. In one, there are quiet minds at rest; in the other, a waking conscience that one might think would trouble the very air. In that close corner where the roofs shrink down and cower together as if to hide their secrets from the handsome street hard by, there are such dark crimes, such miseries and horrors, as could be hardly told in whispers. In the handsome street, there are folks asleep who have dwelt there all their lives, and have no more knowledge of these things than if they had never been, or were transacted at the remotest limits of the world—who, if they were hinted at, would shake their heads, look wise, and frown, and say they were impossible, and out of Nature, — as if all great towns were not.

(*MHC & CHE*, 107-8)

Dickens's last remark is an echo of that traditional sentiment that the city is somehow an unnatural phenomenon; not simply an artificial creation, but a perverted and perverting environment. William Cowper's line 'God made the country and man made the city' is an expression many Victorians would have endorsed.

Although this is a study specifically of Dickens's relationship to his own country, when we come to consider the place of London in that context we are forced to recognise that, although his great city bears all the features (named and unnamed) of England's capital, it also seems often, and strikingly, to be a visionary city. Dickens presents London not as a familiar village that swollen out of proportion, but as a prototype of the modern metropolis with specific consequences for its inhabitants. As Alexander Welsh put it, in his fascinating study *The City of Dickens* (1971), London represents an 'image of moral confusion': and this is why, even if Dickens thinks it a 'vile place', as a novelist of the changing human scene he finds it so compelling. But his impressions of London vary considerably, according to his age and experience of life and according also to the artistic purposes in his fiction.

Dickens knew London early: 'As to my means of observation, they have been pretty extensive. I have been abroad in the world from a mere child' (*Letters P* I, 424. Kuenzel: [? July 1838]). At the age of twelve he was wandering, often alone, in the London streets, as Forster records:

> . . .neglected and miserable as he was, he managed gradually to transfer to London all the dreaminess and all the romance with which he had invested Chatham. There were then at the top of Bayham-street some almshouses, and were still when he re-visited it with me nearly twenty-seven years ago; and to go to this spot, he told me, and look from it over the dustheaps and dock-leaves and fields (no longer there when we saw it together) at the cupola of St. Paul's looming through the smoke, was a treat that served him for hours of vague reflection afterwards. To be taken out for a walk into the real town, especially if it were anywhere about Covent-garden or the Strand, perfectly entranced him with pleasure. But, most of all, he had a profound attraction of repulsion to St. Giles's. If he could only induce whom-soever took him out to take him through Seven-dials, he was supremely happy. "Good Heaven!" he would exclaim, "What wild visions of prodigies of wickedness, want, and beggary, arose in my mind out of that place!"
>
> (Forster, 11)

He knew the coffee shops and pudding shops in the small courts and lanes around St. Martin's and Covent Garden:

> When I had money enough, I used to go to a coffee-shop, and have half-a-pint of coffee, and a slice of bread and butter. When I had no money, I took a turn in Covent-Garden market, and stared at the pineapples. The coffee-shops to which I most resorted were, one in Maiden-lane; one in a court (non-existent now) close to Hungerford-market; and one in St. Martin's-Lane, of which I only recollect that it stood near the church, and that in the door there was an oval glass-plate, with COFFEE-ROOM painted on it, addressed towards the street. If I ever find myself in a very different kind of coffee-room, now, but where there is

such an inscription on glass, and read it backward on the wrong side MOOR-EEFFOC (as I often used to do then, in a dismal reverie), a shock goes through my blood.

(*Ibid.*, p. 28)

His first experience of London is inseparable from his first experiences of great hardship, and this is an association that proves significant throughout his work. These particular childhood memories of London — especially the traumatic months he spent in the blacking factory — stayed with him throughout his life, as is well known. It was over twenty years later before he was able to confide to anyone this part of his personal history:

> Until old Hungerford-market was pulled down, until old Hungerford-stairs were destroyed, and the very nature of the ground changed, I never had the courage to go back to the place where my servitude began. I never saw it. I could not endure to go near it. For many years, when I came near to Robert Warren's in the Strand, I crossed over to the opposite side of the way, to avoid a certain smell of the cement they put upon the blacking-corks, which reminded me of what I was once. It was a very long time before I liked to go up Chandos-Street. My old way home by the borough made me cry, after my eldest child could speak.
>
> In my walks at night I have walked there often, since then, and by degrees I have come to write this.

(*Ibid.*, p. 35)

But at the beginning, there was also the wonder of it all — a child with a fabulous imagination confronted with an immense shop window: he called the city a 'vast emporium' in his description of a childhood wander through London in an 1853 *Household Words* article 'Gone Astray.' Here is Nicholas Nickleby's arrival in London with Smike:

> They rattled on through the noisy, bustling, crowded streets of London, now displaying long double rows of brightly-burning lamps, dotted here and there with the chemists' glaring lights, and illuminated besides with the brilliant flood that streamed from the windows of the shops, where sparkling jewellery, silks and velvets of the richest colours, the most inviting delicacies, and most sumptuous articles of luxurious ornament, succeeded

each other in rich and glittering profusion. Streams of people apparently without end poured on and on, jostling each other in the crowd and hurrying forward, scarcely seeming to notice the riches that surrounded them on every side; while vehicles of all shapes and makes, mingled up together in one moving mass like running water, lent their ceaseless roar to swell the noise and tumult.

As they dashed by the quickly-changing and every-varying objects, it was curious to observe in what a strange procession they passed before the eye. Emporiums of splendid dresses, the materials brought from every quarter of the world; tempting stores of everything to stimulate and pamper the sated appetite and give new relish to the oft-repeated feast; vessels of burnished gold and silver, wrought into every exquisite form of vase, and dish, and goblet; guns, swords, pistols, and patent engines of destruction; screws and irons for the crooked, clothes for the newly-born, drugs for the sick, coffins for the dead, and churchyards for the buried — all these jumbled each with the other and flocking side by side, seemed to flit by in motley dance like the fantastic groups of the old Dutch painter, and with the same stern moral for the unheeding restless crowd.

Nor were there wanting objects in the crowd itself to give new point and purpose to the shifting scene. The rags of the squalid ballad-singer fluttered in the rich light that showed the gold-smith's treasures, pale and pinched-up faces hovered about the windows where was tempting food; hungry eyes wandered over the profusion guarded by one thin sheet of brittle glass — an iron wall to them; half-naked shivering figures stopped to gaze at Chinese shawls and golden stuffs of India. There was a christening party at the largest coffin-maker's, and a funeral hatchment had stopped some great improvements in the bravest mansion. Life and death went hand in hand; wealth and poverty stood side by side; repletion and starvation laid them down together.

(NN, XXXII, 408-9)

The *Sketches by Boz*, Dickens's first publication, may be said to represent his first artistic encounter with London. Nearly all the twenty-five or so 'Scenes' that he wrote in the middle 1830s for the *Morning Chronicle* and *Evening Chronicle* were sketches of London, and here the imagination of the young Dickens is omnivorous. The characters and places that he portrays are astonishingly varied and abundant, and he seems already to have that instinct for telling detail that was to become one of his trademarks. As a kind of centre-piece to this chapter, here is the magnificent description (slightly condensed) from the *Sketches* which traces the slow awakening of the city — the kind of passage that some composer should translate into music:

The appearance presented by the streets of London an hour before sunrise, on a summer's morning, is most striking even to the few whose unfortunate pursuits of pleasure, or scarcely less unfortunate pursuits of business, cause them to be well acquainted with the scene. There is an air of cold, solitary desolation about the noiseless streets which we are accustomed to see thronged at other times by a busy, eager crowd, and over the quiet, closely-shut buildings, which throughout the day are swarming with life and bustle, that is very impressive.

...The drunken, the dissipated, and the wretched have disappeared; the more sober and orderly part of the population have not yet awakened to the labours of the day, and the stillness of death is over the streets; its very hue seems to be imparted to them, cold and lifeless as they look in the grey, sombre light of daybreak. The coach-stands in the larger thoroughfares are deserted; the night-houses are closed; and the chosen promenades of profligate misery are empty.

An occasional policeman may alone be seen at the street corners, listlessly gazing on the deserted prospect before him; and now and then a rakish-looking cat runs stealthily across the road and descends his own area with as much caution and slyness — bounding first on the water-butt, then on the dust-hole, and then alighting on the flagstones — as if he were conscious that his character depended on his gallantry of the preceding night escaping public observation. A partially opened bedroom-window here and there, bespeaks the heat of the weather, and the uneasy slumbers of its occupant; and the dim scanty flicker of the rushlight, through the window blind, denotes the chamber of watching or sickness. With these few exceptions, the streets present no signs of life, nor the houses of habitation.

An hour wears away; the spires of the churches and roofs of the principal buildings are faintly tinged with the light of the rising sun, and the streets, by almost imperceptible degrees, begin to resume their bustle and animation. Market-carts roll slowly along: the sleepy waggoner impatiently urging on his tired horses, or vainly endeavouring to awaken the boy, who, luxuriously stretched on the top of the fruit-baskets, forgets, in happy oblivion, his long-cherished curiosity to behold the wonders of London.

Rough, sleepy-looking animals of strange appearance, something between ostlers and hackney-coachmen, begin to take down the shutters of early public-houses; and little deal tables, with the ordinary preparations for a street breakfast, make their appearance at the customary stations. Numbers of men and women (principally the latter), carrying upon their heads heavy baskets of fruit, toil down the park side of Piccadilly, on their way to Covent Garden, and, following each other in rapid succession, form a long straggling line from thence to the turn of the road at Knightsbridge. . . .

Covent Garden market, and the avenues leading to it, are thronged with carts of all sorts, sizes, and descriptions, from the heavy lumbering waggon, with its four stout horses, to the jingling costermonger's cart, with its consumptive donkey. The pavement is already strewed with decayed cabbage-leaves, broken hay-bands, and all the indescribable litter of a vegetable market; men are shouting, carts backing, horses neighing, boys fighting, basket-women talking, piemen expatiating on the excellence of their pastry, and donkeys braying. . . .

Another hour passes away, and the day begins in good earnest. The servant of all work, who, under the plea of sleeping very soundly, has utterly disregarded "Missis's" ringing for half an hour previously, is warned by Master (whom Missis has sent up in his drapery to the landing-place for that purpose), that it's half-past six, whereupon she awakes all of a sudden, with well-feigned astonishment, and goes down-stairs sulkily, wishing, while she strikes a light, that the principle of spontaneous combustion would extend itself to coals and kitchen range. . . .the passengers who are going out by the early coach, stare with astonishment at the passengers who are coming in by the early coach, who look blue and dismal, and are evidently under the influence of that odd feeling produced by travelling, which makes the events of yesterday morning seem as if they had happened at least six months ago, and induces people to wonder with considerable gravity whether the friends and relations they took leave of a fortnight before, have altered much since they have left them. . . .

Half an hour more, and the sun darts his bright rays cheerfully down the still half-empty streets, and shines with sufficient force to rouse the dismal laziness of the apprentice, who pauses every other minute from his tasks of sweeping out the shop and watering the pavement in front of it, to tell another apprentice similarly employed, how hot it will be today, or to stand with his right hand shading his eyes, and his left resting on the broom, gazing at the "Wonder", or the "Tally-ho", or the "Nimrod", or some other fast coach, till it is out of sight, when he re-enters the shop, envying the passengers on the outside of the fast coach, and thinking of the old red brick house "down in the country", where he went to school: the miseries of the milk and water, and thick bread and scrapings,

fading into nothing before the pleasant recollection of the green
field the boys used to play in, and the green pond he was caned
for presuming to fall into, and other school-boy associations . . . .

The shops are now completely opened, and apprentices and
shopmen are busily engaged in cleaning and decking the
windows for the day. The bakers' shops in town are filled with
servants and children waiting for the drawing of the first batch
of rolls—an operation which was performed a full hour ago in
the suburbs: for the early clerk population of Somers and
Camden Towns, Islington and Pentonville, are fast pouring into
the city, or directing their steps towards Chancery Lane and the
Inns of Court. Middle-aged men, whose salaries have by no
means increased in the same proportion as their families, plod
steadily along, apparently with no object in view but the
counting-house; knowing by sight almost everybody they meet
or overtake, for they have seen them every morning (Sundays
excepted) during the last twenty years, but speaking to no one.
If they do happen to overtake a personal acquaintance, they just
exchange a hurried salutation, and keep walking on, either by
his side or in front of him, as his rate of walking may chance to
be . . . . Small office lads in large hats, who are made men before
they are boys, hurrying along in pairs, with their first coat
carefully brushed, and the white trousers of last Sunday
plentifully besmeared with dust and ink . . . .

Eleven o'clock, and a new set of people fill the streets. The
goods in the shop-windows are invitingly arranged; the shopmen in their white neckerchiefs and spruce coats, look as if they
couldn't clean a window if their lives depended on it; the carts
have disappeared from Covent Garden; the waggoners have
returned, and the costermongers repaired to their ordinary
"beats" in the suburbs; clerks are at their offices, and gigs, cabs,
omnibuses, and saddle-horses, are conveying their masters to
the same destination. The streets are thronged with a vast
concourse of people, gay and shabby, rich and poor, idle and
industrious; and we come to the heat, bustle, and activity of
NOON.

('The Streets — Morning', *SB*, 47-52)

All Dickens's senses are superbly fresh and alert as he
moves from detail to detail to build up his picture,
combining vivid objective description with those occasional sallies of the sympathetic imagination into the
thoughts and feelings of the Londoners. Here, and in the
'Scenes' as a whole, Dickens is exploring the composition
of London.

His relish of the unique individuality of the city people

is, in the early works, stronger than his sense of what on earth it is that they have in common. But it is this latter consideration that he was to develop as one of the principles on which his later studies of the great city operate. In these novels — especially *Bleak House, Little Dorrit,* and *Our Mutual Friend* — contained within massive structures, high and low would be brought together, and casual encounters would begin to spin intricate webs of relationships:

> What connexion can there be, between the place in Lincolnshire, the house in town, the Mercury in powder and the whereabout of Jo the outlaw with the broom, who had that distant ray of light upon him when he swept the churchyard-step? What connexion can there have been between many people in the innumerable histories of this world, who, from opposite sides of great gulfs, have, nevertheless, been very curiously brought together.
>
> (*BH*, XVI, 219).

> It struck me that it would be a new thing to show people coming together, in a chance way, as fellow-travellers, and being in the same place, ignorant of one another, as happens in life; and to connect them afterwards, and to make the waiting for that connection a part of the interest.
>
> (*Letters N* II, 685. Forster: 19 August 1855)

Paradoxically, while it functions superbly as the arena for these significant connexions, Dickens's London is also an agent for the fragmentation of society into small communities, and sometimes threatens even those small communities. In this capacity London often seems to have been designed deliberately to disorientate its people as much morally as geographically. This cluttered labyrinth is nowhere better described than in *Martin Chuzzlewit:*

> Surely there never was, in any other borough, city, or hamlet in the world, such a singular sort of a place as Todgers's. And surely London, to judge from that part of it which hemmed Todgers's round, and hustled it, and crushed it, and stuck its brick-and-mortar elbows into it, and kept the air from it, and stood perpetually between it and the light, was worthy of Todgers's, and qualified to be on terms of close relationship and

alliance with hundreds and thousands of the old family to which Todgers's belonged.

You couldn't walk about Todgers's neighbourhood, as you could in any other neighbourhood. You groped your way for an hour through lanes and bye-ways, and court-yards, and passages; and you never once emerged upon anything that might be reasonably called a street. A kind of resigned distraction came over the stranger as he trod those devious mazes, and, giving himself up for lost, went in and out and round about and quietly turned back again when he came to a dead wall or was stopped by an iron railing, and felt that the means of escape might possibly present themselves in their own good time, but that to anticipate them was hopeless. Instances were known of people who, being asked to dine at Todgers's had travelled round and round for a weary time, with its very chimney-pots in view; and finding it, at last, impossible of attainment, had gone home again with a gentle melancholy on their spirits, tranquil and uncomplaining . . . .

Strange solitary pumps were found near Todgers's hiding themselves for the most part in blind alleys, and keeping company with fire-ladders. There were churches also by dozens, with many a ghostly little churchyard, all overgrown with such straggling vegetation as springs up spontaneously from damp, and graves, and rubbish . . . .

In the throats and maws of dark no-thoroughfares near Todgers's, individual wine-merchants and wholesale dealers in grocery-ware had perfect little towns of their own; and, deep among the foundations of these buildings, the ground was undermined and burrowed out into stables, where cart-horses, troubled by rats, might be heard on a quiet Sunday rattling their halters, as disturbed spirits in tales of haunted houses are said to clank their chains.

                                                              (*MC*, IX, 127-29)

London is, among other things, a great Dickensian eccentric — as odd, angular and unaccountable as any of his more bizarre characters.

In the early novels London's role is firmly established. Shaped perhaps by Dickens's childhood association of the city with the severe and premature hardships of life, those of his central characters who, whatever their age, share a kind of open innocence, all eventually retreat from London into the country: Nicholas Nickleby and his family, Oliver Twist, Little Nell, and Mr. Pickwick (who retires to the genteel semi-rural Dulwich). In the more mature novels London moves to a central position in the moral scheme, where what is wrong with the city is only the most acute symptom of what is wrong with England. Just as Coketown struck the keynote to *Hard Times*, so the description of fog-bound London strikes the keynote in the famous opening to *Bleak House:*

LONDON. Michaelmas Term lately over, and the Lord Chancellor sitting in Lincoln's Inn Hall. Implacable November weather. As much mud in the streets, as if the waters had but newly retired from the face of the earth, and it would not be wonderful to meet a Megalosaurus, forty feet long or so, waddling like an elephantine lizard up Holborn Hill. Smoke lowering down from chimney-pots, making a soft black drizzle, with flakes of soot in it as big as full-grown snowflakes — gone into mourning, one might imagine, for the death of the sun. Dogs, undistinguishable in mire. Horses, scarcely better; splashed to their very blinkers. Foot passengers, jostling one another's umbrellas, in a general infection of ill-temper, and losing their foot-hold at street-corners, where tens of thousands of other foot passengers have been slipping and sliding since the day broke (if this day ever broke), adding new deposits to the crust upon crust of mud, sticking at those points tenaciously to the pavement, and accumulating at compound interest.

Fog everywhere. Fog up the river, where it flows among green aits and meadows; fog down the river, where it rolls defiled among the tiers of shipping, and the waterside pollutions of a great (and dirty) city. Fog on the Essex marshes, fog on the Kentish heights. Fog creeping into the cabooses of collier-brigs; fog lying out on the yards, and hovering in the rigging of great ships; fog drooping on the gunwales of barges and small boats. Fog in the eyes and throats of ancient Greenwich pensioners, wheezing by the firesides of their wards; fog in the stem and bowl of the afternoon pipe of the wrathful skipper, down in his close cabin; fog cruelly pinching the toes and fingers of his shivering little 'prentice boy on deck. Chance people on the bridges peeping over the parapets into a nether sky of fog, with fog all round them, as if they were up in a balloon, and hanging in the misty clouds.

Gas looming through the fog in divers places in the streets, much as the sun may, from the spongy fields, be seen to loom by husbandman and ploughboy. Most of the shops lighted two hours before their time — as the gas seems to know, for it has a haggard and unwilling look.

The raw afternoon is rawest, and the dense fog is densest, and the muddy streets are muddiest, near that leaden-headed old obstruction, appropriate ornament for the threshold of a leaden-headed old corporation: Temple Bar. And hard by Temple Bar, in Lincoln's Inn Hall, at the very heart of the fog, sits the Lord High Chancellor in his High Court of Chancery.

Never can there come fog too thick, never can there come mud and mire too deep, to assort with the groping and floundering condition which this High Court of Chancery, most pestilent of hoary sinners, holds, this day, in the sight of heaven and earth.

(BH, I, 1-2)

Twelve years later, in *Our Mutual Friend*, the fog and filth is, if anything, worse:

> It was a foggy day in London, and the fog was heavy and dark. Animate London, with smarting eyes and irritated lungs, was blinking, wheezing, and choking; inanimate London was a sooty spectre, divided in purpose between being visible and invisible, and so being wholly neither. Gaslights flared in the shops with a haggard and unblest air, as knowing themselves to be night-creatures that had no business abroad under the sun; while the sun itself, when it was for a few moments dimly indicated through circling eddies of fog, showed as if it had gone out, and were collapsing flat and cold. Even in the surrounding country it was a foggy day, but there the fog was grey, whereas in London it was, at about the boundary line, dark yellow, and a little within it brown, and then browner, and then browner, until at the heart of the City — which call Saint Mary Axe — it was rusty-black. From any point of the high ridge of land northward, it might have been discerned that the loftiest buildings made an occasional struggle to get their heads above the foggy sea, and especially that the great dome of Saint Paul's seemed to die hard; but this was not perceivable in the streets at their feet, where the whole metropolis was a heap of vapour charged with muffled sound of wheels, and enfolding a gigantic catarrh.

(OMF, Bk III, i, 420)

In December 1858 Dickens took a foreign friend from Genoa down to the Crystal Palace at Sydenham:

> I asked him to try to imagine the sun shining down through the glass, and making broad lights and shadows. He said he tried very hard, but he couldn't imagine the sun shining within fifty miles of London under any circumstances.

(Letters C, 365-6: 13 December 1858)

Moral and physical health become inseparable in Dickens's attitude towards London in the 1850s, and the novels gain great strength from the structural and thematic integration of such issues. Those features of the metropolis that made it often so appealingly picturesque in the *Sketches* and early novels — the crowds, the bustle, the heterogeneous population, the neglected byways, the profusion of smells and sounds — now seem to be contributing to its disease and slow decay. It took the cholera epidemic of 1848-9 to give any urgent support (and even this was delayed) to Edwin Chadwick's long battle for sanitary reform. Dickens (whose brother-in-law Henry Austin was secretary to the General Board of Health) spoke to this in an 1850 address to the recently formed Metropolitan Sanitary Association:

> Of the sanitary condition of London at the present moment, he solemnly believed it would be almost impossible to speak too ill. He knew of many places in it unsurpassed in the accumulated horrors of their neglect by the dirtiest old spots in the dirtiest old towns, under the worst old governments in Europe. Great contrasts of rank, great contrasts of wealth, and great contrasts of comfort must, as every man of sense was aware exist among all civilised communities; but he sincerely believed that no such contrasts as were afforded by our handsome streets, our railroads and our electric telegraphs, in the year of our Lord 1850, as compared with the great mass of the dwellings of the poor in many parts of this metropolis, had ever before been presented on this earth.
>
> (*Speeches*, 106: London 6 February 1850)

And again in 1851, six months away from penning that November opening to *Bleak House:*

> That no one can estimate the amount of mischief which is grown in dirt; that no one can say, here it stops, or there it stops, either in its physical or its moral results, when both begin in the cradle and are not at rest in the obscene grave, is now as certain as it is that the air from Gin Lane will be carried, when the wind is Easterly, into May Fair, and that if you once have a vigorous pestilence raging furiously in Saint Giles's, no mortal list of Lady Patronesses can keep it out of Almack's.
>
> Twelve or fifteen years ago, some of the first valuable reports of Mr. Chadwick and of Dr. Southwood Smith strengthening

and much enlarging my previous imperfect knowledge of this truth, made me, in my sphere, earnest in the Sanitary Cause. And I can honestly declare tonight, that all the use I have since made of my eyes — or nose — that all the information I have since been able to acquire through any of my senses, has strengthened me in the conviction that Searching Sanitary Reform must precede all other social remedies, and that even Education and Religion can do nothing where they are most needed, until the way is paved for their ministrations by Cleanliness and Decency.

(*Ibid.*, 128-9: London 10 May 1851)

This is one reason why his heroine in *Bleak House* is Esther Summerson, the personification of 'Cleanliness and Decency'; and it is why she must marry Allan Woodcourt, the energetic and dedicated doctor. Fortunately for them, but perhaps unfortunately for London's pressing needs, these two apparently enlightened and able people are to start their secular ministry miles away, in Yorkshire, where their honeysuckle-clad cottage awaits them, and where they are safe from the spread of London's contamination.

The continuing threat of London's encroachment upon the countryside was another of Dickens's themes in these years. He wrote on this matter to Angela Burdett Coutts whose charitable enterprises included plans for the building of cheap apartments designed to house some 200 families in the East End of London:

You never can, for the same money, offer anything like the same advantages in small houses. It is *not* desirable to encourage any small carpenter or builder who has a few pounds to invest, to run up small dwelling houses. If they had been discouraged long ago, London would be an immeasurably healthier place than it can be made in scores of years to come. If you go into any common outskirts of the town now and see the advancing army of bricks and mortar laying waste the country fields and shutting out the air, you cannot fail to be struck by the consideration that if large buildings had been erected for the working people, instead of the absurd and expensive separate walnut shells in which they live, London would have been about a third of its present size, and every family would have had a country walk miles nearer to their own door. Besides this, men would have been nearer to their work — would not have had to dine at public houses — there would have been thicker walls of separation and better means of separation than you can ever give (except at a preposterous cost) in small tenements — and they would have had gas, water, drainage, and a variety of other humanizing things which you can't give them so well in little houses. Further, in little houses, you must keep them near the ground, and you cannot by any possibility afford such sound and wholesome foundations (remedying the objection) in little houses as in large ones. The example of large houses appears to me, in all respects (always supposing their locality to be a great place like London) far better than any example you can set by small houses; and the compensation you give for any overgrown shadow they may cast upon a street at certain hours of the day is out of all proportion to that drawback.

(*Letters* N II, 388-9. Coutts: 18 April 1852)

The sky-scrapers were to come and bring their own set of difficulties. But this does show Dickens's belief in the practical measures he now felt it imperative to take, and it shows the growing frustration at the apparent indifference of those who were officially responsible for these matters. There were some notable exceptions, such as the building of the Embankment in 1869, which won Dickens's approval:

The Thames Embankment is (faults of ugliness in detail apart) the finest public work yet done. From Westminster Bridge to near Waterloo it is now lighted up at night, and has a fine effect. They have begun to plant it with trees, and the footway (not the road) is already open to the Temple. Besides its beauty, and its usefulness in relieving the crowded streets, it will greatly quicken and deepen what is learnedly called the "scour" of the river.

(*Letters* N III, 698. de Cerjat: 4 January 1869)

The Thames through London was another object that excited in Dickens that 'attraction of repulsion', and features particularly in *Our Mutual Friend* where it represents both grave and baptism to a new life. On one outing during a raw winter night in 1853 with the Thames Police, Dickens remarked that the river seemed to him 'an image of death in the midst of the great city's life' ('Down with the Tide', *HW* 5 February 1853: *UT & RP*, 527). Such striking contrasts, which London offered

more readily than most places, were among the chief
sources for Dickens's endless fascination with the city.
Another image of the proximity of life and death,
turbulence and stillness was the prison:

> There, at the very core of London, in the heart of its business
> and animation, in the midst of a whirl of noise and motion:
> stemming as it were the giant currents of life that flow
> ceaselessly on from different quarters and meet beneath its
> walls: stands Newgate.
>
> (*NN*, IV, 29)

Philip Collins, in *Dickens and Crime*, has remarked on the
degree to which, in Dickens's time, prisons must have
dominated the metropolitan scene. Newgate, the Fleet,
the Marshalsea, Horsemonger Lane were sombre pre-
sences no Victorian Londoner could forget. Prisons
abound in Dickens's works, both because they were such
prominent features in the London landscape and because
of Dickens's own unhappy experience with his father's
incarceration. Often, to his mind, like the other ills that
London is heir to — the fog, the labyrinthine streets and
festering alleys — the prison and its accompanying
scenes, particularly the barbarous spectacles of public
executions, become an emblem of all that is worst in the
city:

> I have seen, habitually, some of the worst sources of general
> contamination and corruption in this country, and I think there
> are not many phases of London life that could surprise me. I am
> solemnly convinced that nothing that ingenuity could devise to
> be done in this city, in the same compass of time, could work
> such ruin as one public execution, and I stand astounded and
> appalled by the wickedness it exhibits. I do not believe that any
> community can prosper where such a scene of horror and
> demoralisation as was enacted this morning outside Horse-
> monger Lane Gaol is presented at the very doors of good
> citizens, and is passed by unknown or forgotten. And, when in
> our prayers and thanksgivings for the season, we are humbly
> expressing before God our desire to remove the moral evils of
> the land, I would ask your readers to consider whether it is not a
> time to think of this one, and to root it out.
>
> ('Public Executions', *The Times* 14 November 1849: *NCP* I, 738)

But Dickens was nonetheless continually surprised and appalled by those 'phases of London life' that seemed to him to be a national disgrace; the city's terrible crowding, for instance. In the middle 1850s it was estimated that there were 150,000 families in London each occupying no more than a single room. Mayhew's classic survey *London Labour and the London Poor* belongs to these middle years of the nineteenth century. Many, if not most, of his poor street-sellers are first generation Londoners, drawn to the city for an extraordinary variety of reasons. As the Turf-cutter remarked in interview: 'I think most men when they don't know what in the world to do, come to London'. The consequences of this sort of influx were inevitably harsh:

On the fifth of last November, I, the Conductor of this journal, accompanied by a friend well-known to the public, accidentally strayed into Whitechapel. It was a miserable evening; very dark, very muddy and raining hard.

There are many woeful sights in that part of London, and it has been well-known to me in most of its aspects for many years. We had forgotten the mud and rain in slowly walking along and looking about us, when we found ourselves, at eight o'clock, before the Workhouse.

Crouched against the wall of the Workhouse, in the dark street, on the muddy pavement-stones, with the rain raining upon them, were five bundles of rags. They were motionless, and had no resemblance to the human form. Five great beehives, covered with rags — five dead bodies taken out of graves, tied neck and heels, and covered with rags — would have looked like those five bundles upon which the rain rained down in the public street.

'What is this!' said my companion. 'What *is* this!'

'Some miserable people shut out of the Casual Ward, I think', said I.

We had stopped before the five ragged mounds, and were quite rooted to the spot by their horrible appearance. Five awful Sphinxes by the wayside, crying to every passer-by, 'Stop and guess! What is to be the end of a state of society that leaves us here!'

As we stood looking at them, a decent working-man, having the appearance of a stone-mason, touched me on the shoulder.

'This is an awful sight, sir,' said he, 'in a Christian country!'

'GOD knows it is, my friend,' said I.

('A Nightly Scene in London', HW 26 January 1856: NCP I, 630)

As we shall see in the next chapter, this was the decade when Dickens was most exasperated at the apparent lack of any efficient, organised system, in Government or elsewhere, for coping with such horrors. It is like his general sense of ineptitude in city planning that is reflected in the splendid image of the bored, negligent child that occurs in the description, in *Our Mutual Friend*, of a newly developed area to the south east of London:

> The schools — for they were twofold, as the sexes — were down in that district of the flat country tending to the Thames, where Kent and Surrey meet, and where the railways still bestride the market-gardens that will soon die under them. The schools were newly built, and there were so many like them all over the country, that one might have thought the whole were but one restless edifice with the locomotive gift of Aladdin's palace. They were in a neighbourhood which looked like a toy neighbourhood, taken in blocks out of a box by a child of particularly incoherent mind, and set up anyhow; here, one side of a new street; there, a large solitary public-house facing nowhere; here, another unfinished street already in ruins; there, a church; here, an immense new warehouse; there, a dilapidated old country villa; then, a medley of black ditch, sparkling cucumber-frame, rank field, richly cultivated kitchen-garden, brick viaduct, arch-spanned canal, and disorder of frowsiness and fog. As if the child had given the table a kick and gone to sleep.
>
> (*OMF*, Bk II, i, 218)

Much of London, then, horrified Dickens: 'I wonder what on earth I do there except on obligation.' Obligation, of course, can carry a wide range of reference, and Dickens would presumably include under that heading his family home, his friends and his publishers. But equally important, though perhaps less obvious as an 'obligation', is the nourishment that his particular imagination craves from London. He attributed this, in part, to that 'attraction of repulsion'. He was never so fully aware of this as when he was abroad, struggling to build up creative momentum for the story he was writing. In August 1846 he was in Switzerland, and wrote to Forster complaining of the difficulties he was having with the early numbers of *Dombey and Son*:

You can hardly imagine what infinte pains I take, or what extraordinary difficulty I find in getting on FAST. Invention, thank God, seems the easiest thing in the world; and I seem to have such a preposterous sense of the ridiculous, after this long rest, as to be constantly requiring to restrain myself from launching into extravagances in the height of my enjoyment. But the difficulty of going at what I call a rapid pace, is prodigious: it is almost an impossibility. I suppose this is partly the effect of two years' ease, and partly of the absence of streets and numbers of figures. I can't express how much I want these. It seems as if they supplied something to my brain, which it cannot bear, when busy, to lose. For a week or a fortnight I can write prodigiously in a retired place (as at Broadstairs), and a day in London sets me up again and starts me. But the toil and labour of writing, day after day, without that magic lantern, is IMMENSE!!

(*Letters N* I, 782. Forster: 30 August 1846)

And then, again, a few days later:

The absence of any accessible streets continues to worry me, now that I have so much to do, in a most singular manner. It is quite a little mental phenomenon. I should not walk in them in the day time, if they were here, I dare say: but at night I want them beyond description. I don't seem able to get rid of my spectres unless I can lose them in crowds. However, as you say, there are streets in Paris, and good suggestive streets too: and trips to London will be nothing then.

(*Ibid.*, 787-8. Forster: [September 1846])

As we have seen in considering his thoughts and feelings about rural Britain, Dickens's inspiration is firmly centred in the city, that 'magic lantern'. His night walks through London are almost legendary. Their compulsive nature suggests that the darkened city's sights and sounds are necessary galvanic agents to his imagination:

I have been greatly better at Geneva, though I still am made uneasy by occasional giddiness and headache: attributable, I have not the least doubt, to the absence of streets.

(*Ibid.*, 793. Forster : 3 October 1846)

He would have shared the predilections of his elderly narrator, Master Humphrey, as the opening of *The Old Curiosity Shop* suggests:

Although I am an old man, night is generally my time for walking. In the summer I often leave home early in the morning, and roam about the fields and lanes all day, or even escape for days or weeks together, but, saving in the country, I seldom go out until after dark, though, Heaven be thanked, I love its light and feel the cheerfulness it sheds upon the earth, as much as any creature living.

I have fallen insensibly into this habit, both because it favours my infirmity, and because it affords me greater opportunity of speculating on the characters and occupations of those who fill the streets. The glare and hurry of broad noon are not adapted to idle pursuits like mine; a glimpse of passing faces caught by the light of a street lamp or a shop window, is often better for my purpose than their full revelation in the daylight; and, if I must add the truth, night is kinder in this respect than day, which too often destroys an air-built castle at the moment of its completion, without the smallest ceremony or remorse.

(OCS, I, 1)

Master Humphrey's whimsical taste for the dreamlike visions conjured in the night streets of London might be said to re-emerge, in sinister fashion, thirty years later in Dickens's last novel *The Mystery of Edwin Drood*. John Jasper, the book's enigmatic hero, leads the double life of respectable choirmaster in an ancient English Cathedral Town (the decaying Cloisterham we remarked in Chapter 2), and furtive visitor to London to satisfy his hunger for the opium dreams. The novel opens with an extraordinary montage of exotic and familiar images juxtaposed with a nightmare lack of logic:

An ancient English Cathedral Town? How can the ancient English Cathedral town be here! The well-known massive grey square tower of its old Cathedral? How can that be here! There is no spike of rusty iron in the air, between the eye and it, from any point of the real prospect. What IS the spike that intervenes, and who has set it up? Maybe, it is set up by the Sultan's orders for the impaling of a horde of Turkish robbers, one by one. It is so, for cymbals clash, and the Sultan goes by to his palace in long procession. Ten thousand scimitars flash in the sunlight, and thrice ten thousand dancing-girls strew flowers. Then, follow white elephants caparisoned in countless gorgeous colours, and infinite in number and attendants. Still the Cathedral tower rises in the background, where it cannot be, and still no writhing figure is on the grim spike. (The Mystery of Edwin Drood, ed. M. Cardwell, [Oxford; 1972], p.1).

Jasper's strange commutings between Cloisterham with its 'oppressive respectability' and the East End opium dens are an echo of Dickens's later years, when, among other things, his furtive relationship with Ellen Ternan was taking him up to London from his home at Gad's Hill.

His constitutional restlessness met its match in the metropolis in a way that perhaps no single companion could. A number of the reflective Uncommercial Traveller pieces are the product of his nightly walks through the streets of London, and his descriptions here provide a telling contrast to that narrative from the *Sketches* of London's coming to life in the morning:

> Some years ago, a temporary inability to sleep, referable to a distressing impression, caused me to walk about the streets all night, for a series of several nights. The disorder might have taken a long time to conquer, if it had been faintly experimented on in bed; but, it was soon defeated by the brisk treatment of getting up directly after lying down, and going out, and coming home tired at sunrise.
>
> In the course of those nights, I finished my education in a fair amateur experience of houselessness. My principal object being to get through the night, the pursuit of it brought me into sympathetic relations with people who have no other object every night in the year.
>
> The month was March, and the weather damp, cloudy, and cold. The sun not rising before half-past five, the night perspective looked sufficiently long at half-past twelve: which was about my time for confronting it.
>
> The restlessness of a great city, and the way in which it tumbles and tosses before it can get to sleep, formed one of the first entertainments offered to the contemplation of us houseless people . . . .
>
> Walking the streets under the pattering rain, Houselessness would walk and walk and walk, seeing nothing but the interminable tangle of streets, save at a corner, here and there, two policemen in conversation, or the sergeant or inspector looking after his men. Now and then in the night — but rarely — Houselessness would become aware of a furtive head peering out of a doorway a few yards before him, and, coming up with the head, would find a man standing bolt upright to keep within the doorway's shadow, and evidently intent upon no particular service to society. Under a kind of fascination, and in a ghostly silence suitable to the time, Houselessness and this gentleman

would eye one another from head to foot, and so, without exchange of speech, part, mutually suspicious. Drip, drip drip, from ledge and coping, splash from pipes and water-spouts, and by-and-by the houseless shadow would fall upon the stones that pave the way to Waterloo-bridge; it being in the houseless mind to have a halfpenny worth of excuse for saying "Goodnigh" to the toll-keeper, and catching a glimpse of his fire.

('Night Walks', *UT & RP*, 127-28)

Apart from anything else, Dickens's knowledge of London as a result of such excursions was massive. He is one of London's most accurate and vivid topographers, better qualified than most in 'penetrating the arcana of the Modern Babylon', as Mr. Micawber once put it. But he also sees in this city the shape of things to come — the erosion of community feeling, the closely packed and incompatible human groups, the poverty that can go unheeded until it erupts in crime or cholera. In all of this he shows great social foresight.

There is another curious way in which Dickens's rendering of London has extraordinary clairvoyance. In the January 1921 issue of *The Dial*, Ezra Pound remarked (not in relation to Dickens): 'The life of a village is narrative.... In the city the visual impressions succeed each other, overlap, overcross, they are cinematographic'. The descriptive and narrative techniques that Dickens developed in his fiction in many ways anticipate the cinema. Two of the great pioneers of film, D.W. Griffith and Sergei Eisenstein, both acknowledged a considerable debt to Dickens, particularly in the case of what came to be known as 'montage', a structure dependent on the controlled collision of independent shots. As Pound suggests (and Pound's own pioneer work in Imagism gains much from experiments in poetry with just this kind of 'collision'), this is typically the way in which our impressions of the city are made. As an example, one need only look back to that *Nicholas Nickleby* passage, where the objects 'succeed each other in rich and glittering profusion' in the 'shifting scene'; or one can recall Jasper's opium visions. Dickens's 'magic lantern' proves an uncannily appropriate choice of metaphor.

Any summary of Dickens's creative achievement would have to emphasize his long commitment to making human sense of the strange, 'out of Nature' way of living that the city, and especially the metropolis, imposed on him and on his contemporaries. By the later 1840s he realises London can no longer be seen simply as the glittering shop window or succession of picturesque tableaux. The Dickensian city disperses people and breaks up community; it confuses the senses and offends the sensibility, jolts focus and fractures narrative. To counteract this, the Dickensian Christmas (for example) reunites family, restores the traditional hierarchy of generations and social positions, and, consequently, the traditional narrative patterns. As we saw in the previous chapter and as we recognise in his relationship to London, Dickens is caught in a changing culture. It is a measure of his courage that, unlike his early heroes and heroines, he could not turn his back on London. Seconds before that final stroke at Gad's Hill removed all power of speech, Dickens, sensing what was to come, rose from the dinner table announcing (for reasons none of those present could explain) his intention to go immediately to London.

CHAPTER V

The People Who Govern Us

> My faith in the people governing, is, on the whole, infinitesimal;
> my faith in The People governed, is, on the whole illimitable.
> *(Speeches,* 407. Birmingham: 27 September 1869)

This remark, made in a speech to the Birmingham and Midland Institute in September 1869 can be taken as broadly representative of Dickens's political creed throughout his life. At the time it was made, it proved a highly controversial statement, even though, as Dickens pointed out in a subsequent letter, it was in no way inconsistent with the whole tenor of his writings. He returned to Birmingham in January 1870:

> When I was here last autumn I made... a short confession of my political faith, or perhaps I should better say, want of faith. It imported that I have very little faith in the people who govern us — please to observe 'people' there will be with a small 'p', but that I have great confidence in the People whom they govern: please to observe 'People' there with a large 'P'. This was shortly and elliptically stated; and was, with no evil intention I am absolutely sure, in some quarters inversely explained. Perhaps as the inventor of a certain extravagant fiction, but one which I do see rather frequently quoted as if there were grains of truth at the bottom of it, a fiction called 'The Circumlocution Office', and perhaps also as the writer of an idle book or two, whose public opinions are not obscurely stated — perhaps in these respects I do not sufficiently bear in mind Hamlet's caution to speak by the card lest equivocation should undo me.
> Anyhow I complain of nobody, but simply in order that there may be no mistake as to what I did mean, and as to what I do mean, I will restate my meaning, and I will do so in the words of a great thinker, a great writer, and a great scholar — whose life, unfortunately for mankind, was cut short — in his *History of Civilization in England:*

They . . . may talk as they will about the reforms which government has introduced, and the improvements to be expected from legislation. But whoever will take a wider and more commanding view of affairs, will soon discover that such hopes are chimerical. They will learn that lawgivers are nearly always the obstructors of society, instead of its helpers; and that in the extremely few cases in which their measures have turned out well, their success has been owing to the fact that, contrary to their usual custom, they have implicitly obeyed the spirit of their time, and have been, as they always should be, the mere servants of the people, to whose wishes they are bound to give a public and legal sanction.

(*Ibid.*, 410-1. Birmingham: 6 January 1870)

Although Dickens's complaint that Government and the People were drastically divorced from each other became more acute and explicit in the 1850s (when, among other things, his fiction called "The Circumlocution Office" was invented), this was no sudden change of attitude on his part. He had always had a robust scepticism about those set up in office, especially those who became more careful of their official dignity than of their social responsibility.[1] One of the earliest of such targets is what Dickens was later to refer to as 'that surprising British monster, a beadle':

The beadle of our parish is a splendid fellow . . . .

See him . . . on Sunday in his state coat and cocked hat, with a large-headed staff for show in his left hand, and a small cane for use in his right. How pompously he marshals the children into their places! and how demurely the little urchins look at him askance as he surveys them when they are all seated with a glare of the eye peculiar to beadles! The churchwardens and overseers being duly installed in their curtained pews, he seats himself on a mahogany bracket, erected expressly for him at the top of the aisle, and divides his attention between his prayer-book and the boys. Suddenly, just at the commencement of the communion service, when the whole congregation is hushed into a profound silence, broken only by the voice of the officiating clergyman, a penny is heard to ring on the stone floor

1. Humphry House observes that Dickens 'never once attempted to give one of his benevolent characters any public office' (House, p. 182). House's chapter on 'Politics' remains the best short discussion of Dickens's interests and involvement in this whole area.

of the aisle with astounding clearness. Observe the generalship of the beadle. His involuntary look of horror is instantly changed into one of perfect indifference, as if he were the only person present who had not heard the noise. The artifice succeeds. After putting forth his right leg now and then, as a feeler, the victim who dropped the money ventures to make one or two distinct dives after it; and the beadle, gliding softly round, salutes his little round head, when it again appears above the seat, with divers double knocks, administered with the cane before noticed, to the intense delight of three young men in an adjacent pew, who cough violently at intervals until the conclusion of the sermon.

('Our Parish', *SB*, 2-3)

This character, from the *Sketches by Boz*, is an early version of that eminent 'porochial' officer Mr. Bumble. Many of Dickens's portraits of officialdom are characterised by this combination of pomposity and a somewhat short-sighted sense of responsibility. Dickens's sensitivity to this combination may well have been related to his childhood experience of his own father, for whom, as a 'governor', he developed more amused affection than respect. He was, anyway, throughout his life, wary of paternalistic government at local and national level. But, as his metaphor in praising one aspect of America suggests, an ideal relationship between Government and the People can well reflect a kind of family structure:

The State is a parent to its people; has a parental care and watch over all poor children, women labouring of child, sick persons, and captives.

(*Letters P* III, 135. Forster: 15 March 1842)

But this was certainly not what he found to be the case in England.

Dickens's observation of English Government had started early. He was twenty years old when he sat in the Press Gallery of the House of Commons reporting the debates for *The Mirror of Parliament*. This was at the time of the 1832 Reform Bill, when there were sufficiently stormy ideological confrontations to generate widespread political excitement. But Dickens seems to have been unimpressed:

> ...we have made some few calls at ["the House"] in our time — have visited it quite often enough for our purpose, and a great deal too often for our personal peace and comfort.
>
> ('A Parliamentary Sketch', *SB*, 152)

Over the next thirty years, he evidently saw little to alter this view:

> I suppose it is something peculiar in my constitution, but I *can not* imagine how any man of worth can endure the personal contemplation of the House of Commons.
>
> (*Letters N* III, 541. A.H. Layard: 8 August 1867)

In 'A Parliamentary Sketch' he offers us this unflattering view of the House:

> The order of the serjeant-at-arms will admit you into the Reporters' gallery, from whence you can obtain a tolerably good view of the House. Take care of the stairs, they are none of the best; through this little wicket — there. As soon as your eyes become a little used to the mist of the place, and the glare of the chandeliers below you, you will see that some unimportant personage on the Ministerial side of the House (to your right hand) is speaking, amidst a hum of voices and confusion which would rival Babel, but for the circumstances of its being all in one language.
>
> The "hear, hear," which occasioned that laugh, proceeded from our warlike friend with the moustache; he is sitting on the back seat against the wall, behind the Member who is speaking, looking as ferocious and intellectual as usual. Take one look around you, and retire! The body of the House and the side galleries are full of Members; some, with their legs on the back of the opposite seat; some, with theirs stretched out to their utmost length on the floor; some going out, others coming in; all talking, laughing, lounging, coughing, oh-ing, questioning, or groaning; presenting a conglomeration of noise and confusion, to be met with in no other place in existence, not even excepting Smithfield on a market-day, or a cock-pit in its glory.
>
> ('A Parliamentary Sketch', *SB*, 157)

To pass from general impressions to specific characters, we are introduced in *Nicholas Nickleby* to a notable member of Parliament, one of Dickens's earliest portraits of a politician. Mr. Gregsbury has ' a loud voice, a pompous manner, a tolerable command of sentences with no meaning in them, and, in short, every requisite for a very good member indeed'. Nicholas, having just arrived to apply for the post of secretary, finds Mr. Gregsbury having to confront a deputation from his aggrieved constituents, led by a Mr. Pugstyles:

> 'My conduct, Pugstyles,' said Mr. Gregsbury, looking round upon the deputation with gracious magnanimity — 'My conduct has been, and ever will be, regulated by a sincere regard for the true and real interests of this great and happy country. Whether I look at home, or abroad; whether I behold the peaceful industrious communities of our island home: her rivers covered with steam-boats, her roads with locomotives, her streets with cabs, her skies with balloons of a power and magnitude hitherto unknown in the history of aeronautics in this or any other nation — I say, whether I look merely at home, or, stretching my eyes farther, contemplate the boundless prospect of conquest and possession — achieved by British perseverance and British valour — which is outspread before me, I clasp my hands, and turning my eyes to the broad expanse above my head, exclaim, "Thank Heaven, I am a Briton!"
>
> The time had been when this burst of enthusiasm would have been cheered to the very echo; but now, the deputation received it with chilling coldness. The general impression seemed to be, that as an explanation of Mr. Gregsbury's political conduct it did not enter quite enough into detail; and one gentleman in the rear did not scruple to remark aloud, that, for his purpose, it savoured rather too much of a 'gammon' tendency.
>
> 'The meaning of that term — gammon,' said Mr. Gregsbury, 'is unknown to me. If it means that I grow a little too fervid, or perhaps even hyperbolical, in extolling my native land, I admit the full justice of the remark. I *am* proud of this free and happy country. My form dilates, my eye glistens, my breast heaves, my heart swells, my bosom burns, when I call to mind her greatness and her glory.'
>
> 'We wish, Sir,' remarked Mr. Pugstyles, calmly, 'to ask you a few questions.'
>
> 'If you please, gentlemen; my time is yours — and my country's — and my country's —' said Mr. Gregsbury.
>
> (*NN*, XVI, 192-3)

The deputation's questions are, predictably, received with great complacency, and one by one blown away by these gusts of patriotic rhetoric. Any remaining doubts in the reader's mind of Gregsbury's hypocrisy are finally dispelled by the particulars of the post for which Nicholas is applying:

'With regard to such questions as are not political,' continued Mr. Gregsbury, warming; 'and which one can't be expected to care a curse about, beyond the natural care of not allowing inferior people to be as well off as ourselves — else where are our privileges? — I should wish my secretary to get together a few little flourishing speeches, of a patriotic cast. For instance, if any preposterous bill were brought forward, for giving poor grubbing devils of authors a right to their own property, I should like to say, that I for one would never consent to opposing an insurmountable bar to the diffusion of literature among *the people*, — you understand? — that the creations of the pocket, being man's, might belong to one man, or one family; but that the creations of the brain, being God's, ought as a matter of course to belong to the people at large — and if I was pleasantly disposed, I should like to make a joke about posterity and say that those who wrote for posterity, should be content to be rewarded by the approbation *of* posterity; it might take with the house, and could never do me any harm, because posterity can't be expected to know anything about me or my jokes either — do you see?'

'I see that, Sir,' replied Nicholas.

'You must always bear in mind, in such cases as this, where our interests are not affected,' said Mr. Gregsbury, 'to put it very strong about the people, because it comes out very well at election-time; and you could be as funny as you liked about the authors; because I believe the greater part of them live in lodgings, and are not voters. This is a hasty outline of the chief things you'd have to do, except waiting in the lobby every night, in case I forgot anything, and should want fresh cramming; and, now and then, during great debates, sitting in the front row of the gallery, and saying to the people about — "You see that gentleman, with his hand to his face, and his arm twisted round the pillar — that's Mr. Gregsbury — the celebrated Mr. Gregsbury" — with any other little eulogium that might strike you at the moment. And for salary,' said Mr. Gregsbury, winding up with great rapidity; for he was out of breath — 'And for salary, I don't mind saying at once in round numbers, to prevent any dissatisfaction — though it's more than I've been accustomed to give — fifteen shillings a week, and find yourself. There!'

(*Ibid*., 198-9)

The satirical portrait is overdrawn, and Dickens is clearly using the occasion for some special pleading about the rights of authors. Nonetheless, the type, of which Mr. Gregsbury is an early example, is well established, and Dickens does not significantly depart from it in his representation of 'the people governing' Britain. About fifteen years later, in a *Household Words* article, he extends the following welcome:

> We are delighted to find that he has got in! Our honourable friend is triumphantly returned to serve in the next Parliament. He is the honourable member for Verbosity — the best represented place in England.
>
> Our honourable friend has issued an address of congratulation to the Electors, which is worthy of that noble constituency, and is a very pretty piece of composition. In electing him, he says, they have covered themselves with glory, and England has been true to herself. (In his preliminary address he had remarked, in a poetical quotation of great rarity, that nought could make us rue, if England to herself did prove but true.)
>
> Our honourable friend delivers a prediction, in the same document, that the feeble minions of a faction will never hold up their heads any more; and that the finger of scorn will point at them in their dejected state, through countless ages of time. Further, that the hireling tools that would destroy the sacred bulwarks of our nationality are unworthy of the name of Englishman; and that so long as the sea shall roll around our ocean-girded isle, so long his motto shall be, No surrender.
>
> ('Our Honourable Friend', *UT & RP*, 561)

Dickens's fiction has many such faceless, verbose representatives of English government — the Boodles, Coodles and Doodles, the Buffys, Cuffys and Duffys of *Bleak House* for instance; or the Rt. Hon. Hamilton Veneering, M.P. for Pocket-Breaches, in *Our Mutual Friend*. As usual these are people whom Dickens sees as far more concerned to preserve the power and mystique of their exalted position than to work hard at their proper job:

> Why have six hundred men been trying through several generations to fold their arms? The last twenty Parliaments have directed their entire attention to this graceful art. I have heard it

frequently declared by individual senators that a certain ex-senator still producible, "folded his arms better than any man in the house." I have seen aspirants inflamed with a lofty ambition, studying through whole sessions the folded arms on the Treasury Bench, and trying to fold their arms according to the patterns there presented. I have known neophytes far more distracted about the folding of their arms than about the enunciation of their political views, or the turning of their periods. The injury inflicted on the nation by Mr. Canning, when he folded his arms and got his portrait taken, is not to be calculated. Every member of Parliament from that hour to the present has been trying to fold his arms. It is a graceful, a refined, a decorative art; but, I doubt if its results will bear comparison with the infinite pains and charges bestowed upon its cultivation.

('Why?', *HW* 1 March 1856. *NCP* I, 640-1)

And why... in either house of Parliament must the English language be set to music — bad and conventional beyond any parallel on earth — and delivered, in a manner barely expressible to the eye as follows:

('A Few Conventionalities', *HW* 28 June 1851. *NCP* I, 370)

Among Dickens's early experiences of political life were the local elections he attended as a reporter in the early 1830s. These yielded some rich material for his first novel *Pickwick Papers* in the Eatanswill episode:

It appears, then, that the Eatanswill people, like the people of many other small towns, considered themselves of the utmost and most mighty importance, and that every man in Eatanswill, conscious of the weight that attached to his example, felt himself bound to unite, heart and soul, with one of the two great parties that divided the town — the Blues and the Buffs. Now the Blues lost no opportunity of opposing the Buffs, and the Buffs lost no opportunity of opposing the Blues; and the consequence was, that whenever the Buffs and Blues met together at public meeting, Town-Hall, fair, or market, disputes and high words arose between them. With these dissensions it is almost superfluous to say that everything in Eatanswill was made a party question. If the Buffs proposed to new skylight the market-place, the Blues got up public meetings, and denounced the proceedings; if the Blues proposed the erection of an additional pump in the High Street, the Buffs rose as one man and stood aghast at the enormity. There were Blue shops and Buff shops, Blue inns and Buff inns; — there was a Blue aisle and a Buff aisle in the very church itself . . . .

Never was such a contest known. The Honourable Samuel Slumkey, of Slumkey Hall, was the Blue candidate, and Horatio Fizkin, Esq., of Fizkin Lodge, near Eatanswill, had been prevailed upon by his friends to stand forward on the Buff interest. The Gazette warned the electors of Eatanswill that the eyes not only of England, but of the whole civilised world, were upon them; and the Independent imperatively demanded to know, whether the constituency of Eatanswill were the grand fellows they had always taken them for, or base and servile tools, undeserving alike the name of Englishmen and the blessings of freedom. Never had such a commotion agitated the town before.

The speeches of the two candidates, though differing in every other respect, afforded a beautiful tribute to the merit and high worth of the electors of Eatanswill. Both expressed their opinion that a more independent, a more enlightened, a more public-spirited, a more noble-minded, a more disinterested set of men than those who had promised to vote for him, never existed on earth; each darkly hinted his suspicions that the electors in the opposite interest had certain swinish and besotted infirmities which rendered them unfit for the exercise of the important duties they were called upon to discharge. Fizkin expressed his readiness to do anything he was wanted; Slumkey, his determination to do nothing that was asked of him. Both said that the trade, the manufacturers, the commerce, the prosperity of Eatanswill, would ever be dearer to their hearts than any earthly object; and each had it in his power to state, with the utmost confidence, that he was the man who would eventually be returned.

(*PP*, XIII, from pp. 157-74)

Comedy and contempt are fairly evenly mixed here. But the sense that such proceedings often amounted to a national disgrace is elsewhere put in no uncertain terms. In December 1835 Dickens wrote to his fiancee Kate from

CHARLES DICKENS AND FRIENDS AT GAD'S HILL

DICKENS WITH
DAUGHTERS
KATIE AND
MAMIE

CHILDREN BROUGHT IN TO MEET THE GROWN-UPS

FAMILY GROUP ON STEPS OUTSIDE A MANSION IN THE 1860s

LEAVING HOME
'My son, keep thy
father's commandment,
and forsake not the
law of thy mother'
Proverbs VI, 20

FAMILY DEVOTIONS
'Thy testimonies have
I taken as an
heritage for ever:
For they are the
rejoicing of my heart'
Psalm CXIX, III

HOME INDUSTRIES – SLUM TAILORS, c.1850

DINNER AT A CHEAP LODGING-HOUSE, c.1850

COTTON FACTORIES, MANCHESTER, 1835

THE BLACK COUNTRY, WOLVERHAMPTON, 1866

HULL, YORKSHIRE

THE HAEMATITE IRON AND STEEL WORKS, HINDPOOL, 1867

LEEDS, 1858

THE GREAT *LAND* SERPENT!

CONSTRUCTING KING'S CROSS UNDERGROUND, 1861

THE RAILWAY WORKS AT BLACKFRIARS, 1864

Kettering in Northamptonshire, where he had been reporting the by-election for the *Morning Chronicle:*

> You will see or hear by the Chronicle of yesterday, that we had a slight flare here yesterday morning, just stopping short of murder and a riot. Party feeling runs so high, and the contest is likely to be so sharp a one that I look forward to the probability of a scuffle before it is over. As the Tories are the principal party here, *I* am in no very good odour in the town, but I shall not spare them the more on that account in the descriptions of their behaviour I may forward to head quarters. Such a ruthless set of bloody-minded villains, I never set eyes on, in my life. In their convivial moments yesterday after the business of the day was over, they were perfect savages. If a foreigner were brought here on his first visit to an English town, to form his estimate of the national character, I am quite satisfied he would return forthwith to France, and never set foot in England again. The remark will apply in a greater or less degree to all Agricultural places during the pendency of an Election, but beastly as the electors usually are, these men are superlative blackguards. Would you believe that a large body of horsemen, mounted and armed, who galloped on a defenceless crowd yesterday, striking about them with all directions, and protecting a man who cocked a loaded pistol, were *led* by Clergymen, and Magistrates? Or that I saw one of these fellows with my own eyes, unbuckle one of his stirrup-leathers, and cut about him in the crowd, with the iron part of it — communicating to the blows all the additional force that swinging at the end of the leather could give them? Anything more sickening and disgusting, or anything that roused my indignation so much, I never beheld . . . .
> The polling begins on Friday and then we shall have an incessant repetition of the sounds and sights of yesterday 'till the Election is over — bells ringing, candidates speaking, drums sounding, a band of *eight trombones* (would you believe it?) blowing — men fighting, swearing, drinking, and squabbling — all riotously excited, and all disgracing themselves.
>
> (*Letters P* I, 106-7. Catherine Hogarth: 16 December 1835)

Dickens's life-long distrust of Government is thus partly founded on his knowledge of the corruption, bigotry and clownishness that attended the very procedures whereby the English elected their governors. In the last years of his life little seemed to have changed, to his eyes:

> The madness and general political bestiality of the Elections will come off in the appropriate Guy Fawkes days. It was proposed

to me, under very flattering circumstances indeed, to come in as the Third Member for Birmingham — I replied in what is now my stereotyped phrase "that no consideration on earth would induce me to become a candidate for the representation of any place, in the House of Commons."

(*Letters N* III, 667. T.A. Trollope: 13 September 1868)

This was in 1868. In 1841 he recorded:

I have been greatly importuned by the people of Reading, to stand for the next Parliament, but I can't afford it myself, and don't choose to be bound hand and foot to the Reform Club. Therefore I don't.

(*Letters P* II, 304. A. Fletcher: 15 June 1841)

His visit to America in the following year gave him the opportunity to see another system of government in operation. But, as he confesses in *American Notes*, any reaction he has to Government and its institutions has to be strongly qualified:

In the first place — it may be from some imperfect development of my organ of veneration — I do not remember having ever fainted away, or having even been moved to tears of joyful pride, at sight of any legislative body. I have borne the House of Commons like a man, and have yielded to no weakness, but slumber, in the House of Lords. I have seen elections for borough and county, and have never been impelled (no matter which party won) to damage my hat by throwing it into the air in triumph, or to crack my voice by shouting forth any reference to our Glorious Constitution, to the noble purity of our independent voters, or, the unimpeachable integrity of our independent members.

(*AN & PI*, 118-9)

In rather less equivocal manner, he declared, in 1857:

It appears to me that the House of Commons and Parliament altogether, is just the dreariest failure and nuisance that ever bothered this much bothered world.

(*Letters N* II, 831-2. Bulwer Lytton: 28 January 1857

There are few better satirists of the posturings of Government officialdom than Dickens, but just how politically sophisticated and sensitive was he? Chesterton believed that Dickens was one of a unique national breed: 'a sturdy sentimental English Radical, with a large heart and a narrow mind'. This, with some justice, has remained the popular image of Dickens — that, when it came to political matters, Dickens thought more with his heart than with his head.

'It seems,' George Orwell remarked, 'that in every attack Dickens makes upon society he is always pointing to a change of spirit rather than a change of structure'[1]. Again, broadly speaking, this is fair, if somewhat oversimplified. The belief — memorably expressed by Carlyle[2], among others — that Dickens's solution to all social and political wrongs was to dress up as Father Christmas and dole out enormous turkeys to impoverished families, or slip a couple of guineas to the victims of laissez-faire capitalism, only holds good (if it holds at all) for the first dozen or so years of Dickens's writing career. From the 1850s onwards, both in his art as a novelist and in his scrutiny of the relations between Government and the People, he is considerably more concerned with 'structure'. Impulsive private charity comes to seem not only more or less useless, in the sense of its being a mere drop in the ocean, but positively harmful, in that its continual alleviation of the sores on the surface draws attention away from the chronic internal disorder:

> Let us suppose, to begin with, that there was once upon a time a Baron, who governed his estate not wisely nor too well, and whose dependants sustained in consequence many preventible

1. All quotations from George Orwell are taken from his essay 'Charles Dickens' in *Inside the Whale* (1940), pp. 9-85.

2. 'His [Dickens's] theory of life was entirely wrong. He thought men ought to be buttered up, and the world made soft and accommodating for them, and all sorts of fellows have Turkey for their Christmas dinner.'

       (Sir Charles Duffy *Conversations with Carlyle*, 1892, p. 75)

hardships. Let us suppose that the Baron was of a highly generous disposition, and that when he found a vassal to have been oppressed or maltreated by a hard or foolish steward, who had strained against him some preposterous point of the discordant system on which the estate was administered, he immediately gave that vassal Money. Let us suppose that such munificent action set the noble Baron's mind completely at rest, and that, having performed it, he felt quite satisfied with himself and everybody else; considered his duty done, and never dreamed of so adjusting that point for the future as that the thing could not recur. Let us suppose the Baron to have been continually doing this from day to day and from year to year — to have been perpetually patching broken heads with Money, and repairing moral wrongs with Money, yet leaving the causes of the broken heads and the moral wrongs in unchecked operation. Agreed upon these suppositions, we shall probably agree in the conclusion that the Baron's estate was not in a promising way; that the Baron was a lazy Baron, who would have done far better to be just than generous; and that the Baron, in this easy satisfaction of his noble conscience, showed a false idea of the powers and uses of Money.

Is it possible that we, in England, at the present time, bear any resemblance to the supposititious and misguided Baron? Let us inquire.

A year or so ago, there was a court-martial held at Windsor, which attracted the public attention in an unusual manner; not so much because it was conducted in a spirit hardly reconcileable with the popular prejudice in favour of fair play, as because it suggested very grave defects in our military system, and exhibited us, as to the training of our officers, in very disadvantageous contrast with other countries. The result at which that court-martial arrived, was widely regarded as absurd and unjust. What were we who held that opinion, moved by our honest conviction, to do? To bestir ourselves to amend the system thus exposed? To apply ourselves to reminding our countrymen that it was fraught with enormous dangers to us and to our children, and that, in suffering any authorities whatsoever to maintain it, or in allowing ourselves to be either bullied or cajoled about it, we were imperilling the institutions under which we live, the national liberty of which we boast, and the very existence of England in her place among the nations? Did we go to work to point out to the unthinking, what our valiant forefathers did for us, what their resolute spirit won for us, what their earnestness secured to us, and what we, by allowing work to degenerate into play, were relaxing our grasp of, every hour? Did numbers of us unite into a phalanx of steady purpose, bent upon impressing these truths upon those who accept the responsibility of government, and on having them enforced, in stern and steady practice, through all the vital functions of Great Britain? No. Not quite that. We were highly indignant, we were a little alarmed; between the two emotions we were made, for the moment, exceedingly uncomfortable; so we relieved our uneasy souls by — giving the subject of the court-martial, Money. In putting our hands into our pockets and pulling out our five-pound notes, we discharged, as to that matter, the whole duty of man.

('A Slight Depreciation of the Currency', *HW* 3 November 1855.
NCP I, 619-20)

Humphry House brings a rather more serious charge against Dickens's sense of political responsibility:

In his acceptance of the forms of executive power he was opportunist almost to the point of irresponsibility: the only guiding principle behind this opportunism was his personal belief that what he advocated coincided with the desires and needs of all decent and disinterested men.

(House, 213)

One may wish to query the degree of 'acceptance' implied here, but House's general charge is hard to dismiss. As we have already seen, Dickens clearly does not venerate the formal procedures of English Government: at the same time he does not offer radically different ones, in spite of occasional exhortations to 'amend the system'. As Forster concluded, 'His wish to better what was bad in English institutions carried with it no desire to replace them by new ones'.

It is, however, from that generalised youthful contempt, which we have observed in the first part of this chapter, that a fairly consistent radicalism evolves, profoundly felt if intellectually undisciplined. It is a radicalism compounded chiefly of resentment against political authority founded on inherited privilege, and against the increasing tendency of Government to substitute for individual responsibility a reliance on the impersonality of Boards and Departments. Dickens is, generally, a far more astute critic of the latter than of the former. We might begin by looking at some of his comments on and portraits of the traditional English ruling class:

The humble opinion of the present age, is, that no privileged class should have an inheritance in the administration of the public affairs, and that a system which fails to enlist in the service of the country, the greatest fitness and merit that the country produces, must have in it something inherently wrong.

('The Toady Tree', *HW*, 26 May 1855. *NCP* I, 594)

Dickens's resentment against the power of the ruling classes endured throughout his life. In August of the same year that he was 'importuned' to stand for Parliament by the people of Reading, he published this new version of the famous old song — '"The Fine old English Gentleman' (to be said or sung at all Conservative Dinners)":

I'll sing you a new ballad, and I'll warrant it first-rate,
Of the days of that old gentleman who had that old estate;
When they spent the public money at a bountiful old rate
On every mistress, pimp, and scamp, at ev'ry noble gate,
   In the fine old English Tory times;
   Soon may they come again!

The good old laws were garnished well with gibbets, whips, and chains,
With fine old English penalties, and fine old English pains,
With rebel heads, and seas of blood once hot in rebel veins;
For all these things were requisite to guard the rich old gains
   Of the fine old English Tory times;
   Soon may they come again!

This brave old code, like Argus, had a hundred watchful eyes,
And ev'ry English peasant had his good old English spies,
To tempt his starving discontent with fine old English lies,
Then call the good old Yeomanry to stop his peevish cries,
   In the fine old English Tory times;
   Soon may they come again!

The good old times for cutting throats that cried out in their need,
The good old times for hunting men who held their fathers' creed,
The good old times when William Pitt, as all good men agreed,
Came down direct from Paradise at more than railroad speed...

Oh the fine old English Tory times;
When will they come again!

In those rare days, the press was seldom known to snarl or bark,
But sweetly sang of men in pow'r, like any tuneful lark;
Grave judges, too, to all their evil deeds were in the dark;
And not a man in twenty score knew how to make his mark.
  Oh the fine old English Tory times;
  Soon may they come again!

Those were the days for taxes, and for war's infernal din;
For scarcity of bread, that fine old dowagers might win;
For shutting men of letters up, through iron bars to grin,
Because they didn't think the Prince was altogether thin,
  In the fine old English Tory times;
  Soon may they come again!

But Tolerance, though slow in flight, is strong-wing'd in the main;
That night must come on these fine days, in course of time was plain;
The pure old spirit struggled, but its struggles were in vain;
A nation's grip was on it, and it died in choking pain,
  With the fine old English Tory days,
  All of the olden time.

The bright old day now dawns again; the cry runs through the land,
In England there shall be dear bread — in Ireland, sword and brand;
And poverty, and ignorance, shall swell the rich and grand,
So rally round the rulers with the gentle iron hand,
  Of the fine old English days;
  Hail to the coming time!
              (*The Examiner*, 7 August 1841: *NCP* II, 302-3)

This attack on the 'fine old English Tory days' should
remind us again that any identification of Dickens's
sympathies with good old 'Merrie England' must be
severely qualified. The aristocratic group 'Young England', led by Disraeli, which in the early Victorian years
urged a revival of the near-feudal customs and hierar-

chies of Tudor and earlier times, disgusted the Radical Dickens[1]. One can well imagine his chagrin in an 1865 letter to a friend, written from Gad's Hill:

> We are a small party just now, for my daughter Mary has been decoyed to Andover for the election week, in the Conservative interest; think of my feelings as a Radical parent!
>
> (*Letters* N III, 430. P. Fitzgerald: 7 July 1865)

One of Dickens's finest old English Gentlemen is Sir Leicester Dedlock in *Bleak House:*

Sir Leicester Dedlock is only a baronet, but there is no mightier baronet than he. His family is as old as the hills, and infinitely more respectable. He has a general opinion that the world might get on without hills, but would be done up without Dedlocks. He would on the whole admit Nature to be a good idea (a little low, perhaps, when not enclosed with a park-fence), but an idea dependent for its execution on your great county families. He is a gentleman of strict conscience, disdainful of all littleness and meanness, and ready, on the shortest notice, to die any death you may please to mention rather than give occasion for the least impeachment of his integrity. He is an honourable, obstinate, truthful, high-spirited, intensely prejudiced, perfectly unreasonable man.

Sir Leicester is twenty years, full measure, older than my Lady. He will never see sixty-five again, nor perhaps sixty-six nor yet sixty-seven. He has a twist of the gout now and then, and walks a little stiffly. He is of a worthy presence, with his light grey hair and whiskers, his fine shirt-frill, his pure white waistcoat, and his blue coat with bright buttons always buttoned. He is ceremonious, stately, most polite on every occasion to my Lady, and holds her personal attractions in the highest estimation. His gallantry to my Lady, which has never changed since he courted her, is the one little touch of romantic fancy in him . . . .

Sir Leicester has no objection to an interminable Chancery suit. It is a slow, expensive, British, constitutional kind of thing. To be sure, he has not a vital interest in the suit in question, her part in which was the only property my Lady brought him; and he has a shadowy impression that for his name — the name of Dedlock — to be in a cause, and not in the title of that cause, is a

---

1. For a further discussion of Dickens and 'Young England', in the context of *The Chimes*, see Michael Slater's 'Dickens's Tract for the Times' (esp. pp.110-14) in *Dickens 1970* ed. M. Slater (1970).

most ridiculous accident. But he regards the Court of Chancery, even if it should involve an occasional delay of justice and a trifling amount of confusion as a something devised in conjunction with a variety of other somethings, by the perfection of human wisdom, for the eternal settlement (humanly speaking) of everything. And he is upon the whole of a fixed opinion, that to give the sanction of his countenance to any complaints respecting it, would be to encourage some person in the lower classes to rise up somewhere — like Wat Tyler.

(*BH*, II, from pp. 9-13)

Bleak House appeared early in that decade, the 1850s, when Dickens felt that the deficiencies of English Government had reached crisis proportions. That "Great Dust Heap down at Westminster" he called Parliament in a letter of July 1850, interestingly anticipating the image that dominates his last completed novel, *Our Mutual Friend*. This was the decade when he was most outspoken on matters to do with politics and society. In 1846 he had founded what was intended to be a liberal newspaper *The Daily News:*

The principles advocated by 'The Daily News' will be Principles of Progress and Improvement, of Education, Civil and Religious Liberty, and Equal Legislation.

(Introductory article: quoted in Johnson I, 582)

Dickens's involvement with the newspaper was short-lived, but his appetite for journalistic contact with the public brought about the new weekly *Household Words* in 1850. He planned that all the contributions

...will seem to express the general mind and purpose of the journal, which is the raising up of those that are down, and the general improvement of our social condition.

(*Letters N* II, 202. Mrs Gaskell: 31 January 1850)

Like Charity, Dickens's social and political radicalism begins at Home, and with the Home. His new magazine was to be homely, as the list of suggested titles, and the final choice indicate — for example, *The Hearth, Evergreen Leaves, Home, Home Music, English Bells, The Household Face.* But it was not to be tamely sentimental. Dickens wrote to his sub-editor, W.H. Wills criticising one contribution:

> The fault of Prince's poem, beside its intrinsic meanness as a composition, is, that it goes too glibly with the comfortable idea (of which we have had a great deal too much in England since the Continental commotions) that a man is to sit down and make himself domestic and meek, no matter what is done to him. It wants a stronger appeal to rulers in general to let men do this, fairly, by governing them thoroughly well.
>
> *(Ibid.*, 420. W.H. Willis: 12 October 1852)

Here is the new note that is to be characteristic of Dickens's social and political attitude in the 1850s. *Household Words* is not to be the meek, cosy miscellany that readers might easily have associated with its title. It takes its political responsibility very earnestly: far too earnestly for the comfort of a certain type of reader whom Dickens satirised as Mr. Snoady:

> My objection to London, is, that it is the headquarters of the worst radical sentiments that are broached in England. I consider that it has a great many dangerous people in it. I consider the present publication (if it's *Household Words*) very dangerous, and I write this with the view of neutralising some of its bad effects. My political creed is, let us be comfortable. We are all very comfortable as we are — *I* am very comfortable as I am — leave us alone!
>
> ('Lively Turtle', *HW* 26 October 1850. *NCP* I, 306)

Dickens felt that Snoady-ish complacency was one of the great ills of mid-century England. For one thing, it gave far too broad a license to Government to waste the public money and public patience; and this was something that infuriated Dickens. In an 1855 number of *Household Words* he deftly adapts a recent *Lancet* report to the purposes of political satire:

> The disclosures in reference to the adulteration of Food, Drinks, and Drugs, for which the public are indebted to the vigour and spirit of our contemporary *The Lancet*, lately inspired us with the idea of originating a Commission to inquire into the extensive adulteration of certain other articles which it is of the last importance that the country should possess in a genuine state.

Every class of the general public was included in this large Commission; and the whole of the analyses, tests, observations, and experiments, were made by that accomplished practical chemist, Mr. Bull.

The first subject of inquiry was that article of universal consumption familiarly known in England as "Government". Mr. Bull produced a sample of this commodity, purchased about the middle of July in the present year, at a wholesale establishment in Downing Street. The first remark to be made on the sample before the Commission, Mr. Bull observed, was its excessive dearness. There was little doubt that the genuine article could be furnished to the public, at a fairer profit to the real producers, for about fifty per cent. less than the cost price of the specimen under consideration. In quality, the specimen was of an exceedingly poor and low description; being deficient in flavour, character, clearness, brightness, and almost every other requisite. It was what would be popularly termed wishy-washy, muddled, and flat. Mr BULL pointed out to the Commission, floating on the top of this sample, a volatile ingredient, which he considered had no business there. It might be harmless enough, taken into the system, at a debating-society, or after a public dinner, or a comic song; but in its present connexion it was dangerous. It had come into use as a ready means of making froth, but froth was exactly what ought not to be found at the top of this article, or indeed in any part of it. The sample before the Commission, was frightfully adulterated with immense infusions of the common weed called Talk. Talk, in such combination, was a rank Poison.

('Our Commission', *HW* 11 August 1855, *NCP* I, 322-3)

In 1848 the European revolutions, (the 'Continental commotions' referred to in Dickens's comments to Wills), and the Chartist demonstration and petition of the same year in London spurred social reforms for a while. But, as the 1850s advanced, Dickens grew more frustrated as he watched Government slowly retreating from its responsibilities, and the people relapsing into apathy:

There is nothing in the present time at once so galling and so alarming to me as the alienation of the people from their own public affairs. I have no difficulty in understanding it. They have had so little to do with the game through all these years of Parliamentary Reform, that they have sullenly laid down their cards, and taken to looking on. The players who are left at the table do not see beyond it, conceive that the gain and loss and all the interest of the play are in their hands, and will never be

the wiser until they and the table and the lights and the money
are all overturned together.

> (*Letters N* II, 651. A.H. Layard: 10 April 1855)

This was written to Austen Henry Layard, whose
agitation in Parliament over the gross inefficiency of
Government administration — especially in its handling
of the Crimean War — received warm support from
Dickens. Later in the same year, 1855, when Dickens had
become closely involved with the newly founded
Administrative Reform Association, he wrote to Macready:

> As to the suffrage, I have lost hope even in the ballot. We
> appear to me to have proved the failure of representative
> institutions without an educated and advanced people to
> support them.
>
> (*Ibid.*, 695. W. Macready: 4 October 1855)

But the quiet and sullen nature of the people seemed to
Dickens to mark only a temporary inertia, like the
weather just before a storm breaks:

> I believe the discontent to be so much the worse for smoul-
> dering, instead of blazing openly, that it is extremely like the
> general mind of France before the breaking out of the first
> Revolution, and is in danger of being turned by any one of a
> thousand accidents — a bad harvest — the last strain too much
> of aristocratic insolence or incapacity — a defeat abroad — a
> mere chance at home — into such a devil of a conflagration as
> never has been beheld since.
>
> Meanwhile, all our English tuft-hunting, toad-eating, and
> other manifestations of accursed gentility...ARE expressing
> themselves every day. So, every day, the disgusted millions
> with the unnatural gloom and calm upon them are confirmed
> and hardened in the very worst of moods. Finally, round all this
> is an atmosphere of poverty, hunger, and ignorant desperation,
> of the mere existence of which perhaps not one man in a
> thousand of those not actually enveloped in it, through the
> whole extent of this country, has the least idea.
>
> It seems to me an absolute impossibility to direct the spirit of
> the people at this pass, until it shows itself. If they would begin
> to bestir themselves in the vigorous national manner — it they
> would appear in political reunion — array themselves peace-
> fully, but in vast numbers against a system, that they know to

be rotten altogether — make themselves heard like the Sea all round this Island — I for one should be in such a movement, heart and soul, and should think it a duty of the plainest kind to go along with it (and try to guide it), by all possible means. But you can no more help a people who do not help themselves, than you can help a man who does not help himself. And until the people can be got up from the lethargy which is an awful symptom of the advanced state of their disease, I know of nothing that can be done beyond keeping their wrongs continually before them.

(*Ibid.*, 651-2. A.H. Layard: 10 April 1855)

Dickens recognises that England is a divided nation, and that each half is consciously or unconsciously promoting the division. The people, subsiding into poverty, hunger, lethargy, will do nothing to help themselves: and Government, by averting its eyes from realities, seems content to let the people subside:

There are six hundred and fifty-six gentlemen in the English House of Commons assembling in London. There is not one of those gentlemen who may not, in one week, if he choose, acquire as dismal a knowledge of the Hell upon earth in which he lives, in regard of these children, as this Inspector has — as we have — as no man can by possibility shut out, who will walk this town with open eyes observant of what is crying to GOD in the streets.

('The Metropolitan Protectives', *HW* 26 April 1851)[1]

Here is further evidence of the failed paternalistic duties of Government; for Dickens is talking of those neglected children, whose parents' irresponsibility drives them into juvenile delinquency. In *Bleak House*, written in the following year, Dickens creates his most poignant type of the neglected child, Jo, the crossing-sweeper, whose death is a reproach to his countrymen, high and low:

Dead, your Majesty. Dead, my lords and gentlemen. Dead, Right Reverends and Wrong Reverends of every order. Dead, men and women, born with Heavenly compassion in your hearts. And dying thus around us every day.

(*BH*, XLVII, 649)

1. See Charles Dickens' *Uncollected Writings from Household Words, 1850-1859*, ed. H. Stone (1968) Vol. I, p. 263.

If there is any family feeling to be discovered in the
relationship between Government and the Governed it is
reduced to the simplest and least helpful level. An
example is to be found in the attitude of Parliament
towards Sunday recreations:

> Has it occurred to any of our readers that that is surely an
> unsatisfactory state of society which presents, in the year
> eighteen hundred and fifty-five, the spectacle of a committee of
> the People's representatives, pompously and publicly inquiring
> how the People shall be trusted with the liberty of refreshing
> themselves in humble taverns and tea-gardens on their day of
> rest? Does it appear to any one whom we now address, and
> who will pause here to reflect for a moment on the question we
> put, that there is anything at all humiliating and incongruous in
> the existence of such a body, and pursuit of such an enquiry, in
> this country, at this time of day?
>
> For ourselves, we will answer the question without hesitation.
> We feel indignantly ashamed of the thing as a national scandal.
> It would be merely contemptible, if it were not raised into
> importance by its slanderous aspersions of a hard-worked,
> heavily-taxed, but good-humoured and most patient people,
> who have long deserved far better treatment. In this green
> midsummer, here is a committee virtually enquiring whether
> the English can be regarded in any other light, and domestically
> ruled in any other manner than as a gang of drunkards and
> disorderlies on a Police charge-sheet! O my Lords and Gentle-
> men, my Lords and Gentlemen, have we got so very near
> Utopia after our long travelling together over the dark and
> murderous road of English history, that we have nothing else
> left to say and do to the people but this? Is there nothing
> abroad, nothing at home, nothing seen by us, nothing hidden
> from us, which points to higher and more generous things?
>
> There are two public bodies remarkable for knowing nothing
> of the people, and for perpetually interfering to put them right.
> The one is the House of Commons; the other the Monomaniacs.
> Between the Members and Monomaniacs, the devoted People,
> quite unheard, get harried and worried to the last extremity.
> Everybody of ordinary sense, possessing common sympathies
> with necessities not their own, and common means of obser-
> vation — Members and Monomaniacs knew better, or cared
> nothing about it; and we all know the rest to this time.
>
> Now, the Monomaniacs, being by their disease impelled to
> clamber upon platforms and there squint horribly under the
> strong possession of an unbalanced idea, will of course be out of
> reason and go wrong. But, why the Members should yield to
> the Monomaniacs is another question. And why do they? Is it

because the People is altogether an abstraction to them; a Great Baby, to be coaxed and chucked under the chin at elections and frowned upon at quarter sessions, and stood in the corner on Sundays, and taken out to stare at the Queen's coach on holidays, and kept in school under the rod, generally speaking, from Monday morning to Saturday night? Is it because they have no other idea of the People than a big-headed Baby, now to be flattered and now to be scolded, and now to be sung to and now to be denounced and to old Boguey, now to be kissed and now to be whipped, but always to be kept in long clothes, and never under any circumstances to feel its legs and go about of itself? We take the liberty of replying, yes.

('The Great Baby', *HW* 4 August 1855. *NCP* I, 610-11)

This is an interesting example of the occasional discrepancy in Dickens's attitudes as expressed in his journalism and his letters. In this article he denounces those who treat the People, collectively, as a great Baby; and yet his letters in the same period complain of the meekness, helplessness and general lethargy of the People — conditions only too easy to associate with an infantile state of mind. Quite obviously, Dickens could not risk the alienation of the People by publishing such private views in *Household Words*.

The traditional reassurance that the English middle class would always act as a buffer between the two great national divisions was becoming, according to Dickens, a delusion:

...though we are perpetually bragging of [the middle class] as our safety, it is nothing but a poor fringe on the mantle of the upper.

(*Letters N* II, 695. W. Macready: 4 October 1855)

About a year before this letter, Dickens delivered an address 'To Working Men' from the pages of *Household Words*. Here (in perhaps another instance of that discrepancy between published and private views) he suggests that the middle class, given the right stimulus, could be anything but a 'poor fringe':

If working men will be thus true to themselves and one another,

there never was a time when they had so much just sympathy
and so much ready help at hand. The whole powerful
middle-class of this country, newly smitten with a sense of
self-reproach — far more potent with it, we fully believe than
the lower motives of self-defence and fear — is ready to join
them. The utmost power of the press is eager to assist them. But
the movement, to be irresistible, must originate with themselves, the suffering many. Let them take the initiative, and call
the middle-class to unite with them: which they will do, heart
and soul! Let the working people, in the metropolis, in any one
great town, but turn their intelligence, their energy, their
numbers, their power of union, their patience, their perseverance, in this straight direction in earnest — and by Christmas
they shall find a government in Downing Street and a House of
Commons within hail of it, possessing not the faintest family
resemblance to the Indifferents and Incapables last heard of in
that slumberous neighbourhood.

('To Working Men', *HW* 7 October 1854. *NCP* I, 512)

This is perhaps as close to inciting social revolution as
Dickens ever came. He felt it to be his particular
responsibility to urge the People into loud protest against
their living conditions which Government, by its inac-
tivity, seemed tacitly to condone:

It behoves every journalist, at this time when the memory of an
awful pestilence [the cholera outbreak in the summer of 1854] is
fresh among us, and its traces are visible at every turn in various
affecting aspects of poverty and desolation, which any of us can
see who are not purposely blind, to warn his readers, whatsoever be their ranks and conditions, that unless they set
themselves in earnest to improve the towns in which they live,
and to amend the dwellings of the poor, they are guilty, before
GOD, of wholesale murder.

(*Ibid.*, 510)

A few months later he wrote to Miss Coutts on a more
personal note:

I have made up my mind that what one can do in print to wake
the sleepers [i.e. the public apathy], one is bound to do at such a
serious juncture.

(*Letters C*, 288: 25 January 1855)

He had been careful to point out, in that address 'To

Working Men', that this was no new sense of personal mission in him:

> Long before this journal came into existence, we systematically tried to turn Fiction to the good account of showing the preventible wretchedness and misery in which the mass of the people dwell, and of expressing again and again the conviction, founded upon observation that the reform of their habitations must precede all other reforms; and that without it, all other reforms must fail. Neither Religion nor Education will make any way, in this nineteenth century of Christianity, until a Christian government shall have discharged its first obligation, and secured to the people Homes, instead of polluted dens.
>
> ('To Working Men', *HW* 7 October 1854. *NCP* I, 511)

As we saw in the first chapter, the central concern with Home is nothing new in Dickens. What is new, perhaps, in the middle of the 1850s, is the sense of profound despair in Dickens:

> I do reluctantly believe that the English people are habitually consenting parties to the miserable imbecility into which we have fallen, *and will never help themselves out of it*. Who is to do it, if anybody is, God knows. But at present we are on the down-hill road to being conquered, and the people WILL be content to bear it, sing "Rule Britannia", and WILL NOT be saved.
>
> (*Letters N* II, 695. W. Macready: 4 October 1855)

The great weapon that Government had devised to keep at bay any importunities from its people — short of massive popular demonstrations of the kind Dickens was advocating — was bureaucracy's favourite item of stationery:

> Your public functionary who delights in Red Tape — the purpose of whose existence is to tie up public questions great and small, in an abundance of this official article — to make the neatest possible parcels of them, ticket them, and carefully put them away on a top shelf out of human reach — is the peculiar curse and nuisance of England. Iron, Steel, adamant, can make no such dragchain as Red Tape. An invasion of Red Ants in

innumerable millions would not be half so prejudicial to Great Britain, as its intolerable Red Tape.

Your Red Tapist is everywhere. He is always at hand, with a coil of Red Tape, prepared to make a small official parcel of the largest subject. In the reception-room of a Government Office, he will wind Red Tape round and round the sternest deputation that the country can send to him. In either house of Parliament, he will pull more Red Tape out of his mouth, at a moment's notice, than a conjuror at a Fair. In letters, memoranda, and dispatches, he will spin himself into Red Tape by the thousand yards.

('Red Tape', *HW* 15 February 1851. *NCP* I, 351)

Dickens made elaborate play of this in a *Household Words* piece, written in August 1855, where he adapts the story of Ali Baba and the Forty Thieves:

Accompanied by the Grand Vizier Parmarstoon, and the black mute Mistaspeeka the chief of the Seraglio, Hansardadade again repaired next day to the august presence, and, after making the usual prostrations before the Sultan, began thus:

Sire, there was once a poor relation who lived in a town in the dominions of the Sultan of the Indies, and whose name was Scarli Tapa. He was the youngest son of a Dowajah— which, as your Majesty knows is a female spirit of voracious appetites, and generally with a wig and a carmine complexion, who prowls about old houses and preys upon mankind. This Dowajah had attained an immense age, in consequence of having been put by an evil Genie on the PENSHUNLIST, or Talisman to secure long life; but, at length she very reluctantly died towards the close of a quarter, after making the most affecting struggles to live into the half-year.

Scarli Tapa had a rich elder brother named Cashim, who had married the daughter of a prosperous merchant, and lived magnificently. Scarli Tapa, on the other hand, could barely support his wife and family by lounging about the town and going out to dinner with his utmost powers of perseverance, betting on horse-races, playing at billiards and running into debt with everybody who would trust him — the last being his principal means of obtaining an honest livelihood.

('The Thousand and One Humbugs—II', *HW* 28 April 1855. *NCP* I, 580-1)

The secret charm to open the coveted Robbers' cave (i.e. high office) is the utterance of "Debrett's Peerage. Open Sesame!" The cave is full of plunder, which Scarli Tapa and his family eventually decide to share with the Robbers, and they all live complacently ever after.

But these occasional pieces were small squibs compared with what was to come. Early in 1856 the Congress of Paris established a peace settlement that promised to bring to an end hostilities in the Crimea. Lord Palmerston (the 'Grand Vizier') accepted the conditions of peace for England with what seemed to Dickens to be extraordinarily naive optimism. By the early summer of the same year, Russian Men-of-war were again in the Black Sea:

> I have never doubted Lord Palmerston to be (considering the age in which he lives) the emptiest imposter and the most dangerous delusion ever known. Within three months of the peace, here are its main conditions broken and the whole world laughing at us! I am as certain that these men will get us conquered at last, as I am that I shall die. We have been feared and hated a long time. To become a jest after that, is a very, very serious thing. Nobody knows what the English people will be when they wake up at last and find it out.
>
> (*Letters C*, 326: 13 August 1856)

In this same month, Dickens published an article in *Household Words* entitled 'Nobody, Somebody and Everybody'. It was a full-blooded attack on the abdication of responsibility by the English Government:

> The power of Nobody is becoming so enormous in England, and he is responsible for so many proceedings, both in the way of commission and omission . . .
>
> It is difficult for the mind to span the career of Nobody. The sphere of action opened to this wonderful person, so enlarges every day, that the limited faculties of Anybody are too weak to compass it. Yet, the nature of the last tribunal expressly appointed for the detection and punishment of Nobody may, as a part of his stupendous history, be glanced at without winking.
>
> At the Old Bailey, when a person under strong suspicion of malpractices is tried, it is the custom (the rather as the strong suspicion has been found, by a previous enquiry, to exist), to conduct the trial on stringent principles, and to confide it to impartial hands. It has not yet become the practice of the criminal, or even of the civil courts — but they, indeed, are constituted for the punishment of Somebody — to invite the

prisoner's or defendant's friends to talk the matter over with
him in a cosy, tea-and-muffin sort of way, and make out a
verdict together, that shall be what a deposed iron king called
making things 'pleasant'. But, when Nobody was shown within
these few weeks to have occasioned intolerable misery and loss
in the late war, and to have incurred a vast amount of guilt in
bringing to pass results which all morally sane persons can
understand to be fraught with fatal consequences, far beyond
present calculation, this cosy course of proceeding was the
course pursued. My Lord, intent upon establishing the responsibility of Nobody, walked into court as he would walk into a
ball-room; and My Lord's friends and admirers toadied and
fawned upon him in court, as they would toady him and fawn
upon him in the other assembly. My Lord carried his head very
high, and took a mighty great tone with the common people;
and there was no question as to anything My Lord did or said,
and Nobody to bring any country that the world has ever seen
to defeat and shame, and to lay any head that ever was in it low
were proved beyond question; but, My Lord cried, "On
Nobody's eyes be it!" and My Lord's impaneled chorus cried,
"There is no imposter but Nobody; on him be the shame and
blame!"

We have, it is not to be denied, punished Nobody, with
exemplary rigour. We have, as a nation, allowed ourselves to be
deluded by no influences or insolences of office or rank, but
have dealt with Nobody in a spirit of equal and uncom-
promising justice that has moved the admiration of the world. I
have had some opportunities of remarking, out of England, the
impression made on other peoples by the stern Saxon spirit with
which, the default proved and the wrong done, we have tracked
down and punished the defaulter and wrong-doer. And I do
here declare my solemn belief, founded on much I have seen,
that the remembrance of our frightful failures within the last
three years, and of our retaliation upon Nobody, will be more
vivid and potent in Europe (mayhap in Asia, too, and in
America) for years upon years to come than all our successes
since the days of the Spanish Armada.
('Nobody, Somebody and Everybody', *HW* 30 August 1856. *NCP*
I, 656-8)

The original title for *Little Dorrit*, which had begun to
appear in December of the previous year, was *Nobody's
Fault*. Dickens reported his progress on the novel to a
friend in October 1855:

In No. 3 of my new book I have been blowing off a little of

indignant steam which would otherwise blow me up, and with God's leave I shall walk in the same all the days of my life; but I have no present political faith or hope — not a grain.

(Letters N II, 695. Macready: 4 October 1855)

In No. 3 of *Little Dorrit,* the reader comes to Chapter 10, "Containing the Whole Science of Government":

The Circumlocution Office was (as everybody knows without being told) the most important Department under Government. No public business of any kind could possibly be done at any time, without the acquiescence of the Circumlocution Office. Its finger was in the largest public pie, and in the smallest public tart. It was equally impossible to do the plainest right and to undo the plainest wrong, without the express authority of the Circumlocution Office. If another Gunpowder Plot had been discovered half an hour before the lighting of the match, nobody would have been justified in saving the parliament until there had been half a score of boards, half a bushel of minutes, several sacks of official memoranda, and a family-vault full of ungrammatical correspondence, on the part of the Circumlocution Office.

This glorious establishment had been early in the field, when the one sublime principle involving the difficult art of governing a country, was first distinctly revealed to statesmen. It had been foremost to study that bright revelation, and to carry its shining influence through the whole of the official proceedings. Whatever was required to be done, the Circumlocution Office was before hand with all the public departments in the art of perceiving — HOW NOT TO DO IT.

Through this delicate perception, through the tact with which it invariably seized it, and through the genius with which it always acted on it, the Circumlocution Office had risen to over-top all the public departments; and the public condition had risen to be — what it was.

It is true that How not to do it was the great study and object of all public departments and professional politicians all round the Circumlocution Office. It is true that every new premier and every new government, coming in because they had upheld a certain thing as necessary to be done, were no sooner come in than they applied their utmost faculties to discovering How not to do it. It is true that from the moment when a general election was over, every returned man who had been raving on hustings because it hadn't been done, and who had been asking the friends of the honourable gentleman in the opposite interest on pain of impeachment to tell him why it hadn't been done, and who had been asserting that it must be done, and who had been pledging himself that it should be done, began to devise, How it was not to be done. It is true that the debates of both Houses of Parliament the whole session through, uniformly tended to the protracted deliberation, How not to do it. It is true that the royal speech at the opening of such session virtually said, My lords and gentlemen, you have a considerable stroke of work to do, and you will please to retire to your respective chambers, and discuss, How not to do it. It is true that the royal speech, at the close of such session, virtually said, My lords and gentlemen you have through several laborious months been considering with great loyalty and patriotism, How not to do it, and you have found out; and with the blessing of Providence upon the harvest (natural, not political), I now dismiss you. All this is true, but the Circumlocution Office went beyond it.

Because the Circumlocution Office went on mechanically, every day, keeping this wonderful, all-sufficient wheel of statesmanship How not to do it, in motion. Because the Circumlocution Office was down upon any ill-advised public servant who was going to do it, or who appeared to be by any surprising accident in remote danger of doing it, with a minute, and a memorandum, and a letter of instructions, that extinguished him. It was this spirit of national efficiency in the Circumlocution Office that had gradually led to its having something to do with everything. Mechanicians, natural philosophers, soldiers, sailors, petitioners, memorialists, people with grievances, people who wanted to prevent grievances, people who wanted to redress grievances, jobbing people, jobbed people, people who couldn't get rewarded for merit, and people who couldn't get punished for demerit were all indiscriminately tucked up under the foolscap paper of the Circumlocution Office.

Numbers of people were lost in the Circumlocution Office. Unfortunates with wrongs, or with projects for the general welfare (and they had better have had wrongs at first, than have taken that bitter English recipe for certainly getting them), who in slow lapse of time and agony had passed safely through other public departments, who, according to rule, had been bullied in this, over-reached, by that, and evaded by the other; got referred at last to the Circumlocution Office, and never reappeared in the light of day. Boards sat upon them, secretaries minuted upon them, commissioners gabbled about them, clerks registered, entered, checked and ticked them off, and they melted away. In short, all the business of the country went through the Circumlocution Office, except the business that never came out of it; and *its* name was Legion.

(*LD*, X, 104-6)

This is the 'extravagant fiction' Dickens had modestly referred to in that 1870 speech quoted in the beginning of this chapter. C.P. Snow has pointed out[1] how mistaken Dickens was in many of his specific attacks on the Civil Service in this novel; how, for instance, it had never been the aristocratic preserve Dickens represents it as being, and how, even when he was writing the novel, there was already in operation a system of competitive examinations for admission into the Service. But, as Lord Snow also observes, it is in the general spirit of Dickens's attack on bureaucratic institutions — 'that bitter English recipe' — and on the habit of 'passing the buck' that the Circumlocution Office remains such a splendid 'fiction', the embodied source of so many public and private frustrations.

George Bernard Shaw considered *Little Dorrit* a more seditious book than *Das Kapital*: 'All over Europe men and women are in prison for pamphlets and speeches which are to Little Dorrit as red pepper to dynamite'. He even went so far as to attribute to this novel his own conversion to revolutionary socialism — certainly a remarkable exception to Orwell's generalisation that 'in its attitude towards Dickens the English public has always been a little like the elephant which feels a blow with a walking stick as a delighful tickling'.

In 1855 Dickens had compared the smouldering discontent of the English people to 'the general mind of France before the breaking out of the first Revolution'. At the end of this decade, his vision of such an eruption was recorded in *A Tale of Two Cities*, as clearly designed to be a warning to contemporary England as was Carlyle's monumental history *The French Revolution* (1837), to which Dickens's novel owed a huge debt.[2]

In the last decade of his life, Dickens repeatedly returned to the attack on English Government, but never

1. C.P. Snow 'Dickens and the Public Service' in *Dickens 1970* ed. M. Slater.

2. For an extended discussion of this debt, see e.g. M. Goldberg, *Carlyle and Dickens* (University of Georgia Press, 1972), esp. Chapter 7.

with the sustained energy he had shown in the 1850s. His comments on all such matters in the 1860s are marked more by a resigned disgust that by reformist zeal. His general contempt for English Law never mellowed:

> I have that high opinion of the law of England generally, which one is likely to derive from the impression that it puts all the honest men under the diabolical hoofs of all the scoundrels. It makes me cautious of doing right; an admirable instance of its wisdom!
>
> (*Letters N* III, 773. Mrs. Pollock: 2 May 1870)

The manner of his treatment of old Betty Hidgen in *Our Mutual Friend* shows a somewhat weary indignation with 'my Lords and Gentlemen and Honourable Boards'. The destitute Betty, with her indomitable courage (or her 'tedious pigheadedness', as Humphry House calls it), would rather die than face the parish Poor-house, that demoralising relic of the Poor Law of 1834 which Dickens had attacked long ago in *Oliver Twist*:

> 'Kill me sooner than take me there. Throw this pretty child under cart-horses' feet and a loaded waggon, sooner than take him there. Come to us and find us all a-dying, and set a light to us all where we lie, and let us all blaze away with the house into a heap of cinders, sooner than move a corpse of us there!'
>
> A surprising spirit in this lonely woman after so many years of hard working and hard living, my Lords and Gentlemen and Honourable Boards! What is it that we call it in our grandiose speeches? British independence, rather perverted? Is that, or something like it, the ring of the cant?
>
> (*OMF*, Bk. I, xvi, 199)

Dickens greeted the 1867 Reform Bill, and its limited extension of the franchise with perhaps as little enthusiasm as he had felt, thirty-five years before, for the First Reform Bill, the passage of which through Parliament he must have attended as a young newspaper reporter:

> As to the Reform question, it should have been, and could have been, perfectly known to any honest man in England that the more intelligent part of the great masses were deeply dissatisfied with the state of representation, but were in a very moderate and patient condition, awaiting the better intellectual

cultivation of numbers of their fellows.

> (*Letters N* III, 500. De Cerjat: 1 January 1867)

A year and a half later, he is more optimistic:

> My own strong impression is that whatsoever change the new Reform Bill may effect will be very gradual indeed, and quite wholesome.
>
> Numbers of the middle class who seldom or never voted before will vote now, and the greater part of the new voters will in the main be wiser as to their electoral responsibilities and more seriously desirous to discharge them for the common good than the bumptious singers of "Rule Britannia", "Our dear old Church of England", and all the rest of it.
>
> (*Ibid.*, 664. G.W. Rusden: 24 August 1868)

And a year after this, five months before his death, he made that "short confession of my political faith" with which this chapter began. In the next chapter we turn to the condition of the People — "please to observe People there with a large P" — governed, in whom Dickens protested his faith was illimitable.

His "infinitesimal" faith in Government and governors, as we have seen, is hardly an exaggeration; indeed, his later pessimism is an altogether dispiriting side of Dickens. He had, for a number of reasons, little political aptitude. Humphry House draws attention to a crucial deadlock in Dickens's political stance when he remarks that "an impatient reformer who wants a short-cut to a tolerable world without the risk of violence is always in a weak political postion" (House, p.212). Chesterton's "sturdy sentimental English Radical" was not ultimately a revolutionary. Dickens realised too that his proper allegiance was not to political life but to imaginative literature, and as the last two chapters aim to show, this "impatient reformer's" greatest contribution to making a "tolerable world" of nineteenth-century England was not at all quantifiable in political terms. One of the very best replies to those who criticise Dickens's lack of political sophistication is given by one of his own contemporary reviewers:

We don't blame him for not being a great politician. It would be almost miraculous if a man with such rare power of individualising as he is endowed with, should possess also the power of habitually considering questions in their most comprehensive and abstract bearing.

("Remonstrance with Dickens', *Blackwood's Magazine*, April 1857: *Crit. H.*, p. 361)

CHAPTER VI

A Nation Without Fancy

As we saw in the last chapter, Dickens's attitude towards
'The People governed' is an odd mixture of admiration
and frustration: admiration for their dogged patience and
industriousness, frustration over their lethargy and
excessive deference to authority. He despaired of Government's ever taking the initiative to bring about radical
change in the People's condition; and he despaired of the
People's ever petitioning with enough vigour and controlled purpose for radical reform. What other solutions
were there? George Orwell remarked, a propos of
Dickens, that 'If you hate violence and don't believe in
politics, the only remedy remaining is education. Perhaps
society is past praying for, but there is always hope for
the individual human being, if you can catch him young
enough'.

Dickens's considerable interest in education has been
very fully documented and discussed by Philip Collins in
his excellent study *Dickens and Education*. Collins demonstrates that, in spite of popular belief to the contrary,
Dickens was not a great originator of ideas or even
emphases in educational reform: 'For every one of
Dickens's education beliefs and interests, it is easy to
provide analogues in the writings and activities of his
contemporaries or immediate predecessors' (Collins: *Education*, 211). Nor, at the other end, as Humphry House
and Collins agree, can any specific reformist legislation
be traced directly to the influence of his work. But the
importance of education as a means to the improved
status and well-being of the People was Dickens's
continual preoccupation.

He lived in a period that saw considerable advances in
educational opportunity. Until 1833 there was no State

provision for elementary education. In 1840 the State was contributing some £50,000; and thirty-five years later (five years after Dickens's death) the grant was £1m. There was rapid advance too in the field of adult education. In 1850 England had some seventy Mechanics' Institutes with a total enrolment of over a hundred thousand. The Institutes had begun in the 1820s (in the decade that also saw the founding of London University), and won Dickens's enthusiastic support, in so far as they made available to the hard-pressed labourers in the large manufacturing towns both intellectual recreation as well as some measure of systematic education. The enthusiasm was perhaps reciprocated: in 1841 one of the lecture topics in the Institutes was 'The Writings of Dickens'.

But it was the education of children that more closely concerned Dickens, and which he saw as crucial to the well-being or otherwise of the People. No other novelist of his period invented more schools. No one more earnestly pointed out the importance of education as, for example, a weapon in the fight against crime — particularly juvenile crime. In a letter to the *Daily News* in 1846 Dickens warmly endorses the conclusions of two Prison Governors whom he greatly respected:

> Mr. Chesterton and Lieutenant Tracey (than whom more intelligent and humane Governors of Prisons it would be hard, if not impossible, to find) know, perfectly well, that these children pass and repass through the prisons all their lives; that they are never taught; that the first distinctions between right and wrong are, from their cradles, perfectly confounded and perverted in their minds; that they come of untaught parents, and will give birth to another untaught generation; that in exact proportion to their natural abilities, is the extent and scope of their depravity; and that there is no escape or chance for them in any ordinary revolution of human affairs.
>
> (*Daily News*, 4 February 1846: *NCP* I, 40)

The vicious circle must be broken, and one such attempt (the main subject of the letter) was made in the early 1840s — the Ragged Schools:

The name implies the purpose. They who are too ragged, wretched, filthy, and forlorn, to enter any other place: who could gain admission into no charity-school, and who would be driven from any church door: are invited to come in here, and find some people not depraved, willing to teach them something, and show them some sympathy, and stretch a hand out, which is not the iron hand of Law, for their correction.

(*Ibid.*, 39-40)

Dickens then describes a visit he paid to one of these Schools, located in precisely the district he had chosen for a very different 'school' — Fagin's establishment for the training of young pick-pockets:

It was a hot summer night; and the air of Field Lane and Saffron Hill was not improved by such weather, nor were the people in those streets very sober or honest company. Being unacquainted with the exact locality of the school, I was fain to make some inquiries about it. These were very jocosely received in general; but everybody knew where it was, and gave the right direction to it. The prevailing idea among the loungers (the greater part of them the very sweepings of the streets and station houses) seemed to be, that the teachers were quixotic, and the school upon the whole 'a lark'. But there was certainly a kind of rough respect for the intention, and (as I have said) nobody denied the school or its whereabouts, or refused assistance in directing to it.

It consisted at that time of either two or three — I forget which — miserable rooms, upstairs in a miserable house. In the best of these, the pupils in the female school were being taught to read and write; and though there were among the number, many wretched creatures steeped in degradation to the lips, they were tolerably quiet, and listened with apparent earnestness and patience to their instructors. The appearance of this room was sad and melancholy, of course — how could it be otherwise! — but, on the whole, encouraging.

The close, low, chamber at the back, in which the boys were crowded, was so foul and stifling as to be, at first, almost insupportable. But its moral aspect was so far worse than its physical, that this was soon forgotten. Huddled together on a bench about the room, and shown out by some flaring candles stuck against the walls, were a crowd of boys, varying from mere infants to young men; sellers of fruit, herbs, lucifer-matches, flints; sleepers under the dry arches of bridges; young thieves and beggars — with nothing natural to youth about them; with nothing frank, ingenuous, or pleasant in their faces; low-browed, vicious, cunning, wicked; abandoned of all help

but this; speeding downward to destruction; and UNUT-
TERABLY IGNORANT.

(Ibid., 41)

The Ragged Schools were private enterprises, depending
on voluntary help. As such, they received Dickens's
praise. But the disadvantages of the system were considerable, in his eyes. The squalor of the establishments
themselves was horrible. He also found the substance of
the teaching objectionable:

> So far as I have any means of judging of what is taught there, I
> should individually object to it, as not being sufficiently secular,
> and as presenting too many religious mysteries and difficulties,
> to minds not sufficiently prepared for their reception.
>
> *(Ibid., 42-3)*

He complains bitterly that Government does not take
charge of such places; but, as Philip Collins points out,
Government interference of any kind was inhibited by
religious sectarianism (the Schools were founded largely
by Evangelical or Non-conformist laymen):

> The new exposition I found in this Ragged School, of the
> frightful neglect by the State of those whom it punishes so
> constantly, and whom it might, as easily and less expensively,
> instruct and save; together with the sight I had seen there, in
> the heart of London; haunted me, and finally impelled me to an
> endeavour to bring these Institutions under the notice of the
> Government; with some faint hope that the vastness of the
> question would supersede the Theology of the schools, and that
> the Bench of Bishops might adjust the latter question, after some
> small grant had been conceded. I made the attempt; and have
> heard no more of the subject, from that hour.
>
> *(Ibid., 42)*

This letter contains so much that is fundamental to
Dickens's concerns with education and the social conditions of the poor: Government neglect, religious
monopoly, gloomy and unhygienic environments, lack of
enlightened discipline, starvation of the imagination. It is
not surprising that Dickens's preoccupation with the
education of children should be so urgent and heart-felt.

His own sense of being cheated of such opportunities when he was sent into the blacking factory at the age of twelve was a major part of the general despair he felt:

> It is wonderful to me, . . . how I could have been so easily cast away at such an age. It is wonderful to me, that, even after my descent into the poor little drudge I had been since we came to London, no one had compassion enough on me — a child of singular abilities, quick, eager, delicate, and soon hurt, bodily or mentally — to suggest that something might have been spared, as certainly it might have been, to place me at any common school. Our friends, I take it, were tired out. No one made any sign. My father and mother were quite satisfied. They could hardly have been more so, if I had been twenty years of age, distinguished at a grammar school, and going to Cambridge.
>
> (Forster, 25)

It is no wonder that Dickens felt that 'The simplest and most affecting passage in all the noble history of our Great Master, is his consideration for little children' (*Letters N* II, 672. Mrs. Winter: 13 June 1855). That such neglect as he felt he had suffered in those years should never be allowed to happen to a child, he urged again and again in his fiction and elsewhere. He certainly ensured that it never threatened his own children. His oldest son Charley was sent to Eton (a decision due largely to the moral and financial encouragement of Miss Coutts); his two youngest went to Rochester Grammar School, and one of them, Henry, went on to Cambridge.

Three celebrated schools in Dickens's fiction illustrate what he felt to be cardinal sins in the education of young children: the cruel neglect and exploitation of children in Dotheboys Hall; the more respectable and conscientious, but in some ways equally blighting, Doctor Blimber's Academy where the children are crammed with a heavy diet of the dead languages; and the Utilitarian-oriented system at the Gradgrind school where the pupils are taught to abandon Fancy and to open their minds to receive imperial gallons of Facts.

The proprietor and headmaster of Dotheboys Hall in Yorkshire is Wackford Squeers, whose original, the one-eyed William Shaw, Dickens had met during an incognito trip to Yorkshire specifically to see some of these notorious schools. Edgar Johnson gives some gruesome details of Shaw's establishment:

> William Shaw, who kept an academy at Bowes, near Greta Bridge, was sued by the parents of two children who became totally blind there through infection and gross neglect. During the trial it was testified that the boys were given maggoty food, that as many as five usually slept in a single flea-infested bed, that they were often beaten, that ten boys had lost their sight there and been given no medical treatment. Shaw was convicted and paid damages of £500 but continued to conduct his school. The small churchyard at Bowes has the graves of twenty-five boys from seven to eighteen who died there between 1810 and 1834.
>
> (Johnson I, 217)

Dickens's portrait of Dotheboys is hardly exaggerated. But its horror is mixed with some grotesque comedy, as in this scene where Nicholas is being shown by Squeers the pedagogical methods required by the school:

> Obedient to this summons there ranged themselves in front of the schoolmaster's desk, half-a-dozen scarecrows, out at knees and elbows, one of whom placed a torn and filthy book beneath his learned eye.
>
> 'This is the first class in English spelling and philosophy, Nickleby,' said Squeers, beckoning Nicholas to stand beside him. 'We'll get up a Latin one, and hand that over to you. Now, then, where's the first boy?'
>
> 'Please, sir, he's cleaning the back parlour window,' said the temporary head of the philosophical class.
>
> 'So he is, to be sure,' rejoined Squeers. 'We go upon the practical mode of teaching, Nickleby; the regular education system. C-l-e-a-n, clean, verb active, to make bright, to scour. W-i-n, win, d-e-r, der, winder, a casement. When the boy knows this out of the book, he goes and does it. It's just the same principle as the use of the globes. Where's the second boy?'
>
> 'Please, sir, he's weeding the garden,' replied a small voice.
>
> 'To be sure,' said Squeers, by no means disconcerted. 'So he is. B-o-t, bot, t-i-n, tin, bottin, n-e-y, ney, bottinney, noun substantive, a knowledge of plants. When he has learned that bottinney means a knowledge of plants, he goes and knows 'em. That's our system, Nickleby; what do you think of it?'
>
> 'It's a very useful one, at any rate,' answered Nicholas.

'I believe you,' rejoined Squeers, not remarking the emphasis of his usher. 'Third boy, what's a horse?'

'A beast, sir,' replied the boy.

'So it is,' said Squeers. 'Ain't it, Nickleby?'

'I believe there is no doubt of that, sir,' answered Nicholas.

'Of course there isn't,' said Squeers. 'A horse is a quadruped, and quadruped's Latin for beast, as every body that's gone through the grammar, knows, or else where's the use of having grammars at all?'

'Where indeed!' said Nicholas abstractedly.

'As you're perfect in that,' resumed Squeers, turning to the boy, 'go and look after *my* horse, and rub him down well, or I'll rub you down. The rest of the class go and draw water up, till somebody tells you to leave off, for it's washing-day tomorrow, and they want the coppers filled.'

(*NN*, VII, 90-1)

The definition of a horse also appears to be on the syllabus of the Gradgrind school in *Hard Times*. The prize pupil here, young Bitzer, is a triumph of the Utilitarian philosophy of education.[1] He responds like a computer to Mr. Gradgrind's question on the definition of a horse: 'Quadruped. Graminivorous. Forty teeth, namely twenty-four grinders, four eye-teeth, and twelve incisive. Sheds coat in the spring . . .' etc.

The class continues:

'Now, let me ask you girls and boys, Would you paper a room with representations of horses?'

After a pause, one half of the children cried in chorus, 'Yes, Sir!' Upon which the other half, seeing in the gentleman's face that Yes was wrong, cried out in chorus, 'No, Sir!' — as the custom is, in these examinations.

'Of course, No. Why wouldn't you?'

A pause. One corpulent slow boy, with a wheezy manner of breathing, ventured the answer, Because he wouldn't paper a room at all, but would paint it.

'You *must* paper it,' said the gentleman, rather warmly.

'You must paper it,' said Tomas Gradgrind, 'whether you like it or not. Don't tell *us* you wouldn't paper it. What do you mean, boy?'

'I'll explain to you, then,' said the gentleman, after another

---

1. As with his portrait of Dotheboys, Dickens is not exaggerating here: see David Craig's Introduction to the Penguin English Library *Hard Times* (1969), pp. 22-3.

and a dismal pause, 'why you wouldn't paper a room with
representations of horses. Do you ever see horses walking up
and down the sides of rooms in reality — in fact? Do you?'

'Yes, Sir!' from one half. 'No, Sir!' from the other.

'Of course, No,' said the gentleman, with an indignant look at
the wrong half. 'Why, then, you are not to see anywhere, what
you don't see in fact; you are not to have anywhere, what you
don't have in fact. What is called Taste, is only another name for
Fact.'

(*HT*, Bk. I, ii, 6)

Mr. Gradgrind is aptly likened to a kind of 'cannon
loaded to the muzzle with facts, and prepared to blow
them clean out of the regions of childhood at one
discharge'. Dr. Blimber, in *Dombey and Son*, is equally
guilty of 'Murdering the Innocents' (as Dickens entitled
that *Hard Times* chapter with the schoolroom scene). He
conducts a genteel Academy in Brighton, and is
entrusted with the education of the frail, six-year-old
Paul Dombey:

When ever a young gentleman was taken in hand by Doctor
Blimber, he might consider himself sure of a pretty tight
squeeze. The Doctor only undertook the charge of ten young
gentlemen, but he had, always ready, a supply of learning for a
hundred, on the lowest estimate; and it was at once the business
and delight of his life to gorge the unhappy ten with it.

In fact, Doctor Blimber's establishment was a great hothouse,
in which there was a forcing apparatus incessantly at work. All
the boys blew before their time. Mental green-peas were
produced at Christmas, and intellectual asparagus all the year
round. Mathematical gooseberries (very sour ones too) were
common at untimely seasons, and from mere sprouts of bushes,
under Doctor Blimber's cultivation. Every description of Greek
and Latin vegetable was got off the driest twigs of boys, under
the frostiest circumstances. Nature was of no consequence at all.
No matter what a young gentleman was intended to bear,
Doctor Blimber made him bear to pattern, somehow or other.

This was all very pleasant and ingenious, but the system of
forcing was attended with its usual disadvantages. There was
not the right taste about the premature productions, and they
didn't keep well. Moreover, one young gentleman, with a
swollen nose and an excessively large head (the oldest of the ten
who had 'gone through' everything), suddenly left off blowing
one day, and remained in the establishment a mere stalk.

(*D&S*, XI, 141)

Common to each of these otherwise quite different schools is the absence of any recognition that children are children, with specific emotional, intellectual and imaginative needs. To Squeers they are inconvenient creatures, useful only as menials and sources of income (and, perhaps, as food for his sadistic appetite). To Gradgrind they are guinea-pigs for ideological experiments. To Dr. Blimber, as Dickens's superb extended metaphor makes plain, children are to be 'forced' out of childhood as quickly as possible.

England was making a terrible mistake in allowing her children to be educated in such places, a mistake that would, of course, only be fully realised in the following generation or two:

> I have very seldom seen, in all the strange and dreadful things I have seen in London and elsewhere, anything so shocking as the dire neglect of soul and body exhibited in these children [of the Field Lane Ragged School]. And although I know; and am as sure as it is possible for one to be of anything which has not happened, that in the prodigious misery and ignorance of the swarming masses of mankind in England, the seeds of its certain ruin are sown, I never saw that Truth so staring out in hopeless characters, as it does from the walls of this place.
>
> (*Letters C*, 50-1: 16 September 1843)

It is a terrible vision of England's future. Again and again Dickens calls his country's attention to the 'seeds of its certain ruin' in the neglect of children, which, among the poor particularly, begins before they are even out of the cradle. The Parliamentary Commission enquiring into the 'State of Large Towns and Populous Districts' in 1844 received evidence of the consumption of opium by small children.[1] This was sold openly, as a mixture of treacle and opium known as Godfrey's Cordial, and was usually administered when the child was three to four weeks old: 'A little girl will come to the chemists and ask for a dose of it to give to the baby next day, telling him that her

1. One man giving evidence before this Commission was Dr. Southwood Smith who, on several occasions, furnished Dickens with reports and statistics on the conditions of the labouring poor.

mother is going out to work'. Even the Infant Phenomenon, who is such a lucrative feature of the Crummles
theatrical company in *Nicholas Nickleby*, is more fortunate
than these children: 'she had been kept up late every
night, and put upon an unlimited allowance of gin-
and-water from infancy, to prevent her growing tall'
(*NN*, XXIII, 290), and thereby to ensure her continued
box office appeal.

This stunted creature is grotesquely comical. But there
is a far more serious side to this question of the child's
growing up properly, physically and mentally. No child
should be prevented from maturing physically; rather
should be given every assistance that nourishment, care
and a clean and healthy home can offer. This, as we have
seen in the first chapter, and in Dickens's involvement
with sanitary reform in London, is imperative. But when
it comes to maturity of mind, we are in an altogether
more complicated area. For, in certain respects, Dickens
does not want the child to grow up:

> We received our earliest and most enduring impressions among
> barracks and soldiers, and ships and sailors. We have outgrown
> no story of voyage and travel, no love of adventure, no ardent
> interest in voyagers and travellers. We have outgrown no
> country inn — roadside, in the market-place, or on a solitary
> heath; no country landscape, no windy hill side, no old
> manor-house, no haunted place of any degree, not a drop in the
> sounding sea. Though we are equal (on strong provocation) to
> the Lancers, and may be heard of in the Polka, we have not
> outgrown Sir Roger de Coverley, or any country dance in the
> music-book. We hope we have not outgrown the capacity of
> being easily pleased with what is meant to please us, or the
> simple folly of being gay upon occasion without the least regard
> to being grand.
>
> Right thankful we are to have stopped in our growth at so
> many points — for each of these has a train of its own belonging
> to it — and particularly with the Old Year going out and the
> New Year coming in. Let none of us be ashamed to feel this
> gratitude. If we can only preserve ourselves from growing up,
> we shall never grow old, and the young may love us to the last.
> Not to be too wise, not to be too stately, not to be too rough
> with innocent fancies, or to treat them with too much lightness
> — which is as bad — are points to be remembered that may do
> us all good in our years to come. And the good they do us, may

even stretch forth into the vast expanse beyond those years; for, this is the spirit inculcated by One on whose knees children sat confidingly, and from whom all our years dated.

('Where we Stopped Growing', *HW* 1 January 1853: *NCP* I, 420-1)

This is an amplification of a point made early in *David Copperfield:*

I believe the power of observation in numbers of very young children to be quite wonderful for its closeness and accuracy. Indeed, I think that most grown men who are remarkable in this respect, may with greater propriety be said not to have lost the faculty, than to have acquired it; the rather, as I generally observe such men to retain a certain freshness, and gentleness, and capacity of being pleased, which are also an inheritance they have preserved from their childhood.

(*DC*, II, 13)

Each of these last two passages represents Dickens's slightly simplified and sentimentalised version of Wordsworth's ideas on the relationship between the child and the adult. In Book II of *The Prelude* Wordsworth traces the growth of the 'infant sensibility'. The infant is 'no outcast' — feels no sense of his separateness from the world in which he lives — because, through what Coleridge would have called the 'esemplastic' power and radiance of the mother's love, he feels himself a living part of all that he sees around him:

Emphatically such a Being lives,
An inmate of this *active* universe;
From nature largely he receives; nor so
Is satisfied, but largely gives again,
For feeling has to him imparted strength,
And powerful in all sentiments of grief,
Of exultation, fear, and joy, his mind,
Even as an agent of the one great mind,
Creates, creator and receiver both,
Working but in alliance with the works
Which it beholds. —Such, verily, is the first
Poetic spirit of our human life;
By uniform control of after years
In most abated or suppress'd, in some,

Through every change of growth or of decay,
Pre-eminent till death.
From early days,
Beginning not long after that first time
In which, a Babe, by intercourse of touch,
I held mute dialogues with my Mother's heart
I have endeavour'd to display the means
Whereby the infant sensibility,
Great birthright of our Being, was in me
Augmented and sustain'd.

                    (*The Prelude* [1805] II, ll265-87)

The Wordsworthian sustaining of that 'infant sensibility'
into adult years, and the Dickensian retaining of that
childhood 'inheritance' are closely associated. The 'closeness and accuracy' of Dickens's own 'power of observation' is perhaps proof of the value of not outgrowing
that childhood capacity. But there are obvious confusions
and dangers in such recommendations. Some of Dickens's childish old men, whom we are meant to love for
their 'gentleness and capacity of being pleased' are often
more accurately described in Aldous Huxley's terms as
'gruesome old Peter Pans'. The beaming innocence of
Mr. Pickwick has some little tendency in this direction:
'Blessed if I don't think his heart must ha' been born
five-and-twenty year arter his body, at least', remarks
Sam Weller to himself (*PP*, XXXIX, 556). The eccentric
jolliness of the Cheeryble brothers verges on imbecility.
The elderly Mr. Dick in *David Copperfield* is clearly mad:

> I lifted up my eyes to the window above... where I saw a
> florid, pleasant-looking gentleman, with a grey head, who shut
> up one eye in a grotesque manner, nodded his head at me
> several times, shook it at me as often, laughed, and went
> away...
>
>   (*DC*, XIII, 190)

Dickens mentions Mr. Dick's 'childish delight' when
Aunt Betsey praises him, his love of kite-flying, his
strictly controlled allowance of gingerbread — all of
which are to enhance his attractions by accentuating his
resemblance to a child. The Dickensian eccentric is often
thus conceived in terms of an adult with a child's mind.

It is the comic inversion of that other Dickensian hybrid, the child with the prematurely adult mind.

Whatever odd creatures came into being as a result of Dickens's preoccupations with childhood, the emphasis on that childilke 'capacity for being easily pleased' — 'not to be too wise, not to be too stately' — remained both a primary source for his imaginative power and, in many ways, his chief prescription for the ills of contemporary England. For Dickens lived in a drab age. The middle-class Puritan-Evangelical grip on the moral pulse of England was firm. The shadows of Utilitarianism had lengthened by the mid-century, and colour seemed to be fading from the national life. Numbers of people noticed this, though were not sure how it had come about. Ruskin, for one, lamented it:

> And first, it is evident that the title "Dark Ages," given to the mediaeval centuries, is, respecting art, wholly inapplicable. They were, on the contrary, the bright ages; ours are the dark ones. I do not mean metaphysically, but literally. They were the ages of gold; ours are the ages of umber.
>
> This is partly mere mistake in us; we build brown brick walls, and wear brown coats, because we have been blunderingly taught to do so, and go on doing so mechanically. There is, however, also some cause for the change in our own tempers. On the whole, these are much *sadder* ages than the early ones; not sadder in a noble and deep way, but in a dim wearied way, — the way of ennui, and jaded intellect, and uncomfortableness of soul and body. The Middle Ages had their wars and agonies, but also intense delights. Their gold was dashed with blood; but ours is sprinkled with dust. Their life was inwoven with white and purple: ours is one seamless stuff of brown. Not that we are without apparent festivity, but festivity more or less forced, mistaken, embittered, incomplete — not of the heart. How wonderfully, since Shakespere's time, have we lost the power of laughing at bad jests! The very finish of our wit belies our gaiety.[1]

(*Modern Painters*, Part IV 1856, Ch. XVI, Sect. 8)

1. Cf. Chesterton's comment: 'Upon him [Dickens] descended the real tradition of "Merry England", and not upon the pallid medievalists who thought they were reviving it. The Pre-Raphaelites, the Gothicists, the admirers of the Middle Ages, had in their subtlety and sadness the spirit of the present day. Dickens had in his buffoonery and bravery the Spirit of the Middle Ages.' (*Charles Dickens* 1906, p. 123)

Ruskin's championing of Turner, whose canvases are so often an explosion of colour, and his early support of the Pre-Raphaelites, who, whatever their deficiencies, at least brought glowing colour to the galleries of England's bleak manufacturing towns, can be seen as some effort to challenge the gloom of contemporary England. The *Westminster Review* of April 1856, also noting the prevailing national sombreness, attributed it to the Puritan spirit, and located its stronghold in the lower middle class of English society:

> All that is most peculiar in the English character — its truthfulness, its force, and its melancholy, though ultimately derived from much more remote sources, became crystallised in the Puritan type, and has retained the form there assumed even to the present time.... [The Puritans] infected English society with a vague and unmeaning gloom. Not to be happy became through them a part of the English character.

Emerson's impressions in *English Traits*, witty and succinct, tend to confirm this:

> The Englishman finds no relief from reflection, except in reflection. When he wishes for amusement, he goes to work. His hilarity is like an attack of fever. Religion, the theatre, and the reading the books of his country, all feed and increase his natural melancholy...Their well-known courage is entirely attributable to their disgust of life.

The recognition of this drabness in the lives of the English people is one of the most powerful motives behind Dickens's writing. His own experience told him how invigorating imaginative recreation could be:

> I think that my habit of easy self-abstraction and withdrawal into fancies, had always refreshed and strengthened me in short intervals wonderfully.
>
> (*Letters N* III, 531. W.H. Wills: 6 June 1867)

Surely this resource should not be withheld or so meanly rationed out to the People? Yet it was:

> The English are, so far as I know, the hardest-worked people on

whom the sun shines. Be content if, in their wretched intervals of pleasure, they read for amusement and do no more. They are born at the oar, and they live and die at it. Good God, what would we have of them.

(*Letters N* II, 548. C. Knight: 17 March 1854)

Dickens's ambition as a writer, though more diverse than this, was to afford just this kind of pleasure to a hard-pressed people:

We had sometimes reason to hope that our imaginary worlds afforded an occasional refuge to men busily engaged in the toils of life, from which they came forth none the worse to a renewal of its strivings.

(*Letters N* II, 161. Editor, *Daily News*: 11 July 1849)

In the bosoms of the young and old, of the well-to-do and of the poor, we would tenderly cherish that light of Fancy which is inherent in the human breast; which, according to its nurture, burns with an inspiring flame, or sinks into a sullen glare, but which (or woe betide that day!) can never be extinguished. To show to all, that in all familiar things, even in those which are repellent on the surface, there is Romance enough, if we will find it out: — to teach the hardest workers at the whirling wheel of toil, that their lot is not necessarily a moody, brutal fact, excluded from the sympathies and graces of imagination . . .

('A Preliminary Word', *HW* 30 March 1850: *NCP* I, 223)

Dickens's 'imaginary worlds' supply Fancy to hungry imaginations. This is why he is so angry with the Gradgrind school of Facts, which drove out Fancy from the minds of the children. As he wrote to Miss Coutts in 1850:

It would be a great thing for all of us, if more who are powerfully concerned with Education, thought as you do, of the imaginative faculty.

(*Letters C*, 175: 6 September 1850)

In an 1853 *Household Words* article, deploring the contemporary practice of adapting fairy stories into Temperance tracts, Dickens strongly urges the preservation, unadulterated, of these fanciful imaginary worlds so necessary for the child, and therefore so vital for the nation:

We may assume that we are not singular in entertaining a very great tenderness for the fairy literature of our childhood. What enchanted us then, and is captivating a million of young fancies now, has, at the same blessed time of life, enchanted vast hosts of men and women who have done their long day's work, and laid their grey heads down to rest. It would be hard to estimate the amount of gentleness and mercy that has made its way among us through these slight channels. Forbearance, courtesy, consideration for the poor and aged, kind treatment of animals, the love of nature, abhorrence of tryanny and brute force — many such good things have been first nourished in the child's heart by this powerful aid. It has greatly helped to keep us, in some sense, ever young, by preserving through our worldly ways one slender track not overgrown with weeds, where we may walk with children, sharing their delights.

In an utilitarian age, of all other times, it is a matter of grave importance that Fairy tales should be respected. Our English red tape is too magnificently red ever to be employed in the tying up of such trifles, but every one who has considered the subject knows full well that a nation without fancy, without some romance, never did, never can, never will, hold a great place under the sun. The theatre, having done its worst to destroy these admirable fictions — and having in a most exemplary manner destroyed itself, its artists, and its audiences, in that perversion of its duty — it becomes doubly important that the little books themselves, nurseries of fancy as they are, should be preserved. To preserve them in their usefulness, they must be as much preserved in their simplicity, and purity, and innocent extravagance, as if they were actual fact.

('Frauds on the Fairies', *HW* 1 October 1853: *NCP* I, 463-4)

Dickens argues that such stories are to be treasured not only for their enrichment of the imagination of the People, but also for the moral benefits they bestow. In fact the two — imaginative and moral strength — are mutually dependent, in Dickens's mind, whereas Evangelical opinion, by and large, regarded them as mutually antagonistic. 'A nation without fancy' can never be a great nation. These stories are — like the Dickensian Christmas — rejuvenating influences; and that word 'rejuvenating', with its literal and more general figurative meanings, captures exactly the complex of values Dickens associates with the literature of Fancy.

Colour is closely associated with Fancy. Dickens referred to the 'national dread of colour' in *Our Mutual*

Friend, and, in at least one case, actually took steps to counteract this when he wrote to Miss Coutts on the subject of Dress for the Urania Cottage women:

> Color these people always want, and color (as allied to fancy), I would always give them. In these cast-iron and mechanical days, I think even such a garnish to the dish of their monotonous and hard lives, of unspeakable importance. One color, and that of the earth earthy, is too much with them early and late.[1]
>
> (*Letters C,* 328-9: 15 November 1856)

Dickens's own sartorial protests against the national drabness were often remarked on, usually with some fastidious disapproval — for example, the garish waistcoats he sported during his Public Readings. He has some entertaining and evidently exasperated remarks on the Englishman's conservative attitude towards dress in an 1856 *Household Words* article:

> Our strong English prejudice against anything of this kind that is new to the eye, forms one of our decided insularities. It is disappearing before the extended knowledge of other countries consequent upon steam and electricity, but it is not gone yet. The hermetically-sealed, black, stiff, chimney-pot, a foot and a half high, which we call a hat, is generally admitted to be neither convenient nor graceful; but, there are very few middle-aged gentlemen within two hours' reach of the Royal Exchange, who would bestow their daughters on wide-awakes, however estimable the wearers . . . .
>
> Some years ago, we, the writer, not being in Griggs and Bodger's, took the liberty of buying a great-coat which we saw exposed for sale in the Burlington Arcade, London, and which appeared to be in our eyes the most sensible great-coat we had ever seen. Taking the further liberty to wear this great-coat after we had bought it, we became a sort of Spectre, eliciting the wonder and terror of our fellow creatures as we flitted along the streets. We accompanied the coat to Switzerland for six months; and, although it was perfectly new there, we found it was not regarded as a portent of the least importance. We accompanied it to Paris for another six months; and, although it was perfectly

---

1.   Compare Ruskin's comment in *The Stones of Venice:* 'The purest and most thoughtful minds are those which love colour the most.'

new there too, nobody minded it. This coat so intolerable in
Britain, was nothing more nor less than the loose wide-sleeved
mantle, easy to put on, easy to put off, and crushing nothing
beneath it, which everybody now wears.

('Insularities', *HW* 19 January 1856: *NCP* I, 624-5)

We recall how many of Dickens's fictional characters
subscribe to this kind of rigid conservatism — the
Murdstones, Dombeys and Podsnaps, with their
'buttoned-up' clothing and personalities to match. It is
their influence, compounding the gloomy austerity of
'these cast-iron and mechanical days', that Dickens is
determined to resist.

The one public issue that became a lifelong focus for all
Dickens's preoccupations with Fancy, with the insolence
of conservative office, with English Puritan gloom, with
the childlike capacity for easily pleased, and with the
general need for physical and mental recreation, was the
English Sabbath:

As one half of the world is said not to know how the other half
lives, so it may be affirmed that the upper half of the world
neithers knows nor greatly cares how the lower half amuses
itself.

('The Amusements of the People — I', *HW* 30 March 1850: *NCP*
I, 227)

The Lord's Day Act introduced in the reign of Charles II
still substantially regulated the English Sunday in the
early decades of Victoria's reign. The Evangelical revival
encouraged even stricter measures to ensure that the
Sabbath was protected not only from the performance of
work but even from any form of amusement or recreation. In the early 1830s Sir Andrew Agnew introduced a
very stringent Sabbath Bill, which was repeatedly
delayed, and ultimately failed to be carried through all
the Parliamentary stages: when the death of William IV
in 1837 caused Parliament to be dissolved, Sir Andrew
subsequently lost his seat. But it was specifically to attack
this bill that Dickens wrote his pamphlet entitled *Sunday*

Under Three Heads, published in 1836 under the pseudonym of Timothy Sparks. There Dickens argued that to curtail the harmless pleasures of the lower classes — to prohibit Sunday excursions into the countryside, games of cricket, etc. — was the one sure way to increase their patronage of the city gin-palaces. He was disgusted at the double standards tacitly condoned by those promoting the bill; for the rich were still allowed to enjoy their Sunday dinners and carriage excursions as their servants were exempted from the restrictions on Sabbath work. The idyllic picture of 'Sunday As It Might Be' we have already glimpsed. [See above pp. 39-40]. We have also noticed, in the last chapter, Dickens's indignation in 1855 at 'the spectacle of a committee of the People's representatives, pompously and publicly inquiring how the People shall be trusted with the liberty of refreshing themselves in humble taverns and tea-gardens on their day of rest'. As the title of that article ('The Great Baby') implied, it was an instance of the gross abuse of paternalistic government, and a further example of Tory insolence:

The old school of Tory writers did so pertinaciously labour to cover all easily available recreations and cheap reliefs from the monotony of common life, with ridicule and contempt, that great numbers of the English people got scared into being dull, and are only now beginning to recover their courage. The object of these writers, when they had any object beyond an insolent disparagement of the life-blood of the nation, was to jeer the weaker members of the middle class into making themselves a poor fringe on the skirts of the class above them, instead of occupying their own honest, honourable, independent place. Unfortunately they succeeded only too well, and to this grievous source may be traced many of our present political ills. In no country but England have the only means and scenes of relaxation within the reach of some million or two of people been systematically lampooned and derided. This disgraceful Insularity exists no longer. Still, some weak traces of its contemptuous spirit may occasionally be found, even in very unlikely places. The accomplished Mr. Macaulay, in the third volume of his brilliant History, writes loftily about 'the thousands of clerks and milliners who are now thrown into raptures by the sight of Loch Katrine and Loch Lomond.' No such responsible gentleman, in France or Germany, writing history — writing anything — would think it fine to sneer at any inoffensive and useful class of his fellow subjects. If the clerks and milliners — who pair off arm in arm, by thousands, for Loch Katrine and Loch Lomond, to celebrate the Early Closing Movement, we presume — will only imagine their presence poisoning those waters to the majestic historian as he roves along the banks, looking for Whig Members of Parliament to sympathise with him in admiration of the beauties of Nature, we think they will be amply avenged in the absurdity of the picture.

('Insularities', *HW* 19 January 1856: *NCP* I, 627-8)

This kind of attitude represents one example of what Dickens felt to be a particular national 'misfortune':

It has been, for many years, a misfortune of the English People to be, by those in authority, both over-disparaged and over-praised. The disparagement has grown out of mere arrogance and ignorance; the praise, out of a groundless fear of the people, and a timid desire to keep them well in hand.

('Murderous Extremes', *HW* 3 January 1857: *NCP* I, 666)

Dickens repeatedly asks how it is that the People have acquired such a reputation for degeneracy that they cannot be trusted with devising their own means of recreation:

The English people have long been remarkable for their domestic habits, and their household virtues and affections. They are, now, beginning to be universally respected by intelligent foreigners who visit this country, for their unobstrusive politeness, their good-humour, and their cheerful recognition of all restraints that really originate in consideration for the general good. They deserve this testimony (which we have often heard, of late, with pride) most honourably. Long maligned and mistrusted, they proved their case from the very first moment of having it in their power to do so; and have never, on any single occasion within our knowledge, abused any public confidence that has been reposed in them. It is an extraordinary thing to know of a people systematically excluded from galleries and museums for years, that their respect for such places, and for themselves as visitors to them, dates, without any period of transition, from the very day when their doors were freely opened. The national vices are surprisingly few. The people in general are not gluttons, nor drunkards, nor gamblers, nor addicted to cruel sports, nor to the pushing of any amusement to furious and wild extremes. They are moderate, and easily pleased, and very sensible to all affectionate influences. Any knot of holiday-makers, without a large proportion of women and children among them, would be a perfect phenomenon. Let us go into any place of Sunday enjoyment where any fair representation of the people resort, and we shall find them decent, orderly, quiet, sociable among their families and neighbours.

('The Sunday Screw', *HW* 22 June 1850: *NCP* I, 303)

It was, partly, the continuing Anti-Jacobin mood of government that made it appear necessary to keep the People on as tight a rein as possible. When this was combined with Puritan-Evangelical Sabbatarianism (itself strongly flavoured with Anti-Jacobinism) and with a pervasive Mrs. Grundyism among the middle classes, it is little wonder that those middle years of the nineteenth century in England seemed so bleak. Of all the days in the year, the bleakest was the day of rest. Here is a fine picture of it, as Arthur Clennam in *Little Dorrit* arrives in London after being away from England for some twenty-five years:

It was a Sunday evening in London, gloomy, close and stale. Maddening church bells of all degrees of dissonance, sharp and flat, cracked and clear, fast and slow, made the brick-and-mortar echoes hideous. Melancholy streets in a penitential garb of soot, steeped the souls of the people who were condemned to look at them out of windows, in dire despondency. In every thorough-fare, up almost every alley, and down almost every turning, some doleful bell was throbbing, jerking, tolling, as if the Plague were in the city and the dead-carts were going round. Everything was bolted and barred that could by possibility furnish relief to an overworked people. No pictures, no unfamiliar animals, no rare plants or flowers, no natural or artificial wonders of the ancient world — all *taboo* with that enlightened strictness, that the ugly South Sea gods in the British Museum might have supposed themselves at home again. Nothing to see but streets, streets, streets. Nothing to breathe but streets, streets, streets. Nothing to change the brooding mind, or raise it up. Nothing for the spent toiler to do, but to compare the monotony of his seventh day with the monotony of his six days, think what a weary life he led, and make the best of it — or the worst, according to the probabilities.

(*LD*, III, 28)

There was a current story of the period about a small boy in a

parish school, who, when asked by a Government Inspector
which was the longest day of the year, thought awhile and
then answered 'Sunday'.

Partly through lack of practice, no doubt, the English seemed
peculiarly disinclined to enjoy simple pleasures, and in this
respect compared unfavourably with their neighbours across
the Channel:

> When shall we get rid of the Insularity of being afraid to make
> the most of small resources, and the best of scanty means of
> enjoyment? In Paris (as in innumerable other places and
> countries) a man who has six square feet of yard, or six square
> feet of housetop, adorns it in his own poor way, and sits there
> in the fine weather because he likes to do it; because he chooses
> to do it, because he has got nothing better of his own, and has
> never been laughed out of the enjoyment of what he has got.
> Equally, he will sit at his door, or in his balcony, or out on the
> pavement, because it is cheerful and pleasant and he likes to see
> the life of the city. For the last seventy years his family have not
> been tormenting their lives with continual enquiries and
> speculations whether other families, above and below, to the
> right and to the left, over the way and round the corner, would
> consider these recreations genteel, or would do the like, or
> would not do the like. That abominable old Tyrant, Madame
> Grundy, has never been of his acquaintance. The result is, that,
> with a very small income and in a very dear city, he has more
> innocent pleasure than fifty Englishmen of the same condition;
> and is distinctly, in spite of our persuasion to the contrary (an-
> other Insularity!) a more domestic man than the Englishman, in
> regard of his simple pleasures being, to a much greater extent,
> divided with his wife and children. It is a natural consequence
> of their being easy and cheap, and profoundly independent of
> Madame Grundy.
>
> ('Insularities', *HW* 19 January 1856: *NCP* I, 627)

'We believe these people have a right to be amused',
Dickens protested in his article on 'The Amusements of
the People' in April 1850. This is echoed by the lisping
circus proprietor Mr. Sleary in *Hard Times*, as he
addresses Mr. Gradgrind near the end of that book. The
whole Gradgrind philosophy, of course, has been
directed to the eradication of such frivolous amusements
as circuses:

> 'Thquire, thake handth, firtht and latht! Don't be croth with uth

poor vagabondth. People mutht be amuthed. They can't be alwayth a learning, nor yet they can't be alwayth a working, they an't made for it. You *mutht* have uth, Thquire'

(*HT*, Bk III, viii, 293)

It was not just from cricket and country excursions that the People were excluded on Sundays: it was also art galleries and museums. This was a restriction that must have contributed greatly to the notorious English philistinism towards the fine arts. How could the People acquire any familiarity with, understanding, and appreciation of painting and sculpture if, on moral and religious grounds, they were systematically excluded from galleries on the one day of the week in which they had some leisure? This kind of attitude clearly caused some feedback; for English painting itself had acquired a stultifying kind of moral respectability in subject matter and treatment:

One of our most remarkable Insularities is a tendency to be firmly persuaded that what is not English is not natural. In the Fine Arts department of the French Exhibition, recently closed, we repeatedly heard, even from the more educated and reflective of our countrymen, that certain pictures which appeared to possess great merit — of which not the lowest item was, that they possessed the merit of a vigorous and bold Idea — were all very well, but were 'theatrical'. Conceiving the difference between a dramatic picture and a theatrical picture, to be, that in the former case a story is strikingly told, without apparent consciousness of a spectator, and that in the latter case the groups are obtrusively conscious of a spectator, and are obviously dressed up, and doing (or not doing) certain things with an eye to the spectator, and not for the sake of the story; we sought in vain for this defect. Taking further pains then, to find out what was meant by the term theatrical, we found that the actions and gestures of the figures were not English. That is to say, — the figures expressing themselves in the vivacious manner natural in a greater or less degree to the whole great continent of Europe, were overcharged and out of truth, because they did not express themselves in the manner of our little Island — which is so very exceptional, that it always places an Englishman at a disadvantage, out of his own country, until his fine sterling qualities shine through his external formality and constraint. Surely nothing can be more unreasonable, say, than that we should require a Frenchman of the days of

Robespierre, to be taken out of jail to the guillotine with the calmness of Clapham or the respectability of Richmond Hill, after a trial at the Central Criminal Court in eighteen hundred and fifty-six. And yet this exactly illustrates the requirement of the particular Insularity under consideration.

('Insularities', *HW* 19 January 1856: *NCP* I, 626-7)

Dickens, never himself particularly sensitive to the fine arts, visited the Art Exposition in Paris in 1855, where a number of English painters — some of them, like Clarkson Stanfield ('Stanny'), personal friends of his — had their work exhibited:

> ...The general absence of ideas is horribly apparent; and even when one comes to Mulready, and sees two old men talking over a much-too-prominent table-cloth, and reads the French explanation of their proceedings, 'La discussion sur les principes de Docteur Whiston,' one is dissatisfied. Somehow or other they don't tell. Even Leslie's Sancho wants go, and Stanny is too much like a set-scene. It is of no use disguising the fact that what we know to be wanting in the men is wanting in their works — character, fire, purpose, and the power of using the vehicle and the model as mere means to an end. There is a horrid respectability about most of the best of them — a little, finite, systematic routine in them, strangely expressive to me of the state of England itself....There are no end of bad pictures among the French, but, Lord! the goodness also! — the fearlessness of them; the bold drawing; the dashing conception; the passion and action in them!...
>
> Don't think it a part of my despondency about public affairs, and my fear that our national glory is on the decline, when I say that mere form and conventionalities usurp, in English art, as in English government and social relations, the place of living force and truth.

(*Letters N* II, 700. Forster: [Oct. 1855])

When Dickens announced to Forster in the following spring that, in *Little Dorrit*, 'Society, the Circumlocution Office, and Mr. Gowan [the dilettante painter], are of course three parts of one idea and design' (*Ibid.*, 766. Forster: [April 1856]), he was meaning exactly that: 'mere form and conventionalities usurp, in English art, as in English government and social relations, the place of living force and truth'. This was especially so when comparisons were made with French writers and artists. His son, Henry Fielding Dickens, remarked that 'He had a very strong love of his country, though he himself used to say, laughingly, that his sympathies were so much with the French that he ought to have been born a Frenchman' (Henry Dickens, *op.cit.*, p.28). Dickens associates a passion and boldness with French art. In his own art he particularly regrets the inhibiting moral pressures upon his creativity:

> ...I have always a fine feeling of the honest state into which we have got, when some smooth gentleman says to me or to someone else when I am by, how odd it is that the hero of an English book is always uninteresting — too good — not natural, etc. I am continually hearing this of Scott from English people here [i.e. Paris], who pass their lives with Balzac and Sand. But O my smooth friend, what a shining imposter you must think yourself and what an ass you must think me, when you suppose that by putting a brazen face upon it you can blot out of my knowledge the fact that the same unnatural young gentleman (if to be decent is to be necessarily unnatural), whom you meet in those other books and in mine, *must be* presented to you in that unnatural aspect by reason of your morality, and is not to have, I will not say any of the indecencies you like, but not even any of the experiences, trials, perplexities and confusions inseparable from the making or unmaking of all men!
>
> (*Letters N* II, 797. Forster: 15 August 1856)

The 'horrid respectability' that Dickens recognised in the painting and fiction of his own country was a phenomenon that he himself had contributed to, much earlier in his career. He prided himself, for instance, that, in *Pickwick Papers*,

> no incident or expression occurs which could call a blush into the most delicate cheek, or wound the feeling of the most sensitive person.
>
> ('Preface to the Original Edition': see *PP* ed. R. Patten, Penguin 1972, p. 42)

But nearly thirty years later, in *Our Mutual Friend*, he is heavily satirizing the complacent jingoism of Mr. Podsnap:

> '...there is in the Englishman a combination of qualities, a
> modesty, an independence, a responsibility, a repose, combined
> with an absence of everything calculated to call a blush into the
> cheek of a young person, which one would seek in vain among
> the Nations of the Earth.'
>
> (*OMF*, Bk I, xi, 133)

Respectability, like red tape, can strangle a people. Mr.
Podsnap magnificently incarnates the objects of Dickens's
scorn in the 1850s and early '60s: the arrogant insularity,
the lack of any Fancy, buttoned-up respectability, 'the
little, finite, systematic routine', and the degeneration of
English art:

> Mr. Podsnap's world was not a very large world, morally; no,
> nor even geographically: seeing that although his business was
> sustained upon commerce with other countries, he considered
> other countries, with that important reservation, a mistake, and
> of their manners and customs would conclusively observe, 'Not
> English!' when, PRESTO! with a flourish of the arm, and a flush
> of the face, they were swept away. Elsewise, the world got up at
> eight, shaved close at a quarter-past, breakfasted at nine, went
> to the City at ten, came home at half-past five, and dined at
> seven. Mr. Podsnap's notions of the Arts in their integrity might
> have been stated thus. Literature; large print, respectively
> descriptive of getting up at eight, shaving close at a quarter-
> past, breakfasting at nine, going to the City at ten, coming home
> at half-past five, and dining at seven. Painting and Sculpture;
> models and portraits representing Professors of getting up at
> eight, shaving close at a quarter-past, breakfasting at nine,
> going to the City at ten, coming home at half-past five, and
> dining at seven. Music; a respectable performance (without
> variations) on stringed and wind instruments, sedately expres-
> sive of getting up at eight, shaving close at a quarter-past,
> breakfasting at nine, going to the City at ten, coming home at
> half-past five, and dining at seven. Nothing else to be permitted
> to those same vagrants the Arts, on pain of excommunication.
> Nothing else To Be — anywhere!
>
> (*Ibid.*, 128-9)

Mr. Podsnap would certainly have approved of Miss
Twinkleton. This lady — obviously a close relative of that
'abominable old Tyrant, Madame Grundy' — is reading
to the young heroine of *Edwin Drood*, Rosa Budd; but her
Bowdler-inspired approach towards romantic literature

involves some strange falsifications:

> But Rosa soon made the discovery that Miss Twinkleton didn't read fairly. She cut the love-scenes, interpolated passages in praise of female celibacy, and was guilty of other glaring pious frauds. As an instance in point, take the glowing passage: 'Ever dearest and best adored, — said Edward, clasping the dear head to his breast, and drawing the silken hair through his caressing fingers, from which he suffered it to fall like golden rain, — ever dearest and best adored, let us fly from the unsympathetic world and the sterile coldness of the stony-hearted, to the rich warm Paradise of Trust and Love.' Miss Twinkleton's fraudulent version tamely ran thus: 'Ever engaged to me with the consent of our parents on both sides, and the approbation of the silver-haired rector of the district, — said Edward, respectfully raising to his lips the taper fingers so skilful in embroidery, tambour, crochet, and other truly feminine arts, — let me call on thy papa ere to-morrow's dawn has sunk into the west, and propose a suburban establishment, lowly it may be, but within our means, where he will be always welcome as an evening guest, and where every arrangement shall invest economy, and constant interchange of scholastic acquirements, with the attributes of the ministering angel to domestic bliss.'
>
> (*ED*, XXII, 259-60)

In an England threatened by such manifestations of philistinism, Dickens's sense of his own responsibility as an artist was considerable. We have seen how one of his main concerns was to provide imaginative recreation for a hard-pressed people. He took his art more seriously than is often assumed. When Thackeray died in December 1863 Dickens was invited to write an obituary in the *Cornhill Magazine* (which Thackeray himself had established). In an otherwise generous and eulogistic tribute to his fellow writer, Dickens had this reservation:

> I though that he too much feigned a want of earnestness, and that he made a pretence of undervaluing his art, which was not good for the art that he held in trust.
> ('In Memoriam: W.M. Thackeray', *Cornhill Magazine*, Feb. 1864: NCP I, 98)

As to his own practice, he wrote to Miss Coutts a few years earlier:

I have as great a delight in it as the most enthusiastic of my
readers; and the sense of my trust and responsibility in that
wise, is always upon me when I take pen in hand. If *I* were
soured, I should still try to sweeten the lives and fancies of
others.

(*Letters C*, 370: 8 April 1860)

Dickens was one of a number of distinguished writers
who inaugurated a Guild of Literature and Art in 1850,
designed to give financial support to struggling writers,
and to make some change in the status of the literary
man in England. The Guild (whose funds came largely
from the profits of Dickens's various theatrical enterprises in the early 1850s) was incorporated in 1854, and
continued to receive Dickens's interest and support
through to the end of his life. The image of the struggling
artist held no romantic attractions for Dickens. As he
demonstrated in his own life, the artist could, and no
doubt should be a figure of solid bourgeois respectability:

There had been, and perhaps were, those of certain conventional ideas, who present Art as a mere child: a poor
moon-stricken creature unable to take care of itself waiting as it
were, to be safely conducted over the great crossings of life by
some professional sweepers; as a miserable, slovenly slattern,
down-at-heel and out-at-elbows, with no appreciation of the
value of a home, no knowledge whatever of the value of money
— and so on; but with these popular and still lingering
hallucinations he [Dickens] had nothing whatever to do. He
altogether renounced them. He represented the artist in a
widely different light. Yes! as a reasonable creature; a sensible,
practical, responsible gentlemen; as one quite as well acquainted
with the value of his own time and money as though he were
'on high "Change"' every day; as steadfast and methodical as if
he had even a Bank or Life-office of his own to attend to; who
lived in a house as well as others who were not artists; who
enjoyed the pleasures of his wife, and home, and children, as
other men; the former of whom not only attended properly to
the ordinary matters of dress and curling of hair but, in short,
was usually to be found marked by an association with a
decorous amount of drapery. On the other hand he presented
the artist as one to whom the finest and frailest of the five
senses was essential to the achievement of every business of his
life. He could not gain wealth or fame by buying something he
never touched or saw, or selling to another man something he

might never touch or see. No! he must strike out of himself
every spark of the fire which warmed and lighted — aye, and
perhaps consumed him. He must win the great battle of life
with his own hands and by his own eyes, and he could not
choose but be in the hot encounter, General Commander-
in-Chief, Captain, Ensign, non-commissioned-officer, private,
drummer, all, in one short word, in his own unaided self.

> (*Speeches*, 303-4. London: 28 March 1862)

There was no reason, Dickens suggests, why such
respectable English values should be incompatible with
the creation of imaginary worlds: but, of course, they
were frequently, as this self-portrait of the artist in the act
of creation suggests:

> Your note finds me settling myself to Little Dorrit again, and in
> the usual wretchedness of such settlement — which is unsettle-
> ment. Prowling about the rooms, sitting down, getting
> up, stirring the fire, looking out of window, tearing my hair,
> sitting down to write, writing nothing, writing something and
> tearing it up, going out, coming in, a Monster to my family, a
> dread Phaenomenon to myself, etc. etc. etc.
>
> (*Letters C*, 316: 19 February 1856)

Dickens actually says little about his own art: he is, in
this respect as in many others, like his fictionalised self,
David Copperfield, who grows up to become a famous
author, but has a kind of reticence about his work which
baffles readers of that novel: could David Copperfield
really have written *David Copperfield?* George Dolby,
Dickens's Manager for the later Reading Tours, remarked
on Dickens's 'singular habit... of regarding his own
books as the productions of some one else, and [how he]
would almost refer to them as such' (George Dolby,
Charles Dickens as I Knew Him, Philadelphia 1885, p. 19).
Dickens spoke more readily about his art in his earlier
years; but I do not suppose that, at the end of his life, he
would have wanted to make many changes to this
statement of his artistic creed:

> It is not easy for a man to speak of his own books. I daresay that
> few persons have been more interested in mine than I; and if it
> be a general principle in nature that a lover's love is blind, and

that a mother's love is blind, I believe it may be said of an author's attachment to the creatures of his own imagination, that it is a perfect model of constancy and devotion, and is the blindest of all. But the objects and purposes I have in view are very plain and simple, and may easily be told. I have always had, and always shall have, an earnest and true desire to contribute, as far as in me lies, to the common stock of healthful cheerfulness and enjoyment. I have always had, and always shall have, an invincible repugnance to that mole-eyed philosophy which loves the darkness, and winks and scowls in the light. I believe that Virtue shows quite as well in rags and patches, as she does in purple and fine linen. I believe that she and every beautiful object in external nature, claim some sympathy in the breast of the poorest man who breaks his scanty loaf of daily bread. I believe that she goes barefoot as well as shod. I believe that she dwells rather oftener in alleys and by-ways than she does in courts and palaces, and that it is good, and pleasant, and profitable to track her out, and follow her.

(*Speeches*, 19-20. Boston: 1 February 1842)

His 'faith in the People' — especially in the poor — is here. So too is his concern to brighten the lives of his readers. In the final chapter we shall see some of the fruits of this endeavour — his great characters, drawn from the English scene, and presented in heightened colours to take their place in the novels and in the imaginations of millions.

CHAPTER VII

Anno Dombei – and Son

> I have an idea (really founded on the love of what I profess),
> that the very holding of popular literature through a kind of
> popular dark age, may depend on such fanciful treatment.
>
> (Dickens quoted in Forster, p. 728)

For the ills of England Dickens prescribed fairy stories
and proper sanitation: but as the creator of imaginary
worlds he dispensed something altogether richer. His
genius lay in his comedy, and in his ability to make the
ordinary extraordinary. It is difficult to think of a period
in English history when those two particular gifts were
more needed than in the middle decades of the
nineteenth century — those 'cast-iron and mechanical
days'. That is not to say that the need was a consciously
expressed demand from the public. On the contrary,
many a critic then, as now, complained that Dickens's
characters, incidents and settings were grotesquely
exaggerated versions of reality.[1] Dickens's reply is what
we might expect from someone who was so conscious of
the general drabness of the age:

> What is exaggeration to one class of minds and perceptions, is
> plain truth to another....I sometimes ask myself...whether it
> is *always* the writer who colours highly, or whether it is now and
> then the reader whose eye for colour is a little dull?
>
> (MC, xv: 'Preface' [1868])

As we saw in the last chapter, colour in Dickens is allied
to fancy, and fancy to the child's capacity for wonder;

1. Two discussions of this kind of criticism of Dickens are of particular interest: the chapter 'Dickens as a Novelist', in Forster's biography;
and George Ford's *Dickens and His Readers* (1955), esp. Ch. 7 'The Poet
and the Critics of Probability'.

and all of these had become dulled by the middle of the nineteenth century.

As previous chapters will have made fairly clear, the changing character of England during Dickens's lifetime will not allow any single characterisation to represent satisfactorily the national identity over this period. John Bull, for example, is typical only of the sturdy middle-class Englishman, and has little to do with the urban proletariat or the English aristocrat. So, in the case of Dickens's vast range of fictional characters, there is no single figure to which we can point and say, there is the quintessential Englishman or Englishwoman. But there are many in whom one can recognise typically English traits. As befits a society so heterogeneous as the English in Dickens's period, only some kind of composite character will be an adequate representation of his notion of the national identity; and this character, as I shall suggest later, is composed chiefly of two strains.

But the most appropriate starting point for a survey of the national character in Dickens is with the Englishman's sense of himself as, first and foremost, an Englishman. Dickens has some fine portraits of patriotic chauvinism — those characters for whom it is clear that the only proper attitude towards foreigners is one of more or less tolerant condescension. They range from the redoubtable Miss Pross in *A Tale of Two Cities* to the 'Little England' complacencies of Mr. Meagles in *Little Dorrit*, and beyond to the higher reaches of jingoistic xenophobia in Mr. Podsnap. As Orwell observed, 'one of the very striking things about Dickens, especially considering the time he lived in, is his lack of vulgar nationalism'. He might have added that Dickens not only lacked that vulgarity, but expressly deplored it:

> It is more or less the habit of every country — more or less commendable in every case — to exalt itself and its institutions above every other country, and be vain-glorious. Out of the partialities thus engendered and maintained, there has arisen a great deal of patriotism, and a great deal of public spirit. On the other hand, it is of paramount importance to every nation that its boastfulness should not generate prejudice, conventionality,

and a cherishing of unreasonable ways of acting and thinking, which have nothing in them deserving of respect, but are ridiculous or wrong.

We English people, owing in a great degree to our insular position, and in a small degreee to the facility with which we have permitted electioneering lords and gentlemen to pretend to think for us, and to represent our weaknesses to us as our strength, have been in particular danger of contracting habits which we will call for our present purpose, Insularities.

('Insularities', *HW* 19 January 1856: *NCP* I, 624)

While free from vulgar nationalism, Dickens was nonetheless patriotic. Love of country was important to him in the same way (though perhaps not to the same degree) that love of hearth and home was important. He was jealous of his country's reputation abroad, as we noticed in his disgust at Palmerston's diplomacy over the Crimean War, when he felt England was in danger of being ridiculed. He was also proud of the material progress his country had made and was making. However indigestible he found some of the fruits of contemporary civilisation, he abhorred current Romantic notions of the Noble Savage:

> To come to the point at once, I beg to say that I have not the least belief in the Noble Savage. I consider him a prodigious nuisance, and an enormous superstition. His calling rum firewater, and me a pale face, wholly fail to reconcile me to him. I don't care what he calls me. I call him a savage, and I call a savage a something to be civilised off the face of the earth. I think a mere gent (which I take to be the lowest form of civilisation) better than a howling, whistling, clucking, stamping, jumping, tearing savage . . . .
>
> Yet it is extraordinary to observe how some people will talk about him, as they talk about the good old times; how they will regret his disappearance, in the course of this world's development, from such and such lands where his absence is a blessed relief and an indispensable preparation for the sowing of the very first seeds of any influence that can exalt humanity.
>
> ('The Noble Savage', *UT & RP*, 467)

The same detestation of the tendency to glamourise barbarity occurs in Dickens's 1868 Uncommercial Traveller article 'The Ruffian', where he chastises the

Police for their dilatoriness in taking action against London's street-bandits — 'muggers', as they would now be called. He is severe in his suggestions for appropriate punishment:

> I demand to have the Ruffian kept out of my way, and out of the way of all decent people. I demand to have the Ruffian employed, perforce, in hewing wood and drawing water somewhere for the general service, instead of hewing at her Majesty's subjects and drawing their watches out of their pockets....When he infamously molests women coming out of chapel on Sunday evenings...I would have his back scarified often and deep.
>
> ('The Ruffian', *AYR* 10 October 1868: *UT & RP*, 302)

The violence of this proposed retribution often comes as a nasty surprise to those only familiar with the sentimental, genial, compassionate Dickens. It is not to be accounted for by Dickens's crusty old age (he was a crusty old fifty-six at the time): one has, for example, only to read his description in *The Old Curiosity Shop* (1840-1) of the violent death of Quilp, who 'infamously molests' (or would if he had the chance) the beautiful, helpless Little Nell, to see the singular brutality Dickens designs for those who seem beyond the pale of civilisation. There is nothing noble, but plenty that is savage about Quilp.

A related instance of this less endearing side of Dickens's concern to safeguard what he regards as the values of decent civilisation arose over the Governor Eyre incident in 1865. The Governor's reprisals against the Jamaican uprising in October of that year involved the establishment of martial law, the flogging of more than six hundred Jamaicans, and the shooting of between four and five hundred others. Dickens condoned the promptness of the Governor's action (as we would expect from one so impatient with the dilatoriness of his own country's police), and seemed also to approve of his measures. He was certainly infuriated by those at home who insisted at some length on the prosecution of the Governor for this action. It seemed to him of a piece with the misplaced missionary zeal promoted by Exeter Hall philanthropy:

So we are badgered about New Zealanders and Hottentots, as if they were identical with men in clean shirts at Camberwell, and were to be bound by pen and ink accordingly.

(*Letters N* III, 445. De Cerjat: 30 November 1865)

However distasteful these outbursts may seem, they are not instances of the kind of 'vulgar nationalism' that Orwell referred to — though they are not of course thereby excused. That kind of vulgarity has more to do with the manifestations of jingoism among his contemporaries, and Dickens has a sharp eye for this 'insularity'. Mr. Podsnap is his finest portrait here, as the following scene from *Our Mutual Friend* demonstrates. The Podsnaps are giving a lavish dinner, to which, after many reservations on Mr. Podsnap's part, they have invited a foreign gentleman:

'How Do You Like London?'' Mr. Podsnap now inquired from his station of host, as if he were adminstering something in the nature of a powder or potion to the deaf child; 'London, Londres, London?'

The foreign gentleman admired it.

'You find it Very Large?' said Mr. Podsnap, spaciously.

The foreign gentleman found it very large.

'And Very Rich?'

The foreign gentleman found it, without doubt, *enormement riche*.

'Enormously Rich. We say,' returned Mr. Podsnap, in a condescending manner. 'Our English adverbs do Not terminate in Mong and We Pronounce the "ch" as if there were a "t" before it. We Say Ritch.'

'Reetch,' remarked the foreign gentleman.

'And Do You Find, Sir' pursued Mr. Podsnap, with dignity, 'Many Evidences that Strike You, of our British Constitution in the Streets Of The World's Metropolis, London, Londres, London?'

The foreign gentleman begged to be pardoned, but did not altogether understand.

'The Constitution Britannique,' Mr. Podsnap explained, as if he were teaching in an infant school. 'We Say British, But You Say Britannique, You Know' (forgivingly, as if that were not his fault). 'The Constitution, Sir.'

The foreign gentleman said, 'Mais, yees; I know eem.'

A youngish sallowish gentleman in spectacles, with a lumpy forehead, seated in a supplementary chair at a corner of the table, here caused a profound sensation by saying, in a raised voice, 'ESKER,' and then stopping dead.

'Mais oui,' said the foreign gentleman, turning towards him. 'Est-ce que? Quoi donc?'

But the gentleman with the lumpy forehead having for the time delivered himself of all that he found behind his lumps, spake for the time no more.

'I Was Inquiring,' said Mr. Podsnap, resuming the thread of his discourse, 'Whether you Have Observed in our Streets as We should say, Upon our Pavvy as You would say, any Tokens —'

The foreign gentleman with patient courtesy entreated pardon: 'But what was tokenz?'

'Marks' said Mr. Podsnap: 'Signs, you know, Appearances — Traces.'

'Ah! Of a Orse?' inquired the foreign gentleman.

'We call it Horse,' said Mr. Podsnap, with forbearance. 'In England, Angleterre, England, We Aspirate the "H" and We Say "Horse." Only our Lower Classes Say "Orse!"'

'Pardon,' said the foreign gentleman: 'I am alwiz wrong!'

'Our Language', said Mr. Podsnap, with a gracious consciousness of being always right, 'is Difficult. Ours is a Copious Language, and Trying to Strangers. I will not Pursue my Question.'

But the lumpy gentleman, unwilling to give it up, again madly said 'ESKER,' and again spake no more.

'It merely referred,' Mr. Podsnap explained, with a sense of meritorious proprietorship, 'to Our Constitution, Sir. We Englishmen are Very Proud of our Constitution, Sir. It Was Bestowed Upon Us By Providence. No Other Country is so Favoured as This Country.'

'And ozer countries? —' the foreign gentleman was beginning, when Mr. Podsnap put him right again.

'We do not say Ozer; we say Other: the letters are "T" and "H"; you say Tay and Aish, You Know;' (still with clemency). 'The sound is "th" — "th!"'

'And *other* countries,' said the foreign gentleman. 'They do how?'

'They do, Sir,' returned Mr. Podsnap, gravely shaking his head: 'they do — I am sorry to be obliged to say it —*as* they do.'

(*OMF*, Bk I xi, 131)

The exchange ends with Mr. Podsnap's favourite gesture, the dismissive right-arm flourish, with which 'he put the rest of Europe and the whole of Asia, Africa, and America nowhere.'

Xenophobia is not restricted to the pompous middle-class circles of society. It is also found, in rather different form, among the wary, good-natured, impoverished community of Bleeding Heart Yard in *Little Dorrit*, where the vivacious little Italian John Baptist Cavalletto (recently lamed in an accident) takes up residence:

> It was up-hill work for a foreigner, lame or sound, to make his way with the Bleeding Hearts. In the first place, they were vaguely persuaded that every foreigner had a knife about him; in the second, they held it to be sound constitutional national axiom that he ought to go home to his own country. They never thought of inquiring how many of their own countrymen would be returned upon their hands from divers parts of the world, if the principle were generally recognised; they considered it practically and peculiarly British. In the third place, they had a notion that it was a sort of Divine visitation upon a foreigner that he was not an Englishman, and that all kinds of calamities happened to his country because it did things that England did not, and did not do things that England did.
>
> (*LD*, XXV, 302)

As in those general comments about English insularities quoted earlier, Dickens here goes on to blame much of the People's ingrained distrust on the propaganda of electioneering lords and gentlemen (in this case the Barnacles and Stiltstalkings).

> However, the Bleeding Hearts were kind hearts; and when they saw the little fellow cheerily limping about with a good-humoured face, doing no harm, drawing no knives, committing no outrageous immoralities, living chiefly on farinaceous and milk diet, and playing with Mrs. Plornish's children of an evening, they began to think that although he could never hope to be an Englishman, still it would be hard to visit that affliction on his head. They began to accommodate themselves to his level, calling him 'Mr Baptist,' but treating him like a baby, and laughing immoderately at his lively gestures and his childish English — more, because he didn't mind it, and laughed too. They spoke to him in very loud voices as if he were stone deaf. They constructed sentences, by way of teaching him the language in its purity, such as were addressed by the savages to Captain Cook, or by Friday to Robinson Crusoe. Mrs. Plornish was particularly ingenious in this art; and attained so much celebrity for saying 'Me ope you leg well soon,' that it was considered in the Yard, but a very short remove indeed from speaking Italian. Even Mrs. Plornish herself began to think that she had a natural call towards that language. As he became

more popular, household objects were brought into requisition for his instruction in a copious vocabulary; and whenever he appeared in the Yard ladies would fly out at their doors crying 'Mr. Baptist — tea-pot!' 'Mr. Baptist — dust-pan!' 'Mr. Baptist — flour-dredger!' 'Mr. Baptist — coffee-biggin!' At the same time exhibiting those articles, and penetrating him with a sense of the appalling difficulties of the Anglo-Saxon tongue.

(*Ibid.*, 303-4)

Both Mr. Podsnap and the Bleeding Hearts were showing 'hospitality' to the foreigners on their home ground. But the English abroad could be equally arrogant, as Dickens noted in a very funny scene witnessed during his stay in Geneva in 1846:

There are two men standing under the balcony of the hotel in which I am writing, who are really good specimens, and have amused me mightily. An immense Frenchman, with a face like a bright velvet pincushion, and a very little Englishman, whose head comes up to about the middle of the Frenchman's waistcoat. They are travelling together. I saw them at Mont Blanc, months ago. The Englishman can't speak a word of French, but the Frenchman can speak a very little English, with which he helps the Englishman out of abysses and ravines of difficulty. The Englishman, instead of being obliged by this, condescends good humouredly to correct the Frenchman's pronunciation, patronises him, would pat him on the head if he could reach so high, and screeches at his mistakes. There he is now, staggering over the stones in his little boots, and falling up against a watchmaker's window, in perfect convulsions of joy, because the beaming giant, without whom he couldn't get a single necessary of life, has made some mistake in the English language! I never saw such a fellow. The last time I met them was at the other end of the Lake by Chillon, disembarking from the steamer. It is done in little boats, the water being shallow close in shore, and in the confusion, the Giant had gone into one boat and the Dwarf in another. A hairy sailor on board the steamer found the Dwarf's greatcoat on deck and gave a great roar to him; upon which the Dwarf, standing up in the boat, cried out (in English): "Put it down. Keep it. I shall be back in an hour." The hairy sailor, of course not understanding one word of this, roared again and shook the coat in the air. "Oh you damned fool!" said the Dwarf (still in English). "Oh you precious jackass! Put it down, will you?" The Giant, perceiving from the other boat what was the matter, cried out to the hairy sailor what it was necessary for him to know, and then called

OPENING OF THE CORNWALL RAILWAY 1859

THIRD CLASS 'PARLIAMENTARY' TRAIN, 1858

SLUMS, LONDON, 1870

WATER SUPPLY, BETHNAL GREEN, 1863

LONDON, c.1860s

OLD HOUSES IN DRURY LANE, 1876

MANUFACTURE OF STOCKINGS AT OWEN AND UGLOW'S
FACTORY AT TEWKESBURY, 1860

SHEFFIELD STEEL INDUSTRIES, 1866

THE PEN GRINDING ROOM, 1851

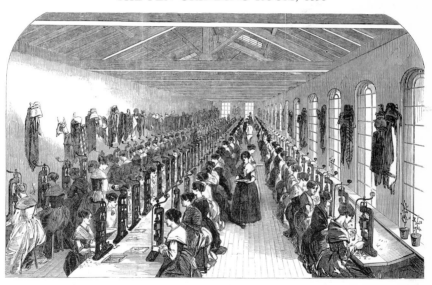

THE PEN SLITTING ROOM, 1851

CHILD CHIMNEY SWEEP, 1866

TREMENDOUS SACRIFICE!

SWEATED LABOUR 1830s

'HOUSELESS AND HUNGRY', 1869

HIRING FAIR AT SPITALFIELDS, 1850

Held on Mondays and Thursdays when young children hired themselves
for work for the ensuing week. Girls of 9 and 10 undertook to clean, wash,
nurse and cook for families who were at work and required temporary
servants. The wages ranged from 1s. to 1s. 4d. a week, and no food given.

COFFEE SHOP AT MIDNIGHT, 1820

LONDON DOCKS – NIGHT SCENE

out to the Dwarf: "I have tell him to cap it!" I thought the Dwarf would have died with delight. "Oh my God!" he said to himself. "You're a nice man! Tell him to cap it, have you? Yes, yes. Ha ha ha! Cap it, indeed! Oh Lord!" And never left off chuckling till he landed.

> (*Letters N* I, 800-1. T. Beard: 21 October 1846)

A splendid portrait of the eccentric Englishman abroad — this time not a xenophobe — comes in Dickens's account of a certain Lord Vernon, with whom he became acquainted in Switzerland in 1846:

> Another curious man is backwards and forwards here — a Lord Vernon, who is well-informed, a great Italian scholar deep in Dante, and a very good-humoured gentleman, but who has fallen into the strange infatuation of attending every rifle-match that takes place in Switzerland, accompanied by two men who load rifles for him, one after another, which he has been frequently known to fire off, two a minute, for fourteen hours at a stretch, without once changing his position or leaving the ground. He wins all kinds of prizes; gold watches, flags, teaspoons, teaboards, and so forth; and is constantly travelling about with them, from place to place, in an extraordinary carriage, where you touch a spring and a chair flies out, touch another spring and a bed appears, touch another spring and a closet of pickles opens, touch another spring and disclose a pantry! while Lady Vernon (said to be handsome and accomplished) is continually cutting across this or that Alpine pass in the night, to meet him on the road for a minute or two, on one of his excursions; these being the only times at which she can catch him. The last time he saw her, was five or six months ago, when they met and supped together on the St. Gothard!
>
> (*Ibid.*, 779-80. Forster: [Aug. 1846])

Part of the national distrust of foreigners that Dickens deplores depends on the sense that the Englishman has that, just as England is the centre of civilisation (as London is the 'world's metropolis'), so the Englishman himself represents the moral norm for civilised man. Other countries are judged as deviations in varying degrees from this norm. It is the same kind of attitude that is involved in the matter of eccentricity, traditionally an English affliction — or proud prerogative, depending on how you regard it. The delight in eccentricity relies to a large extent on a confident consensus about what forms the 'centre': that this same confidence may be absurdly misplaced is beside the question. 'Eccentricity', observed one of the shrewdest of our eccentrics, Edith Sitwell, 'exists particularly in the English, and partly, I think, because of that peculiar and satisfactory knowledge of infallibility that is the hallmark and birthright of the British nation'.[1]

Dickens's great eccentrics, in many minds the triumph of his fiction, were for his contemporaries and remain for us today ' a medicine for our melancholy', to use Miss Sitwell's phrase. They are disconcerting, capricious, extravagant and, by and large, harmless. They offer relief from the sobriety, conformity and drabness that seemed to be overtaking England in the middle of the nineteenth century. 'The world is too much with us, early and late', complained Dickens in his article 'Frauds on the Fairies', in echo of Wordsworth. Even Dickens's nomenclature has a kind of eccentricity. Think of the rigid, ponderous dissyllables that compose his names for those who represent the Englishman's formality and constraint: Dombey, Murdstone, Dedlock, Podsnap. Then compare this selection of names drawn up by Dickens, but, as far as I recall, not used in any of the novels:

> Towndling, Mood, Guff, Treble, Gannerson, Chinkerble, Queedy, Musty, Grout, Drowvey, Warbler, Tricklebank, Foggy, Bremmidge, Blodget, Slingo, Glibbery, Doolge.
>
> (Forster, 758-9)

The very sounds of the names evoke a kind of grotesque freakishness and vitality that challenge the austerity of the earlier list.

In *David Copperfield*, a novel in which (like England in 1850) the growing earnestness makes the eccentric presence more than usually attractive, Dickens creates a brilliant range of such characters: Mr. Dick (whom we glimpsed in the last chapter), Barkis, the younger

---

1. Edith Sitwell, *English Eccentrics*, New York: Vanguard Press 1957, pp.20-1

Traddles, Aunt Betsey, Mr Micawber. Some of these are characters whose eccentricity and freedom of movement are somewhat curtailed in the later, more sober stages of the novel, because they are important participants in the developing story. But there is a splendid example of a grotesque eccentric who has no such responsibility — the alarming owner of the slop-shop where young David tries to sell his jacket:

He was a dreadful old man to look at, in a filthy flannel waistcoat, and smelling terribly of rum. His bedstead, covered with a tumbled and ragged piece of patchwork, was in the den he had come from, where another little window showed a prospect of more stinging-nettles, and a lame donkey.

'Oh, what do you want?' grinned this old man, in a fierce, monotonous whine. 'Oh, my eyes and limbs, what do you want? Oh, my lungs and liver, what do you want? Oh, goroo, goroo!'

I was so much dismayed by these words, and particularly by the repetition of the last unknown one, which was a kind of rattle in his throat, that I could make no answer; hereupon the old man, still holding me by the hair, repeated:

'Oh, what do you want? Oh, my eyes and limbs, what do you want? Oh, my lungs and liver, what do you want? Oh, goroo!' — which he screwed out of himself, with an energy that made his eyes start in his head.

'I wanted to know', I said, trembling, 'if you would buy a jacket.'

'Oh, let's see the jacket!' cried the old man. 'Oh, my heart on fire, show the jacket to us! Oh, my eyes and limbs, bring the jacket out!'

With that he took his trembling hands, which were like the claws of a great bird, out of my hair; and put on a pair of spectacles, not at all ornamental to his inflamed eyes.

'Oh, how much for the jacket?' cried the old man, after examining it. 'Oh — goroo! — how much for the jacket?'

'Half-a-crown,' I answered, recovering myself.

'Oh, my lungs and liver', cried the old man, 'no! Oh, my eyes, no! Oh, my limbs, no! Eighteenpence. Goroo!'

Every time he uttered this ejaculation, his eyes seemed to be in danger of starting out; and every sentence he spoke, he delivered in a sort of tune, always exactly the same, and more like a gust of wind, which begins low, mounts up high, and falls again, than any other comparison I can find for it.

'Well,' said I, glad to have closed the bargain, 'I'll take eighteenpence.'

'Oh, my liver!' cried the old man, throwing the jacket on a shelf. 'Get out of the shop! Oh, my lungs, get out of the shop! Oh, my eyes and limbs — goroo! — don't ask for money; make it an exchange.'

(DC, XIII, 184-5)

This is one of Dickens's simple eccentrics, simple in that sense mentioned earlier: he does not have to become incorporated into the developing design of the novel, and therefore modified. Another example is the lunatic gentleman in small clothes in *Nicholas Nickleby*, who woos Mrs. Nickleby by hurling vegetables over the wall into her garden, in one of the most hilarious scenes in all Dickens.

Mr. Micawber, though, is a complex eccentric. He is complex not only because Dickens requires of him some slight change of character as the novel nears its climax; but he is complex in the very nature of his personality. We are introduced to him when, one lunchtime at the Murdstone and Grinby bottling warehouse, young David is called into the counting-house:

I went in, and found there a stoutish, middle-aged person, in a brown surtout and black tights and shoes, with no more hair upon his head (which was a large one, and very shining) than there is upon an egg, and with a very extensive face, which he turned full upon me. His clothes were shabby, but he had an imposing shirt-collar on. He carried a jaunty sort of a stick, with a large pair of rusty tassels to it; and a quizzing-glass hung outside his coat, — for ornament, I afterwards found, as he very seldom looked through it, and couldn't see anything when he did.

(Ibid, XI, 155-6)

David soon notices that Micawber has 'a certain condescending roll in his voice, and a certain indescribable air of doing something genteel'. Dickens is always fascinated by the shabby-genteel, but never gave as rich a portrait of the type as here. Micawber's general demeanour of pompous respectability, so naively belied by those traces of simple shabbiness, is also expressed in his famous conversational manner as a kind of linguistic shabby-gentility: he launches into those magnificent latinate polysyllabic periods, then seems to run out of steam abruptly and ends, 'in short', with blunt Anglo-Saxon simplicities — 'crushed', 'floored', 'in the lurch'. Dickens himself draws attention to correspondences between dress and language, and went so far as to compare Mr. Micawber's superfluity of words with a failure on the national level:

> we are fond of having a large superfluous establishment of words to wait upon us on great occasions; we think it looks important, and sounds well. As we are not particular about the meaning of our liveries on state occasions, if they be but fine and numerous enough, so the meaning or necessity of our words is a secondary consideration, if there be but a great parade of them. And as individuals get into trouble by making too great a show of liveries, ... so I think I could mention a nation that has got into a great many difficulties, and will get into many greater, from maintaining too large a retinue of words.
>
> (*Ibid.*, LII, 754)

I mentioned earlier that the English character, for Dickens, seemed to be composed chiefly of two strains. This may be illustrated in the case of Mr. Micawber. He is an odd and peculiarly English combination of buttoned-up respectability and spontaneous effusiveness. Many of Dickens's great portraits of the English are characterised precisely by the degree to which their personalities reveal one or other of these strains. *Dombey and Son*'s very title directs one to the heart of this peculiarity in the English character. One might re-phrase the title as a question of psychological alternatives: Dombey *or* Son? Dombey's forbidding reserve, rigid respectability and arrogance, or Son's frank affections, rich imagination and tenderness? These are alternatives with which Dickens again and again confronted his public in his portraits of the English. Dombey's ultimate redemption is significantly in terms of a loving reconciliation with Son (the little Paul of the succeeding generation). Dickens also creates a number of characters who appear to be eccentric amalgamations of these two strains, like Mr. Micawber; or, in the later works, divided personalities of more alarming complexity, like John Jasper.

But let us now consider the former of these two characteristics, the buttoned-up respectability, and concentrate on Mr. Micawber. Mr. Micawber's assumptions of gentility are almost always transparent and comical. There is a fine moment in the novel when the icily formal Littimer intrudes on a dinner given by David, and catches the company relaxed and off-guard. Mr. Micawber is among the guests who have been served with an exceptionally *saignant* leg of mutton, and it is he who has suggested the brilliant though scarcely genteel remedy of slicing and toasting the leg. In this situation, Littimer's sudden presence nearly paralyses the company:

> Mr. Micawber, humming a tune, to show that he was quite at ease, subsided into his chair, with the handle of a hastily concealed fork sticking out of the bosom of his coat as if he had stabbed himself.
>
> (*Ibid*., XXVIII, 414)

But perhaps his most endearing and characteristic moment comes with his parting bestowal of advice on young David:

> 'My dear young friend,' said Mr. Micawber, 'I am older than you; a man of some experience in life, and — and of some experience, in short, in difficulties, generally speaking. At present, and until something turns up (which I am, I may say, hourly expecting), I have nothing to bestow but advice. Still my advice is so far worth taking that — in short, that I have never taken it myself, and am the' — here Mr. Micawber, who had been beaming and smiling, all over his head and face, up to the present moment, checked himself and frowned — 'the miserable wretch you behold.'
> 'My dear Micawber!' urged his wife.
> 'I say', returned Mr. Micawber, quite forgetting himself, and smiling again, 'the miserable wretch you behold. My advice is, never do to-morrow what you can do to-day. Procrastination is the thief of time. Collar him!'
> 'My poor papa's maxim,' Mrs. Micawber observed.
> 'My dear, said Mr. Micawber, 'your papa was very well in his way, and Heaven forbid that I should disparage him. Take him for all in all, we ne'er shall — in short, make the acquaintance,

probably, of anybody else possessing, at his time of life, the
same legs for gaiters, and able to read the same description of
print, without spectacles. But he applied that maxim to our
marriage, my dear; and that was so far prematurely entered
into, in consequence, that I never recovered the expense.'

Mr. Micawber looked aside at Mrs. Micawber, and added:
'Not that I am sorry for it. Quite the contrary, my love.' After
which he was grave for a minute or so.

'My other piece of advice, Copperfield,' said Mr. Micawber,
'you know. Annual income twenty pounds, annual expenditure
nineteen nineteen six, result happiness. Annual income twenty
pounds, annual expenditure twenty pounds ought and six,
result misery. The blossom is blighted, and the leaf is withered,
the God of day goes down upon the dreary scene, and — and in
short you are for ever floored. As I am!'

To make his example the more impressive, Mr. Micawber
drank a glass of punch with an air of great enjoyment and
satisfaction, and whistled the College Hornpipe.

(*Ibid.*, XII, 174-5)

The rapid changes of mood here are as remarkable as the
weird synchronisation of very grave sentiments with a
beaming countenance. In spite of the 'imposing shirt
collar', the 'condescending roll in his voice', and his 'air
of doing something genteel', Mr. Micawber has as little
control over himself as over his family's finances.

The condescending, genteel and somewhat starched
strain in Mr. Micawber's personality provides basic
material for some of Dickens's most formidable characters. The combination gives us, for example, Messrs
Pecksniff, Murdstone, Dorrit, and Podsnap, as well as
those fearsome frozen women Mrs. Pipchin and Mrs.
Clennam. These are all different characters in many
ways, but all are preoccupied with sustaining an image of
rigid respectability:

Mr. Pecksniff was a moral man: a grave man, a man of noble
sentiments and speech ....

Perhaps there never was a more moral man than Mr.
Pecksniff: especially in his conversation and correspondence. He
was a most exemplary man: fuller of virtuous precept than a
copybook. Some people likened him to a direction-post, which
is always telling the way to a place, and never goes there: but
these were his enemies; the shadows cast by his brightness; that

was all. His very throat was moral. You saw a good deal of it. You looked over a very low fence of white cravat (whereof no man had ever beheld the tie, for he fastened it behind, and there it lay, a valley between two jutting heights of collar, serene and whiskerless before you. It seemed to say, on the part of Mr. Pecksniff, 'There is no deception, ladies and gentlemen, all is peace, a holy calm pervades me.' So did his hair, just grizzled with an iron-grey, which was all brushed off his forehead, and stood bolt upright, or slightly drooped in kindred action with his heavy eyelids. So did his person, which was sleek though free from corpulency. So did his manner, which was soft and oily. In a word, even his plain black suit, and state of widower, and dangling double eyeglass, all tended to the same purpose, and cried aloud, 'Behold the moral Pecksniff!'

(*MC*, II, 12-13)

Mr. Dombey, 'stiff with starch and arrogance' (*D&S*, VII, 91), lacks Pecksniff's unctuosity, but has in many ways an even more forbidding respectability. This is never more clearly demonstrated than when Dickens sets father and son side by side, and makes Dombey seem to belong not so much to a different generation as to an altogether different world. Mr. Dombey cannot cope with children, nor indeed with any relationship that makes emotional demands on him:

Dombey was about eight-and-forty years of age. Son about eight-and-forty minutes. Dombey was rather bald, rather red, and though a handsome well-made man, too stern and pompous in appearance, to be prepossessing. Son was very bald, and very red, and though (of course) an undeniably fine infant, somewhat crushed and spotty in his general effect, as yet. On the brow of Dombey, Time and his brother Care had set some marks, as on a tree that was to come down in good time — remorseless twins they are for striding through their human forests, notching as they go . . . .

He had risen, as his father had before him, in the course of life and death, from Son to Dombey, and for nearly twenty years had been the sole representative of the firm. Of those years he had been married, ten — married, as some said, to a lady with no heart to give him; whose happiness was in the past, and who was content to bind her broken spirit to the dutiful and meek endurance of the present. Such idle talk was little likely to reach the ears of Mr. Dombey, whom it nearly concerned; and probably no one in the world would have received it with such utter incredulity as he, if it had reached

him. Dombey and Son had often dealt in hides, but never in
hearts. They left that fancy ware to boys and girls, and
boarding-schools and books. Mr. Dombey would have
reasoned: That a matrimonial alliance with himself *must*, in the
nature of things, be gratifying and honourable to any woman of
common sense. That the hope of giving birth to a new partner in
such a house, could not fail to awaken a glorious and stirring
ambition in the breast of the least ambitious of her sex. That
Mrs. Dombey had entered on that social contract of matrimony:
almost necessarily part of a genteel and wealthy station, even
without reference to the perpetuation of family firms: with her
eyes fully open to these advantages.

(D&S, I, 1-2)

Mrs. Pipchin, to whom young Paul is entrusted later, is
one of Dickens's monstrous incarnations of Mrs. Grundyism:

This celebrated Mrs. Pipchin was a marvellous ill-favoured,
ill-conditioned old lady, of a stooping figure, with a mottled
face, like bad marble, a hook nose, and a hard grey eye, that
looked as if it might have been hammered at on an anvil without
sustaining any injury. Forty years at least had elapsed since the
Peruvian mines had been the death of Mr. Pipchin; but his relict
still wore black bombazeen, of such a lustreless, deep, dead,
sombre shade, that gas itself couldn't light her up after dark,
and her presence was a quencher to any number of candles. She
was generally spoken of as "a great manager" of children; and
the secret of her management was, to give them everything that
they didn't like, and nothing that they did — which was found
to sweeten their dispositions very much.

(Ibid, VIII, 99)

Dickens's very first published 'character', Mr. Minns
from the sketch 'Dinner at Poplar Walk', belongs to this
same family. Though not as fierce as Mrs. Pipchin nor as
imposing as Dombey, he is similarly starched, and
incapable of dealing with children (always in Dickens a
sure sign of some maladjustment):

MR. AUGUSTUS MINNS was a bachelor of *about* forty, as he
said — of about eight-and-forty, as his friends said. He was
always exceedingly clean, precise, and *tidy,* perhaps somewhat
priggish, and the most "retiring man in the world." He usually
wore a brown frock-coat without a wrinkle, light inexplicables

without a spot, a neat neckerchief with a remarkably neat tie, and boots without a fault; moreover, he always carried a brown silk umbrella with an ivory handle. He was a clerk in Somerset House, or, as he said, he held "a responsible situation under Government." He had a good and increasing salary, in addition to some £10,000. of his own (invested in the funds), and he occupied a first floor in Tavistock-street, Covent Garden, where he had resided for twenty years, having been in the habit of quarrelling with his landlord the whole time, regularly giving notice of his intention to quit on the first day of every quarter, and as regularly countermanding it on the second. He had but two particular horrors in the world, and those were dogs and children. His prejudice arose from no unamiability of disposition, but that the habits of the animals were continually at variance with his love of order, which might be said to be equally as powerful as his love of life.

('Dinner at Poplar Walk', *The Monthly Magazine*, Dec. 1833)[1]

Selfish, fastidious, reserved, respectable: Edith Sitwell thought that one of the chief components of eccentricity was a 'rigidity', a term implying either a refusal or an inability to adapt socially — an inflexibility. This rigidity can issue in comedy — as in many of the Dickensian eccentrics — or in the more serious emotional limitations of those starched middle-class characters. In either case, the rigidity seems to give to these characters a massiveness almost in proportion to their inflexibility. This massiveness and a peculiar immobility that often goes with it makes many of them seem like some endangered species of animal life. Anyone writing a Natural History of the English People would have to account for these extraordinary creatures, who seem larger than life and yet are unmistakeably drawn from life. Chesterton said of these characters that they 'live for ever because they never really live at all': it is an oversimplification, but one which catches a truth. Some of these figures seem to have an existence curiously independent of the novels in which they appear. 'They start off as magic-lantern slides

1. Reprinted in F.J. Harvey Darton, *Charles Dickens: Positively The First Appearance* (1933). The story appeared under a different title (and slightly revised) as 'Mr. Minns and His Cousin' in *Sketches by Boz* (SB, 312-22).

and they end by getting mixed up in a third-rate movie':
Orwell's remark catches well this sense of the imaginative autonomy of these characters.

The capacity for psychological development in many of
these characters seems very limited, although Dickens
makes great demands on them. Old Scrooge converted, or
the formidable Dombey redeemed and penitent may seem
less to have grown morally than to have shrunk physically,
or suddenly been seized with senile disintegration.
Dickens, I think, would have us understand these
transformations less as an access of senile benignity than as
a recovery of childhood simplicities. Certainly Scrooge and
Dombey's reformations are signalled largely by their newly
discovered delight in children: Scrooge becomes a devoted
second father to Tiny Tim, and our last glimpse of Dombey
shows him playing fondly with his grandchild on the
sea-shore. This latter scene is an interesting, if uncon-
scious, echo of Wordsworth's metaphor for the adult's
intimations of immortality from recollections of early
childhood:

> Though inland far we be,
> Our Souls have sight of that immortal sea
> Which brought us hither,
> Can in a moment travel thither,
> And see the children sport upon the shore,
> And hear the mighty waters rolling evermore.

The broken link in the continuity of love and family feeling
between the generations is thus repaired, as child and adult
come together again. As we have seen, Dickens so often
diagnoses the condition of England in terms of this sort of
imagery: Government becomes a kind of negligent parent
who treats its People with gross condescension ('the Great
Baby') or irrational authoritarianism; and it establishes a
buttoned-up Civil Service to keep its People at bay with
red-tape formalities, much as Mr. Dombey's demeanour
forbids intimacies from Florence:

> Not to be too wise, not to be too stately, not be too rough with
> innocent fancies, or to treat them with too much lightness — which

is as bad — are points to be remembered that may do us all good in
our years to come.

('Where We Stopped Growing', *HW* 1 January 1853: *NCP* I, 421)

Whatever Dickens may have felt in principle about the
human capacity for moral regeneration, his fictional
performances of redemption do not easily carry conviction,
though there are notable exceptions such as Pip. The
rigidity of his characters involves something more than just
an artistic limitation in Dickens — perhaps a deeper
pessimism than he is inclined to admit to himself. Philip
Collins's conclusions about Dickens's attitudes towards the
treatment of the criminal point in this direction: 'For all his
gaiety and high spirits, Dickens was not at bottom very
optimistic about human nature. To adopt the reformative
policy in prison discipline [as opposed to a deterrent
policy], obviously one must believe that at least a
substantial number of prisoners are reclaimable; Dickens
on the whole did not' (Collins: *Crime*, p.82)[1].

As I suggested earlier, rigidity in its comic manifestations
contributes to the great eccentrics. Its graver and more fully
developed form is to be seen in those daunting representatives of English respectability. These middle-class
habits of reserve were bred largely by the Puritan-
Evangelical movement in England in the earlier nineteenth
century. We recall Dickens's complaints in 1855 about the
'horrid respectability' of English art, when compared with
the 'passion and action' evident in the work of the French
painters. In the same period, the French historian and critic
Hippolyte Taine described what he understood to be the
priorities in English public taste, as derived particularly
from a reading of Dickens's novels:

> Be moral. All your novels must be such as may be read by young
> girls. We are practical minds, and we would not have literature
> corrupt practical life. We believe in family life, and we would not
> have literature paint the passions which attack family life. We are
> Protestants, and we have preserved something of the severity of
> our fathers against enjoyment and passions. Amongst these, love
> is the worst. Beware of resembling in this respect the most
> illustrious of our neighbours.   (*Crit.H.*, p.340)

1. Collins also develops briefly the connection between Dickens's
attitudes to reformative policy in prisons and his fictional characters'
limited capacity for reformation.

Beware particularly of sexual passion. We have seen how Dickens himself chafed under the restrictions of his own country's moral code and admired the boldness and passion of the French ('the most illustrious of our neighbours' in Taine's wry phrase): but it is not by any means easy to guess how his own artistic treatment of passionate love would have developed had that inhibiting code been lifted. Sexual passion in the later fiction is an awesome thing. Miss Wade, Bradley Headstone and John Jasper are formidable figures when their frustrated passions are wrought up to greatest intensity; all the more formidable perhaps because their demeanour otherwise seems as respectably buttoned-up as the characters we have already noticed:

> The wild energy of the man, now quite let loose, was absolutely terrible. He stopped and laid his hand upon a piece of the coping of the burial-ground enclosure, as if he would have dislodged the stone.
>
> 'No man knows till the time comes what depths are within him. To some men it never comes; let them rest and be thankful! To me you brought it; on me, you forced it; and the bottom of this raging sea,' striking himself upon the breast, 'has been heaved up ever since.'
>
> *(OMF*, Bk II, xv, 396)

This is Bradley Headstone with Lizzie in the scene where his fury and frustration brings him to pound that coping stone until his fist is raw and bleeding. But one has only to compare it with the scene in *Wuthering Heights* where Heathcliff in fury and despair at Catherine's death beats his head against a tree until the blood comes, to feel the strain in Dickens's writing and how his heightening of emotion has a touch of melodrama that eventually acts as an anodyne. One might have expected that the Dickens who fulminates against English respectability would find in the Brontes' portrayals of passion a welcome exception to the prevailing moral tenor of English fiction. But this does not seem to be the case. Not only had he probably not read *Wuthering Heights* and *Jane Eyre*, but he seems even to have disapproved of that kind of literature.[1]

1. See J. Meckier's discussion of a contemporary account of Dickens's conversation, *The Dickensian* LXXI (1975), pp.5-20.

Sexuality in Dickens's fiction is usually more compelling and convincing when it is displaced, issuing obliquely and indirectly. John Carey has commented, for instance, that 'Dickens can allow himself to convey the physicality of sex with a more brutal frankness when talking about textiles and furniture than when talking about bodies'.[1] Psychoanalytic criticism of Dickens's fiction in the last forty years, though much of it tends to be too reductive and schematic, has illuminated the abundant covert sexuality in the novels, expressed, as so much is always powerfully expressed in his fictional world, through the rich symbolic imagery.[2] I would be inclined to distrust Dickens's attributing inhibitions in his own work to the prevailing Victorian code. Even supposing those restrictions were lifted, there seems to be in Dickens sufficient fear and distrust of sexuality to disable his artistic exploration of this area of human experience. Sexual innocence is one of the greatest moral positives in his fictional world. For all his francophilia, there is enough of the English anti-Jacobin in Dickens to prompt him to distrust sexual passion as much as violent social revolution. His little women heroines — Nell, Esther Summerson, Little Dorrit, etc — are the fictional issue of such fears, given form and substance by his idealised memories of his sister-in-law Mary Hogarth. One characteristic that they share (though to a lesser degree) with the group of buttoned-up middle-class adults is a distinctively English reserve. The fastidious love of order, for example, that was comically exaggerated in Mr. Minns, is given to these heroines as an assurance of their security and moral stability. They are neat, orderly, self-controlled and fortified against all muddle and passion; for the love of order is (like the English reserve) as much a safeguard against emotional disturbance as it is a guarantee of a sound domestic economy. Mr. Micawber, it

1. John Carey, *The Violent Effigy* (1973), p.168.
2. Steven Marcus's *Dickens: from Pickwick to Dombey* (1965) is one of the best studies to approach Dickens in this way. His book *The Other Victorians* (1966), a fascinating examination of Victorian sexuality as seen in its pornography, enables us to reconsider Dickens in relation to the moral climate of his age.

may be noted, is an instance of conspicuous failure in both respects.

The portrait of the English that we have been considering so far seems pretty forbidding: but it is only partial. How, for example, could Turgenev have remarked that it was largely through his reading of Dickens's works that he came to appreciate the underlying warmth of the un-demonstrative British character?[1]

Let us now follow the direction pointed by that other strain in Mr. Micawber's character, the man that openly laughs and cries, grows greatly convivial over the punch-bowl, and whistles the College Hornpipe. That strain distinguishes a host of characters, jovial, voluble, and frank: the Wellers, Dick Swiveller, Captain Cuttle, many of the Bleeding Hearts, and, one might add, the converted Scrooge and the Walworth Wemmick. These people are very little concerned at all with respectability; indeed, they are often placed in the novel precisely to counterbalance the ponderous presence of the former group (the later Scrooge has, of course, the unreformed Scrooge to counterbalance). Most of them, it will be noticed, come from the lower fringes of the middle class, or from the working class. These are the people whom Dickens considers 'the life-blood of the nation'. Charac-ters like these swarm through the pages of Dickens's first book *Sketches by Boz,* which he held to be 'Illustrative of Every-Day Life and Every-Day People'.Consider this portrait of Cockney life from the *Sketches,* where a fierce encounter takes place in London's Seven Dials:

> On one side, a little crowd had collected round a couple of ladies, who having imbibed the contents of various "three-outs" of gin and bitters in the course of the morning, have at length differed on some point of domestic arrangement, and are on the eve of settling the quarrel satisfactorily, by an appeal to blows,

1. See P. Waddington, 'Dickens, Pauline Viardot, Turgenev', *The New Zealand Slavonic Journal* (September 1974).

greatly to the interest of other ladies who live in the same house, and tenements adjoining, and who are all partisans on one side or other.

"Vy don't you pitch into her, Sarah?" exclaims one half-dressed matron by way of encouragement. "Vy don't you? if *my* 'usband had treated her with a drain last night, unbeknown to me, I'd tear her precious eyes out — a wixen!"

"What's the matter, ma'am?" inquires another old woman, who has just bustled up to the spot.

"Matter!" replies the first speaker, talking *at* the obnoxious combatant, "matter! Here's poor dear Mrs. Sulliwin, as has five blessed children of her own, can't go out a-charing for one afternoon, but what hussies must be a-comin', and 'ticing avay her oun' 'usband, as she's been married to twelve year come next Easter Monday, for I see the certificate ven I vas a-drinkin' a cup o'tea with her, only the werry last blessed Ven'sday as ever vas sent. I 'appen'd to say promiscuously, 'Mrs. Sulliwin,' says I —"

"What do you mean by hussies?" interrupts a champion of the other party, who has evinced a strong inclination through-out to get up a branch fight on her own account ("Hooroar," ejaculates a pot-boy in parenthesis, "put the kye-bosk on her, Mary!") "What do you mean by hussies?" reiterates the champion.

"Niver mind," replies the opposition expressively "niver mind; *you* go home, and, ven you're quite sober, mend your stockings."

This somewhat personal allusion, not only to the lady's habits of intemperance, but also to the state of her wardrobe, rouses her utmost ire, and she accordingly complies with the urgent request of the bystanders to "pitch in," with considerable alacrity. The scuffle became general, and terminates, in minor play-bill phraseology, with "arrival of the policeman, interior of the station-house, and impressive *denouement.*"

('Seven Dials', SB, 70-1)

It is the total carelessness of respectability and reserve that attracts Dickens here. His own stilted, elaborately formal narrative style is designed precisely to throw into greater relief the rapid, freewheeling cockney speech rhythms as passions mount in the scene. The nature of the comic discrepancy between the two styles is strongly Micawberish.

If Dickens owed his early success to any single character, it was to one drawn from just such a milieu —

Sam Weller. Sam's first appearance in July 1836, in the fourth monthly number of Dickens's first novel *Pickwick Papers*, rapidly attracted the public interest. Before long sales had risen from around four hundred copies per number in the first four months to some forty thousand, and Dickens's name was made. Sam and his father upstage nearly all the other characters in this novel (and there are some three hundred of them) with scenes such as the composition of the Valentine letter in the parlour of the Blue Boar Inn. Sam, proud of his literary skills, reads the letter aloud to his highly critical father:

"'Lovely creetur,'" repeated Sam.

"'Tain't in poetry, is it?' interposed his father.

'No, no,' replied Sam.

'Werry glad to hear it,' said Mr. Weller. 'Poetry's unnat'ral; no man ever talked poetry 'cept a beadle on boxin' day, or Warren's blackin', or Rowland's oil, or some o' them low fellows; never you let yourself down to talk poetry, my boy. Begin agin, Sammy.'

Mr. Weller resumed his pipe with critical solemnity, and Sam once more commenced, and read as follows:

"'Lovely creetur i feel myself a dammed"' —.'

'That ain't proper,' said Mr. Weller, taking his pipe from his mouth.

'No; it ain't "dammed",' observed Sam holding the letter up to the light, 'it's "shamed," there's a blot there — "I feel myself ashamed...and completely circumscribed in a dressin' of you, for you *are* a nice gal and nothin' but it.'"

'That's a werry pretty sentiment,' said the elder Mr. Weller, removing his pipe to make way for the remark.

'Yes, I think it is rayther good,' observed Sam, highly flattered.

'Wot I like in that 'ere style of writin',' said the elder Mr. Weller, 'is, that there ain't no callin' names in it, — no Wenuses, nor nothin' o' that kind. Wot's the good o' callin' a young 'ooman a Wenus or a angel, Sammy?'

'Ah! what indeed?' replied Sam.

'You might jist as well call her a griffin, or a unicorn, or a king's arms at once, which is werry well known to be a col-lection o' fabulous animals,' added Mr. Weller.

'Just as well,' replied Sam.

'Drive on, Sammy,' said Mr. Weller.

Sam complied with the request, and proceeded as follows: his father continuing to smoke, with a mixed expression of wisdom and complacency, which was particularly edifying.

"'Afore I see you, I thought all women was alike.'"

'So they are,' observed the elder Mr. Weller, parenthetically.

"'But now,'" continued Sam, "'now I find what a reg'lar soft-headed, inkred'lous turnip I must ha' been; for there ain't nobody like you, though *I* like you better than nothin' at all." I thought it best to make that rayther strong,' said Sam, looking up.

Mr. Weller nodded approvingly, and Sam resumed.

"'So I take the privilidge of the day, Mary, my dear — as the gen'l'm'n in difficulties did, ven he valked out of a Sunday, — to tell you that the first and only time I see you, your likeness was took on my hart in much quicker time and brighter colours than ever a likeness was took by the profeel macheen (wich p'raps you may have heerd on Mary my dear) altho it *does* finish a portrait and put the frame and glass on complete, with a hook at the end to hang it up by, and all in two minutes and a quarter.'"

'I am afeerd that werges on the poetical, Sammy,' said Mr. Weller, dubiously.

'No it don't,' replied Sam, reading on very quickly, to avoid contesting the point:

"'Except of me Mary my dear as your walentine and think over what I've said. — My dear Mary I will now conclude." That's all,' said Sam.

'That's rather a sudden pull up, ain't it, Sammy?' inquired Mr. Weller.

'Not a bit on it,' said Sam; 'she'll vish there wos more, and that's the great art o' letter writin'.'

'Well,' said Mr. Weller, 'there's somethin' in that; and I wish your mother-in-law 'ud only conduct her conwersation on the same genteel principle.'

(PP, XXXIII, 452-4)

The comedy depends on the tensions between the strict proprieties involved in the Valentine enterprise, of which both Wellers are earnestly aware, and their native impulse to reduce the thing to unpretentious commonsense — e.g. Old Weller's allergy to anything that 'werges on the poetical'.

To Dickens, the Wellers seemed to be members of a disappearing race in England. Tony Weller's occupation, coachman, was already threatened by the coming of the railways: he is a sad casualty of those 'shiftings and changes'. But, more generally, the particular colourful idiosyncracies of these people seemed to have a limited future. At the end of one of the *Sketches* describing a cab-driver and an omnibus 'cad' called Mr. Barker, Dickens reflects on the future of such people:

> We have spoken of Mr. Barker and of the red-cab-driver, in the past tense. Alas! Mr. Barker has again become an absentee; and the class of men to which they both belonged are fast disappearing. Improvement has peered beneath the aprons of our cabs, and penetrated to the very innermost recesses of our omnibuses. Dirt and fustian will vanish before cleanliness and livery. Slang will be forgotten when civility becomes general: and that enlightened, eloquent, sage, and profound body, the Magistracy of London, will be deprived of half their amusement, and half their occupation.
>
> ('The Last Cab-Driver and the First Omnibus Cad', *SB*, 151)

This mock-elegy is only half in mockery. There is the same sort of ambivalence about Dickens's feelings towards these people as he showed in his description of the new railway development's transformation of old Staggs's Garden in *Dombey and Son*.

To suggest that the lower classes in Dickens are always free from the kinds of hypocrisies usually associated with the middle class is to fall into the old trap of believing Dickens always idealised the poor. With Sarah Gamp's grossly transparent assumptions of a delicate sensibility, we are aware of being in the presence of a great hypocrite, for whom middle-class gentility is the only respectable demeanour. She was, as Dickens observed in his 1868 Preface to *Martin Chuzzlewit*, 'four-and-twenty years ago, a fair representative of the hired attendant on the poor in sickness'. Mrs. Gamp remains one of the greatest of Dickens's portraits of lower-class life in England:

> She was a fat old woman, this Mrs. Gamp, with a husky voice and a moist eye, which she had a remarkable power of turning up, and only showing the white of it. Having very little neck, it cost her some trouble to look over herself, if one may say so, at those to whom she talked. She wore a very rusty black gown,

rather the worse for snuff, and a shawl and bonnet to correspond. In these dilapidated articles of dress she had, on principle, arrayed herself, time out of mind, on such occasions as the present; for this at once expressed a decent amount of veneration for the deceased, and invited the next of kin to present her with a fresher suit of weeds: an appeal so frequently successful, that the very fetch and ghost of Mrs. Gamp, bonnet and all, might be seen hanging up, any hour in the day, in at least a dozen of the second-hand clothes shops about Holborn. The face of Mrs. Gamp — the nose in particular — was somewhat red and swollen, and it was difficult to enjoy her society without becoming conscious of a smell of spirits. Like most persons who have attained to great eminence in their profession, she took to hers very kindly; insomuch that, setting aside her natural predilections as a woman, she went to a lying-in or a laying-out with equal zest and relish.

'Ah!' repeated Mrs. Gamp; for it was always a safe sentiment in cases of mourning. 'Ah dear! When Gamp was summoned to his long home, and I see him a-lying in Guy's Hospital with a penny-piece on each eye, and his wooden leg under his left arm, I thought I should have fainted away. But I bore up.'

If certain whispers current in the Kingsgate Street circles had any truth in them, she had indeed borne up surprisingly; and had exerted such uncommon fortitude as to dispose of Mr. Gamp's remains for the benefit of science. But it should be added, in fairness, that this had happened twenty years before; and that Mr. and Mrs Gamp had long been separated on the ground of incompatibility of temper in their drink.

'You have become indifferent since then, I suppose?' said Mr. Pecksniff. 'Use is second nature, Mrs. Gamp.'

'You may well say second natur, sir,' returned that lady. 'One's first ways is to find sich things a trial to the feelings, and so is one's lasting custom. If it wasn't for the nerve a little sip of liquor gives me (I never was able to do more than taste it), I never could go through with what I sometimes has to do. "Mrs. Harris," I says, at the very last case as ever I acted in, which it was but a young person, "Mrs. Harris," I says, "leave the bottle on the chimley-piece, and don't ask me to take none, but let me put my lips to it when I am so dispoged, and then I will do what I'm engaged to do, according to the best of my ability." "Mrs. Gamp," she says, in answer, "if ever there was a sober creetur to be got at eighteen pence a day for working people, and three and six for gentlefolks — night watching,"' said Mrs. Gamp, with emphasis, '"being a extra charge — you are that inwallable person." "Mrs. Harris," I says to her, "don't name the charge, for if I could afford to lay all my feller creeturs out for nothink, I would gladly do it, sich is the love I bears'em. But what I always says to them as has the management of matters, Mrs. Harris:"'

here she kept her eye on Mr. Pecksniff: "'be they gents or be they ladies, is, don't ask me whether I won't take none, or whether I will, but leave the bottle on the chimley-piece, and let me put my lips to it when I am so dispoged.'"

(MC, XIX, 313-4)

Mrs. Gamp's assumed gentility deceives no one, except perhaps herself and Mrs. Harris. Like Mr. Micawber and Sam Weller, she has become one of the great Dickensian characters, and she shares with them much of her creator's wild imaginative energy and verbal resourcefulness. Indeed, one of the traits of the Dombeys and Murdstones in Dickens's world is the poverty of their speech, which is as stiff and reserved as their general demeanour.

Sarah Gamp's professional connection with the dying and the dead accentuates her grotesqueness as a comic character. Her gentility has been strenuously cultivated because of the pressure of contemporary conventions in the attitude towards death. The national appetite for gloom and drabness, which we noted in the last chapter, indulged itself with extraordinary extravagance in the formalities of the funeral. The public parade of gravity, the hypocritical displays of grief, the mercenary excesses of the undertakers, all became targets for Dickens's satire, particularly here in *Martin Chuzzlewit*. It was a peculiar manifestation of the national character in its fierce pieties and competitive respectability:

> Several years have now elapsed since it began to be clear to the comprehension of most rational men, that the English people had fallen into a condition much to be regretted, in respect of their Funeral customs. A system of barbarous show and expense was found to have gradually erected itself above the grave, which, while it could possibly do no honour to the memory of the dead, did great dishonour to the living, as inducing them to associate the most solemn of human occasions with unmeaning mummeries, dishonest debt, profuse waste, and bad example in an utter oblivion of responsibility . . . . The competition among the middle classes for superior gentility in Funerals — the gentility being estimated by the amount of ghastly folly in which the undertaker was permitted to run riot — descended even to the very poor: to whom the cost of funeral customs was so

ruinous and so disproportionate to their means, that they formed
clubs among themselves to defray such charges.

('Trading in Death' *HW,* 27 November 1852:
NCP I,405)

Dickens talked of the 'inconsistencies, monstrosities,
horrors and ruinous expenses, that...beset all classes of
society in connexion with Death' (*Letters N* II, 415-6. Coutts:
23 September 1852). The extravagance of the greatest public
funeral of the age, that of the Duke of Wellington in 1852,
horrified Dickens: 'The whole Public seem to me to have
gone mad...a relapse into semi-barbarous practices' (*ibid*).

His own novels, of course, are notorious for their
lingering, lugubrious death scenes which dissolved the
Victorian family reading circle in tears, and felled even the
more austere critic. Their contemporary appeal is a
puzzling characteristic of the age. Humphry House has
offered one of the most plausible explanations:

> Their popularity at the time is partly explained by the fact that a
> religion in a state of transition from supernatural belief to
> humanism is very poorly equipped to face death, and must dwell
> on it for that very reason.

(House, 132)

When Dickens decided to kill Little Nell he said that he
'resolved to try and do something which might be read by
people about whom Death had been, — with a softened
feeling, and with consolation' (*Letters P* II, 188. Forster:
[?17] January 1841). One may guess that the same purpose
applies to all his sentimental child deaths, even though he
was not always so intensely involved emotionally as he had
been with Nell. Sometimes he can seem privately quite
business-like, if not jovial, when approaching such
moments in the novels. During the composition of *Dombey
and Son* he reports:

> Paul, I shall slaughter at the end of number five.

(*Letters N* I, 820. Forster: 6 December 1846)

And in a bulletin on the next novel:

> I have been very hard at work these three days, and have still Dora
> to kill. But with good luck, I may do it to-morrow.

(*Ibid.* II, 228. Forster: 20 August 1850)

That his death scenes did actually afford some consolation in an age too familiar with child mortality is amply attested[1]. One notable instance may be given here. In 1852 Dickens received a request from Byron's daughter Ada Augusta, then Lady Lovelace, to pay her a visit. She was on her death bed, and wanted to meet the man whose narrative of Paul Dombey's death had greatly soothed her.

It might be just as interesting, if not more so, to speculate on why such scenes move us so little today, or move us to aesthetic distaste sooner than to sympathetic tears. It cannot be that we are any more reconciled to death than were the Victorians — perhaps less so in many ways. Possibly as death develops into a more private, clinical, antiseptic occasion (we are at least spared the likes of Mrs. Gamp now), there is less allowance for the public expression of grief. At any rate some such correlation is likely. Dickens's death scenes overflow with sincere private grief partly to counteract the posturings of mourning — the 'unmeaning mummeries' — which Victorian convention required in the public funeral, and which so excited his indignant satire.

Satire and sentimentality work in their different ways towards the same end. The sense Dickens has of the threat posed by the English middle-class standards of respectability to the vitality of the nation became particularly acute in his fiction from the middle 1840s onwards. In novel after novel he lays siege to those strongholds of English rigidity: Mr. Dombey, the Murdstones, Chancery and the code of the Dedlocks, Gradgrindism, the Barnacle-bound Circumlocution Office, Pip's parvenu gentility, Podsnappery. Dickens's siege weapons are, principally, three: they are designed to melt the enemy, to deflate, or to bombard. He melts with his sentimental ammunition, — his young children and little heroines. He deflates by bringing into confrontation with his pompous enemy his range of vivacious, unsophisticated characters: this is essentially a comic device, and much more frequent in his earlier novels. Finally he bombards the stronghold, whether it be a

[1]See George Ford's discussion of the extraordinary public response to Nell's death in *Dickens and His Readers*, Chapter IV.

character or an institution, with the heavy artillery of his own satire or angry remonstrance. Each one can be very effective, though modern tastes tend to shy away from his exploitation of the first. The combination of all three in operation in one novel is what gives Dickens's fiction its distinctive character.

As I said earlier, no single type can adequately represent the national character, because it is a far from settled and homogeneous society that Dickens portrays. But it is this tension, this interaction between not necessarily two classes of society but two different kinds of temperament, the two dominant strains already discussed, that distinguished Dickens's view of the English character.

This focus was perhaps inevitable for Dickens, who was himself shaped by some of the social pressures he dramatises. He certainly associates himself with some of the traditional middle-class values: he is earnest, industrious, somewhat puritanical, anti-bohemian, a self-made man and proud of it. But equally certainly he is remarkably free from other characteristics: acquisitiveness, hypocrisy, lack of imagination, snobbery. One can think of instances of each of these, but not, I think, enough to suggest that these are at all characteristic habits of mind in Dickens. He was also, as we have seen, too radical both in his political attitudes and in his sympathy with the poor ever to be fully comfortable with the middle-class establishment. On the other hand, his horror of financial insecurity and his fastidious habits made him determined to live with traditional middle-class comfort.

He was, as Edmund Wilson points out in the main argument of his classic pioneering essay on Dickens,[1] in a very good position as an artist to understand that the English character was composed of two strains in particular, with which his personality and circumstances were closely identified. He was a man with the kind of

1. Edmund Wilson, 'Dickens: The Two Scrooges', *The Wound and The Bow* (1941).

passionate nature, wild sense of humour and high imaginative powers that he often associates with characters from the lower, less rigidified, classes of society. Genius and industriousness launched him abruptly into upper middle-class circles, a traumatic move perhaps, and one that many a critic and biographer have claimed to be crucially significant in understanding his character and art. But, both by nature and experience Dickens was not, psychologically, altogether unprepared to meet some of that class's demands, and to live by its code of values.

Let us take just two characteristics. Dickens preserved a stiff upper lip that was much more akin to Dombeyan rigid self-discipline than to, say, Sam Weller's breezy stoicism; and, secondly, he had an obsession with domestic order, neatness and punctuality that would have greatly endeared him to Mr. Minns. The strict emotional self-control could of course collapse under great pressure, and for a man with as passionate a nature as Dickens's the strain must have been terrible sometimes. He himself attributed what he called his 'habit of suppression' to the early disappointment in love that he experienced with Maria Beadnell. Years later he confided to her:

> My entire devotion to you, and the wasted tenderness of those hard years which I have ever since half loved, half dreaded to recall, made so deep an impression on me that I refer to it a habit of suppression which now belongs to me, which I know is no part of my original nature, but which makes me chary of showing my affections, even to my children, except when they are very young.
>
> (*Letters N* II, 633. Mrs. Winter: 22 February 1855)

His son, Henry, remarked on his father's intense dislike of 'letting himself go', and gave one instance of it:

> In the year 1869, after I had been at college about a year, I was fortunate enough to gain one of the principal scholarships at Trinity Hall, Cambridge — not a great thing, only £50 a year; but I knew that this success, slight as it was, would give him intense pleasure, so I went to meet him at Higham Station upon his arrival from London to tell him of it. As he got out of the train I told him the news. He said, "Capital! capital!" — nothing more.

Disappointed to find that he received the news apparently so lightly, I took my seat beside him in the pony carriage he was driving. Nothing more happened until we had got half-way to Gad's Hill, when he broke down completely. Turning towards me with tears in his eyes and giving me a warm grip of the hand, he said, "God bless you, my boy; God bless you!" That pressure of the hand I can feel now as distinctly as I felt it then, and it will remain as strong and real until the day of my death.

(Henry Fielding Dickens, *op.cit.*, 19-20)

This is a change of mood that is almost Micawberish.

Dickens's obsessive neatness, of which again he was fully aware, is mentioned in passing in a fine tribute to John Forster:

I desire no better for my fame, when my personal dustiness shall be past the control of my love of order, than such a biographer and such a critic.

(*Letters N* II, 84. Forster: 22 April 1848)

His daughter Mamie recorded that 'there never existed, I think, in all the world, a more thoroughly tidy or methodical creature than was my father. He was tidy in every way — in his mind, in his handsome and graceful person, in his work, in keeping his writing table drawers, in his large correspondence, in fact in his whole life' (Mamie Dickens, *op.cit.*, 15). The love of tidiness and the 'habit of suppression' are presumably related psychologically. But how were these rigidities to be reconciled with the man who laughed and cried as he wrote *A Christmas Carol*, who would prowl the dark streets of London through the early hours of the morning, and who ultimately became obsessed with the indulgence of what he called his 'murderous instincts', when, in those 'Sikes and Nancy' public readings, he determined to 'tear myself to pieces' (the supremely *un*tidy act)?

These tensions were not to be reconciled in Dickens's own life. Nor were the related tensions and complexities which he saw writ large in English society to be resolved in his imaginary worlds. On the contrary, the character of John Jasper, the central figure in the last, uncompleted novel *The Mystery of Edwin Drood*, suggests that these two strains became more mutually irreconcilable than ever.

But that is hardly the point. We no more properly expect Dickens to resolve such matters in his private life or published work than we demand that he prove himself a more sophisticated politician. His achievement lay in highlighting the forces within English society that were breeding moral confusion, apathy and rigidity; and this he does with an extraordinary eye for colour, accomplishing

> The fusion of the graces of the imagination with the realities of life, which is vital to the welfare of any community, and for which I have striven . . . as honestly as I could . . . .
>
> (Announcement of *AYR*, *HW* 28 May 1859: *NCP* I, 225)

As a result, we can hardly imagine the early Victorian age without him. The ambiguity in that statement is worth pointing up: for we both greatly depend on his imaginative insights for our portrait of the English then, and we also have the sense that he is himself inseparably a part of that age, however anomalous he often seems. And he was an anomalous presence. Although he was very much a man of his time, chronicling his time, he also stood out as a wayward poetic spirit in those increasingly prosaic years. What he said of his aim in *Bleak House* might well remain as a clue to the source of that fabulous legacy he left us:

> I have purposely dwelt upon the romantic side of ordinary things.
>
> (BH, xiv: 'Preface')

INDEX